Elder Mistreatment: Ethical Issues, Dilemmas, and Decisions

Elder Mistreatment: Ethical Issues, Dilemmas, and Decisions

Tanya Fusco Johnson, MDiv, PhD
Editor

The Haworth Press, Inc.,
New York • London

Elder Mistreatment: Ethical Issues, Dilemmas, and Decisions has also been published as *Journal of Elder Abuse & Neglect*, Volume 7, Numbers 2/3 1995.

The development, preparation, and publication of this work has been undertaken with great care. However, the publisher, employees, editors, and agents of The Haworth Press and all imprints of The Haworth Press, Inc., including the Haworth Medical Press and Pharmaceutical Products Press, are not responsible for any errors contained herein or for consequences that may ensue from use of materials or information contained in this work. Opinions expressed by the author(s) are not necessarily those of The Haworth Press, Inc.

The Haworth Press, Inc., 10 Alice Street, Binghamton, NY 13904-1580 USA

Library of Congress Cataloging-in-Publication Data

Elder Mistreatment: ethical issues, dilemmas, and decisions/Tanya Fusco Johnson, editor
     p. cm.
   Includes bibliographical references and index.
   ISBN 1-56024-770-3 (alk. paper)
   1. Social work with the aged–United States. 2. Aged–United States–Abuse of–Prevention. I. Johnson, Tanya F.
HV1465.E434 1995
362.6–dc20
                                             95-40700
                                                CIP

The authors of this volume dedicate this book to Mr. Paul Blanton, an Adult Protective Services specialist in the Texas Department of Human Services. His untimely death in 1987 silenced a strong voice for the welfare of older adults. We pay tribute to his courage to seek justice for all of those who cannot help themselves. Now, through our own voices, we continue his goal of strengthening the ethical conduct of human services professionals in their day-to-day efforts to protect older adults.

INDEXING & ABSTRACTING

Contributions to this publication are selectively indexed or abstracted in print, electronic, online, or CD-ROM version(s) of the reference tools and information services listed below. This list is current as of the copyright date of this publication. See the end of this section for additional notes.

- *Abstracts in Social Gerontology: Current Literature on Aging,* National Council on the Aging, Library, 409 Third Street SW, 2nd Floor, Washington, DC 20024

- *AgeLine Database,* American Association of Retired Persons, 601 E Street, NW, Washington, DC 20049

- *Behavioral Medicine Abstracts,* University of Washington, School of Social Work, Seattle, WA 98195

- *Brown University Geriatric Research Application Digest "Abstracts Section,"* Brown University, Center for Gerontology & Health Care Research, c/o Box G-B 235, Providence, RI 02912

- *Cambridge Scientific Abstracts, Risk Abstracts,* Cambridge Information Group, 7200 Wisconsin Avenue #601, Bethesda, MD 20814

- *caredata CD: the social and community care database,* National Institute for Social Work, 5 Tavistock Place, London WC1H 9SS, England

- *Communication Abstracts,* Temple University, 303 Annenberg Hall, Philadelphia, PA 19122

- *Criminal Justice Abstracts,* Willow Tree Press, 15 Washington Street, 4th Floor, Newark, NJ 07102

- *Criminal Justice Periodical Index,* University Microfilms, Inc., 300 North Zeeb Road, Ann Arbor, MI 48106

- *Current Contents* . . . . . see: Institute for Scientific Information

- *Family Violence & Sexual Assault Bulletin,* Family Violence & Sexual Assault Institute, 1310 Clinic Drive, Tyler, TX 75701

(continued)

- *Human Resources Abstracts (HRA),* Sage Publications, Inc., 2455 Teller Road, Newbury Park, CA 91320

- *Index to Periodical Articles Related to Law,* University of Texas, 727 East 26th Street, Austin, TX 78705

- *Institute for Scientific Information,* 3501 Market Street, Philadelphia, Pennsylvania 19104. Coverage in:
  b) Research Alerts (current awareness service)
  c) Social SciSearch (magnetic tape)
  d) Current Contents/Social & Behavioral Sciencies (weekly current awareness service)

- *INTERNET ACCESS (& additional networks) Bulletin Board for Libraries ("BUBL"), coverage of information resources on INTERNET, JANET, and other networks.*
  - JANET X.29:UK.AC.BATH.BUBL or 00006012101300
  - TELNET: BUBL.BATH.AC.UK or 138.38.32.45 login 'bubl'
  - Gopher: BUBL.BATH.AC.UK (138.32.32.45). Port 7070
  - World Wide Web: http: //www.bubl.bath.ac.uk./BUBL/home.html
  - NISSWAIS: telnetniss.ac.uk (for the NISS gateway), The Andersonian Library, Curran Building, 101 Saint James Road, Glasgow G4 ONS, Scotland

- *Inventory of Marriage and Family Literature (online and hard copy),* National Council on Family Relations, 3989 Central Avenue NE, Suite 550, Minneapolis, MN 55421

- *Mental Health Abstracts (online through DIALOG),* IFI/Plenum Data Company, 3202 Kirkwood Highway, Wilmington, DE 19808

- *Social Planning/Policy & Development Abstracts (SOPODA),* Sociological Abstracts, Inc., P. O. Box 22206, San Diego, CA 92192-0206

- *Social Science Citation Index ....* see: Institute for Scientific Information

- *Social Work Abstracts,* National Association of Social Workers, 750 First Street NW, 8th Floor, Washington, DC 20002

- *Sociological Abstracts (SA),* Sociological Abstracts, Inc., P. O. Box 22206, San Diego, CA 92192-0206

- *Violence and Abuse Abstracts: A Review of Current Literature on Interpersonal Violence (VAA),* Sage Publications, Inc., 2455 Teller Road, Newbury, Park, CA 91320

(continued)

SPECIAL BIBLIOGRAPHIC NOTES

related to special journal issues (separates)
and indexing/abstracting

☐ indexing/abstracting services in this list will also cover material in any "separate" that is co-published simultaneously with Haworth's special thematic journal issue or DocuSerial. Indexing/abstracting usually covers material at the article/chapter level.

☐ monographic co-editions are intended for either non-subscribers or libraries which intend to purchase a second copy for their circulating collections.

☐ monographic co-editions are reported to all jobbers/wholesalers/approval plans. The source journal is listed as the "series" to assist the prevention of duplicate purchasing in the same manner utilized for books-in-series.

☐ to facilitate user/access services all indexing/abstracting services are encouraged to utilize the co-indexing entry note indicated at the bottom of the first page of each article/chapter/contribution.

☐ this is intended to assist a library user of any reference tool (whether print, electronic, online, or CD-ROM) to locate the monographic version if the library has purchased this version but not a subscription to the source journal.

☐ individual articles/chapters in any Haworth publication are also available through the Haworth Document Delivery Services (HDDS).

Elder Mistreatment:
Ethical Issues, Dilemmas, and Decisions

CONTENTS

∞ ALL HAWORTH BOOKS AND JOURNALS
   ARE PRINTED ON CERTIFIED
   ACID-FREE PAPER

ABOUT THE EDITOR

Tanya Fusco Johnson, PhD, is Lecturer in the Department of Sociology at the University of Hawaii, Hilo. She has over 20 years of experience teaching at the college level on such subjects as child development, gerontology, race and ethnicity, sociology of childhood and youth, urban sociology, and social psychology. The author of *Elder Mistreatment: Deciding Who Is at Risk*, Ms. Johnson has also written numerous articles, book chapters, and professional reports on topics including elder neglect and abuse, elder guardianship, elder health and well-being, and gifted children. Among her many professional involvements have been the American Public Health Association, the American Public Welfare Association, the American Society on Aging, the British Gerontology Society, the Gerontological Society of America, and The National Committee for the Prevention of Elder Abuse.

Preface

The Administration on Aging funded the National Center on Elder Abuse (Center) to serve as a comprehensive resource for professionals and practitioners concerned with elder abuse. The Center is operated collaboratively by four organizations: the American Public Welfare Association, The National Association of State Units on Aging, the University of Delaware's College of Human Resources, and the National Committee for the Prevention of Elder Abuse (NCPEA).

NCPEA is using its official publication, *Journal of Elder Abuse & Neglect,* to conduct the work of the Center. This volume examines a vital issue for state and local program administrators as well as practitioners and the clients they serve: the ethical questions and dilemmas that surround the daily practice of professionals involved in elder abuse prevention and intervention. Discussion of "elder mistreatment: ethical issues, dilemmas, and decisions" is relevant and timely for all of us who are concerned about the nationwide increase in reports of elder abuse, neglect, and exploitation and the attending need to take preventive and remedial action in response to the reports while at the same time protecting the rights of vulnerable older persons.

The 1992 Amendments to the Older Americans Act call upon states to carry out vulnerable elder rights protection activities. Chapter 3 of Title VII emphasizes protection of elder rights as an integral part of the expanded State Programs for the Prevention of Elder Abuse, Neglect and Exploitation. Chapter 3 specifies that states use funds for conducting training with particular focus on prevention and enhancement of individual rights, self-determination, and autonomy. Succeeding sections of Chapter 3 of Title VII call upon states to promote development of state elder abuse, neglect, and exploitation systems of coordinated prevention and treatment programs that include prompt investigation to substantiate the accuracy of reported instances of abuse and, upon substantiation, to take steps to protect the health and welfare of the abused, neglected, and exploited older individual.

For some time experts in the field of elder abuse have been concerned about conflicting rights involved in elder abuse case work. In 1991, the National Aging Resource Center on Elder Abuse (NARCEA) gave voice to this concern. In discussing legal and ethical concerns as they relate to the development of a research agenda, NARCEA pointed out that the identification and investigation of elder abuse and neglect, and the many intervention programs and procedures designed to protect the health and welfare of the abused older person, may potentially involve a violation of the person's right to self-determination. NARCEA noted that when an elderly client is unable to protect himself or herself from abuse, neglect, and exploitation, all practitioners who intervene and provide services for that client find themselves faced with the difficult ethical dilemma of balancing the individual's right to autonomy with the individual's right to receive protection from the government. NARCEA observed that any intervention system imposed by government that potentially infringes on an individual's rights must be seen by society as fair and benevolent; and as preventing harm to, as well as promoting the welfare of, both the individual and society.

Elder Mistreatment: Ethical Issues, Dilemmas, and Decisions should serve as a valuable preparation to program administrators in developing training programs on protecting elder rights and to practitioners in preserving elder rights. Experts from a wide range of disciplines analyze three cases from their own professional perspective and discuss the application of ethical principles in practice. They do not always agree on the questions to be asked, the dilemmas to be faced, or the actions to be taken. But the reader gains a clearer understanding of these differences, which is one of the strengths of the volume. The reader is provided a comprehensive review of the ethical issues involved in developing and providing coordinated elder abuse prevention and treatment services.

The case studies also give a human face to elder mistreatment. The reader is moved beyond the abstract world of ethics into the concrete world of individual lives. Mary and Martha, John and Manny, and Bonnie come alive. As we follow the discussions by representatives of the various disciplines, we care about what happens to the people in the case studies.

I want to applaud the individual authors and Tanya Fusco Johnson, PhD, Editor, who volunteered to participate in the creation of what is indeed a special collection.

Fernando M. Torres-Gil, PhD
Assistant Secretary for Aging
U.S. Department of Health and Human Services

Chapter One

Ethics and Elder Mistreatment: Uniting Protocol with Practice

Tanya Fusco Johnson, MDiv, PhD

SUMMARY. This chapter focuses on the meaning of ethics in elder mistreatment. More specifically, ethical issues are distinguished from non-ethical issues and ethical dilemmas. The primary objective is to demystify ethics for elder-serving practitioners and to show how ethics can be a part of the treatment decision-making process. This process details "doing" ethics in the practice setting. It proposes a method for developing ethical practice at the multidisciplinary level. The multidisciplinary level starts with the client and professional and ends with the community-based multidisciplinary team. The latter include human services professionals who have the important task of transforming ethical protocols into practice. *[Article copies available from The Haworth Document Delivery Service: 1-800-342-9678.]*

INTRODUCTION

Harry Moody comments in the opening chapters of his new book, *Ethics in an Aging Society*. The growing interest in questions of

Tanya Fusco Johnson is Family Sociologist, Department of Sociology, University of Hawaii-Hilo, 200 West Kauili Street, Hilo, HI 96720.

The author would like to thank the colleagues who have reviewed this chapter. Special thanks go to Carol Thornhill, Project Officer at the Administration on Aging and to Rosalie Wolf, President of the National Committee for the Prevention of Elder Abuse, for their guidance and helpful critiques of all of the chapters in this publication.

[Haworth co-indexing entry note]: "Ethics and Elder Mistreatment: Uniting Protocol with Practice." Johnson, Tanya Fusco. Co-published simultaneously in *Journal of Elder Abuse & Neglect* (The Haworth Press, Inc.) Vol. 7, No. 2/3, 1995, pp. 1-18; and: *Elder Mistreatment: Ethical Issues, Dilemmas, and Decisions* (ed: Tanya Fusco Johnson) The Haworth Press, Inc., 1995, pp. 1-18. [Single or multiple copies of this are available from The Haworth Document Delivery Service: 1-800-342-9678, 9:00 a.m. - 5:00 p.m. (EST)].

ethics and aging in recent years has been stimulated by two broad trends: advances in medical technology that have led to dilemmas in clinical bioethics . . . and the coming of an aging society with rising numbers of dependent elderly people whose care raises far-reaching questions of social policy."

To his analysis we might add an increasing awareness of the ethical implications of professional and corporate behavior. . . . As awareness heightens, there seems to be a vague uneasiness about "doing ethics" in public.

–Msgr. Charles J. Fahey,
"Ethics Comes out of the Closet"
Aging Today, Nov./Dec., 1992

This chapter and those that follow address ethics and elder neglect and abuse–terms not likely to be defined by everyone in the same way. In fact, we may never have consensus on the meanings of ethics and elder mistreatment. This latter term will be used in the following pages to include both abuse and neglect. Definitions of ethics and elder mistreatment vary among cultures, subcultures, political jurisdictions, and even among members of the same professional group. Since American society is more heterogeneous than homogeneous with respect to role differentiation, regions, religions, legislation, allocations, and aspirations, we do not expect agreement on what is ethical or the nature and scope of elder mistreatment. Therefore, from the start, the authors want to make it clear that our objective is not to achieve consensus on which ethical theory is best or what specific circumstances constitute elder mistreatment either in theory or in practice.

Having differences in meaning, however, should not prevent us from discussing ethics and elder mistreatment and the issues they imply with any less urgency than other important, but more uniformly defined, issues. What elder serving human services professionals do agree on is the need to be "ethical" when they work with those involved in potential or actual abuse and neglect. This need is clearly stated in the recently completed doctoral dissertation of Britt-Inger Saveman entitled, *Formal Carers in Health Care and the Social Services Witnessing Abuse of the Elderly in Their Homes* (1994). Dr. Saveman's goal and ours is to encourage professionals to "do ethics in public" and, thus, to approach a level of care in which ethical practice is an integral part of our work. More specifically, in the chapters that follow, the authors will lay the groundwork for the process of ethical decision-making in cases of elder mistreatment. Each professional discipline looks to ethics as a means of preserving and protecting older adults' rights. When viewed in this way, ethics is central to the practitioner's role.

Ethics, as a subject of study, belongs to the field of philosophy. However, the practice of ethics is a part of every aspect of our lives whether personal or professional. First and last, philosophers are not expected to be practitioners, and practitioners do not have the leisure to study philosophical theories to any great length. Therefore, we need a bridge between the two worlds if we are to benefit from the contributions of both. This volume is intended to do this very thing–to identify principles in ethics and elder mistreatment, on the one hand, and practices on the other, in order to propose a unifying framework that incorporates both. This chapter introduces the process for joining theory with practice.

The chapters that follow will provide the reader with a variety of multidisciplinary ethical perspectives. These include medical, mental health, social welfare, legal, and religious ethics. The final chapter centers on ways to link the varieties of professional starting points to approach consensus in multidisciplinary ethical decision-making in cases of elder mistreatment.

Ethics has developed a reputation for being abstract, if not esoteric, and, thus, removed from ordinary life. At the same time much of our behavior is rooted in the ethical realm. It is our task in this chapter to demystify ethics as a concept, to identify ethical concerns that arise in serving older adults, and to show practitioners concrete ways of applying ethics in their cases of elder mistreatment. An important question to begin with is how one learns ethics. It may seem that practitioners need formal coursework in order to "do ethics." Certainly, special training is always helpful and should be encouraged. However, the authors of this book want to show how one can do ethics in the practice setting without formal coursework. Since ethics is a part of everyday life, each of us has developed some level of expertise although we may not be conscious of having done so. Our goal is to provide a way to strengthen the skills we already possess and suggest ways to further develop them. Before we begin to clarify this process, we must make it clear that this volume does not pursue a debate about whether elder mistreatment is ethical or not or a critique of how ethical the victims and violators are. Rather, it addresses how elder-serving human services professionals may use ethics in their work with victims and violators of elder mistreatment as well as one another.

We will begin the discussion of doing ethics by including a basic ethics vocabulary. This vocabulary provides a general framework in which to understand ethical issues, dilemmas, and decision-making.

ON THE MEANING OF ETHICS

The root of the word ethics comes from the Greek "ethos" or "ethikos" meaning moral or character. Morals, in turn, fall within the sphere of "mores" or cultural rules. Here, culture does not refer to a specific culture. Rather, it refers to the development of a script for good conduct that takes place in ongoing organized groups to signal right from wrong. The script lays the foundation for what the group "ought to do" in our conduct as compared with what we may actually "choose to do." The "mores" of our group provide a marker to show us the degree of congruence between what is expected in our conduct and our performance. John Hospers, in his book *Human Conduct: An Introduction to the Problems of Ethics,* observed that ethics is a qualitative concept.

> Ethics not merely describes moral ideals held by human beings, but asks which ideal is better than others. . . . Two people might agree on the empirical facts of the case and yet disagree about what course of action to follow in view of the facts. Here lies the great difference between ethics . . . on the one hand and the empirical sciences–physics, chemistry, biology, psychology, and so on–on the other. (1961, pp. 6-7)

As a legal guardian for an older relative, we may have wished to have given better care to help preserve that relative's health. However, we may not have had the time, energy, resources, or motivation to carry out what we fully intended to do–what we believed we ought to have done according to our ethical script for caregiving. Ethics is a guide for right conduct, but there is no guarantee that we will measure up to the expectations contained in these ethics as we exercise our everyday rights and duties. If we do not measure up to the standards, it does not, necessarily, mean that we are unethical. Ethical conduct includes both a measure of degree and a kind of conduct. With regard to degree, one may be extremely ethical, moderately ethical or minimally ethical. In the context of offering adequate care, if one is extremely ethical, one may do everything possible, and more, for the care-receiver. Or, that individual may be only moderately involved with care decisions. Or, perhaps, one does as little as possible, but, nevertheless, still provides care. In the case of the latter, we would not consider minimal care unethical. It is merely inadequate to meet the other person's needs.

Further, we cannot say that, if one does not do what is prescribed for the care of the dependent older adult, one's conduct is unethical. Failing to do something because of personal or material circumstances is not necessarily a sign of being unethical. We might consider this an unmet obligation, but this failure might signal a legitimate limitation rather than unethical conduct. Returning to the example of guardianship for the relative who needs care, one may engage substitutes to offer the needed care. Finding substitutes is one way to preserve the ethical conduct prescribed by the group's expectations in the face of insufficient personal resources. The latter could be in the form of asking others to volunteer their help in the care of the older adult or paying others to help. On the other hand, individuals may be considered unethical if they consciously and purposefully violate what the group expects they "ought to do" when nothing is preventing them from compliance with the rules. If a person deliberately chooses to do nothing to help when that individual should and could, we may consider that behavior to be unethical.

Ethical conduct is based on values–words or phrases that signal what one "ought to do or be." Examples of values that pertain to older adults in American culture include autonomy, personal safety, trust, adequate care, accountability, and least restrictive alternatives. Values like these are essential for the group's ongoing social existence. They tend to be codified into rules and expressed repeatedly in a number of communication mediums–songs, stories, pictures, formal gatherings, and conversations. Ethical rules need not always be in written form; however, clearly delineated, recorded values typify the ethics of most groups.

There is one final qualification for the meaning of ethics. Every action does not constitute an ethical action. There are a number of behaviors that do not represent ethical conduct. Routine behaviors to supply basic needs and personal preferences would be included among them. Where we shop for clothing or how we carry out household tasks illustrate the former. How much money we spend on clothes or "the styles" are in the arena of the non-ethical. Choosing a particular color for a nightgown we purchase for a friend who is hospitalized, the kind of food we prepare for the disabled adult, or how we do that person's laundry do not require ethical decisions. They are simply examples of personal preferences or taste. These are matters of partiality, rather than expectations rooted in particular values. Therefore, at the outset of our work as practitioners in "doing ethics in public," we need to identify which actions are in the ethical realm and which are not.

ETHICS AND ELDER MISTREATMENT

In American society, when ethics is used by professionals in the context of elder mistreatment, we are speaking broadly of a common value of preventing unnecessary suffering (Johnson, 1991). In some instances, suffering may be necessary to maintain one's quality of life. We must be clear, therefore, about how we decide what is necessary and what is not. For example, it may be necessary to restrain someone in a chair or bed to prevent falls. One may be over-medicated or under-medicated causing dizziness, nausea, or some other problems, but these side effects may, nevertheless, be "necessary" to preserve one's quality of life. Therefore, we must call these experiences necessary suffering and, as such, they are not unethical. Ethical conduct is measured by the degree to which one's actions, directly or indirectly, protect individuals from unnecessary suffering.

While each professional may identify different circumstances as mistreatment or use different words to describe elder mistreatment in their professional jurisdiction, the common goal is protecting citizens from suffering. This includes suffering unnecessary to the maintenance of the quality of life of older adults either at their own hands or the hands of others. While some professionals may disagree that both self and other abuse and neglect are appropriate categories to include in the elder mistreatment population, others do include these varieties. Therefore, to provide for all possibilities, this chapter and those that follow, cover self and other neglect, and self and other abuse as well as combinations of the four.

Having stated that ethics refers to right conduct and that conduct for elder-serving professionals means preventing unnecessary suffering, the next step is to identify the sources for the values we adopt. The starting point for such an exercise must inevitably be context-specific. In American society, we are not likely to have universal values–a price we pay for diversity. Therefore, we may anticipate a range of ethical rules. The substantive content of ethics depends on the mores (morality) of the communities in which we participate–home, school, religion, physical and mental health care, legal care, social welfare, the educational system, the workplace, interpersonal relations, and our own personal standards. It is because of these multiple settings and the variety of circumstances they produce that ethical conduct has so many meanings. Certainty is further compromised by our awareness that there is not, necessarily, consensus on what is right conduct among communities in the same subculture or among members of the same communities. For example, elder serving human services professionals may agree that older adults should have control over their environment, even those who are dependent, but there may be considerable disagreement on how that control is defined.

Ethics in cases of elder mistreatment may operate in two spheres. It may center on issues or dilemmas (or both). Joan Callahan (1988, p. 6) defines issues as "questions" arising from singular values, and dilemmas as "questions" that emerge because two or more values are in conflict. For example, adequate care, guardianship for mentally disabled adults, and protecting vulnerable adults are *values*. The *issues* tied to these three might be: Can the son provide adequate care for his elderly dependent parents? Should community volunteers serve as legal guardians for an older adult? Is a moderately dementing adult, living alone, able to protect herself? These are singular points of concern in which decisions are based on the unit values.

On the other hand, ethical *dilemmas* refer to those situations in which there are conflicts among two or more values. These values may be found within an individual or between or among individuals. An example of a dilemma within the individual would be a desire to protect oneself from a mistreating relative while at the same time, wishing to preserve the relationship with the offender because of the broader benefits of kinship. By remaining in that relationship, the competent older adult is fully aware that the choice may make that individual vulnerable to victimization.

Ethical dilemmas may also occur between individuals, between professionals and their clients, or among professionals. An example that illustrates this web of interpersonal dilemmas is the conflict between the client's happiness and safety (in circumstances where one must choose one or the other). Should one be allowed to live in his/her own home because it is the individual's preference even if that individual may be vulnerable to falls, burns, or other harm? There are some who might say one should seek happiness at all costs, even if the individual becomes vulnerable to harm by doing so. There are others who might say one cannot be happy until or unless that individual is safe. Still others might say, the determination should be made by the group, not a specific individual, to decide what will give happiness to the members involved in the relationship as a whole. Another ethical interpretation might be to defer to some impartial authority, letting the individual or agency in authority decide for the client, even if the latter is able to make decisions competently. Another viewpoint might suggest that how happiness and safety are evaluated depends on the specific situation. In this approach, every case and, subsequently, every outcome would be unique. Finally, there may be some who would not consider happiness to be a part of the ethical domain at all. Thus, in this particular case, if happiness is removed from the equation, the ethical dilemma is resolved since there are no longer conflicting values.

While it may be relatively easy for practitioners to give their opinions on what they believe to be right in the case of choosing happiness or safety, other parties in the situation may have difficulty agreeing. Family members, friends, others in the informal network, and other helping professionals, even those in the same profession or same workplace may have different views on what is right conduct in this ethical dilemma. In fact, more likely than not, we may expect different starting points when deciding what to do when there are ethical dilemmas. How, then, can we work toward consensus in the face of such ethical diversity? This is the task we have set for ourselves in the book. In the remainder of this chapter, we will formulate a means for managing this diversity by (1) identifying the varieties of ethical starting points; (2) distinguishing between ethical protocols and ethical practice; and (3) proposing a way for multidisciplinary teams to approach agreement in ethical decision-making in abuse and neglect.

VARIETIES OF ETHICAL STARTING POINTS

The field of ethics includes three major branches–metaethics, ideology, and application. All three are important bedfellows in our understanding of how we develop our ethical standards both as laypersons and professionals.

Metaethics

Metaethics centers on raising questions about the ethical domain and the varieties of ethical conceptualizations it has spawned. It is not the job of the metatheoretician to espouse a particular theory or ethical judgment. Rather, metaethics is limited to the study of how we decide what is ethical. The function of metaethics is to ask how individuals and groups arrive at different ethical starting points. This branch of ethics continually reminds us that "ethics" is a relative concept. Observations of how people come to adopt certain ethical standards shows the importance of this aspect of their lives. At the same time we recognize that the phenomenon of ethics is subjective. Therefore, we do not look to metaethics for unifying standards.

Ideology

Ideology, the second branch of ethics, includes the ethical theories that have been systematically constructed to make judgments of right conduct and to explicitly or implicitly state beliefs that are wrong. Most of us are familiar with a number of broader system ideologies–Christianity, Judaism, Democracy, Utilitarianism, Existentialism, Hedonism, and the norms of subcultures such as African Americans or Japanese Americans. Ideologies can be divided into sacred and secular. The sacred refers to religious belief systems. Secular includes ideologies that are beliefs in the areas of political, social, and ethnic ethics. These categories point out the fact that one may embrace a number of ideologies at the same time. Therefore, we may expect individuals and groups to draw from several systems in the management of their daily lives. This fact makes it difficult to track the bases for one's ethical conduct. Finally, ideologies are theories, but not solutions. Therefore, they remain couched in speculation rather than the specifying solutions. May and Sharratt (1994) make this point in their book *Applied Ethics.* "Each of these theories may give a different answer to questions. . . . In our view, ethics is not a science that provides such solutions; rather the study of ethics enriches one's deliberations but leaves the conclusion of those deliberations often unresolved" (p. 8).

Applied

The third branch of ethics is called applied ethics. In this form, theory is translated into practice by means of interpretation. There are two broad contexts in the practice setting–private ethics and public ethics. Private ethics refer to guidelines we personally employ in the informal setting. The informal setting is an environment that allows for flexibility and latitude in beliefs with little censure from those in authority in the formal system (unless private ethics violates public interpretation based on the law). Private ethics may be further divided into personal and interpersonal categories. Personal ethics are what each of us as individuals may create in the privacy of our thoughts and actions, especially actions over which we have considerable control. These ideologies may be congruent with those of one's subculture, but they may also be in conflict. For example, an adult child may believe he has no obligation to help his frail father. Meanwhile, the rest of the family may operate from a different ethic that expects his help.

Interpersonal ethics includes actions intended to promote right conduct between and among two or more individuals in the informal setting. Sometimes, there may be clashes between personal and interpersonal ethics. In the company of others, one may dominate, capitulate, subordinate, or negotiate ethical differences. In the case of the son and his frail father, he would be in conflict with his sister who provides most of the care for the father. She expects him to share in the care. Private ethics, whether personal or interpersonal, are difficult to discern because they are subjective. However, this fact does not diminish the importance of discovering one's private ethics, whether a client or a professional. Private ethics have as much power and impact as ethics originating in the formal sector.

Therefore, professionals must discover the private ethics of the clients whom they serve along with their publicly expressed beliefs.

Public ethics refers to formal protocols and clearly defined plans for action. Principles have been established systemically and recorded by those who have been authorized to establish and preserve them. With public ethics, one is held accountable for one's actions because there are clear sanctions. Clients turn to their sacred and secular ideologies and the rules that have been generated in those spheres. Professionals in the practice setting turn to ethical protocols stipulated by their professions. Typical guidelines for ethical practice include (1) governing policies for the discipline, (2) professional codes of ethics, and (3) agency or workplace policy. These three types of protocols constitute the foundations for ethical practice.

ETHICAL PROTOCOL AND ETHICAL PRACTICE

Each elder serving discipline has its own protocols. They include policies to protect individuals and groups from mistreatment. These policies are designed as safeguards should others not treat older adults ethically. For example, the legal system turns to the law. Social welfare systems have procedural manuals that reflect the law and that are designed to protect individuals from themselves and others; religion is based on some "polity" or recorded rules for right conduct in religious behavior; an illustration of the Judeo-Christian polity would be the Bible; and the mental and physical health care systems turn to practice manuals, informed consent, and advance directives. In addition, each of the disciplines has its own codes of ethics governing the conduct of the practitioner. Third, agencies and organization may also have specific policies on ethics tailored to their particular program. These sets of protocols are what the practitioner brings to the elder mistreatment setting. They will be central in decision-making, but protocols do not translate automatically into ethical decisions.

Ethical decisions are much more than protocols. They transcend the protocol and, at the same time, give this ethical script meaning. Protocols describe what is ethical, but they cannot take on the process necessary for deciding how to achieve the ethical ends dictated by the protocol. This process is what we call ethical practice. Least restrictive behaviors, adequate care, etc., are common values put forth in professional protocols. To achieve these goals, however, one must apply these values to the specific context of the client. Least restrictive behaviors and adequate care only take on meaning when embodied in the circumstances of a particular case.

Ethical practice (the doing of ethics) is the process of translating the scripted protocol into individuals' social conduct with all of their particularities. The task of ethical practice is to interpret the protocol and apply its essential meaning case by case.

The goal of ethical practice is to arrive at a decision or decisions that will protect older adults from mistreatment. To move toward this goal, one must, of course, start with protocols. The professional must identify all of the ethical policy sources operating and, in the process, clarify the ethical issues and dilemmas that may be present in a particular case. This practice phase of ethics leads professionals into dynamic, demanding, and unpredictable situations. The certainty we derive from the protocol fades as the relationships with clients and colleagues become more involved. Ethics and its practice is an intimate experience so professionals must be prepared to probe but to be patient with a process that, in contrast with protocol, has no delineated script.

The process of ethical practice identifies values, issues, and dilemmas, and then proceeds to find points of agreement and disagreement among the parties in the case. There are three basic steps in this process: information, deliberation, and negotiation. In the first step, one gathers information about ethical starting points. The practitioner asks who believes what, and why, and by whose authority. The second step is to deliberate. In this phase, all parties clarify meaning, listen to each other's ethical concerns, discuss, and, perhaps, debate differences. The primary objective is to know the ethical orientation of all parties. Finally, after deliberation, there is the phase of negotiation. This last step calls for the development of consensus by means of give and take, compromise, reconciliation, and revision with a view to meeting everyone's needs, not as absolutely as perhaps they were first stated but, nevertheless, arriving at a mutually crafted decision that respects the equanimity of each ethical starting point. This last step of negotiation cannot be achieved without cooperation and commitment to create a truly joint outcome. Rigidity, stubbornness, and silence must be absent from a negotiated decision. Finally, negotiation is not "compromise," it is a created agreement.

This approach to decision-making is similar to the "communicative ethics" of Jurgen Habermas (1990). Thomas McCarthy summarizes the notion of Habermas's communicative ethics in much the same language as stated above:

> What Habermas calls "communicative ethics" is grounded in the "fundamental norms of rational speech." Communication that is oriented toward reaching understanding inevitably involves the reciprocal rising and recognition of validity claims. Claims to truth and

rightness, if radically challenged, can be redeemed only through argumentative discourse leading to rationally motivated consensus. (1978, p. 325)

Harry Moody in *Ethics in an Aging Society* has adopted the communicative ethic as his model:

In both clinical and social ethics, I have stressed that I favor the replacement of abstract principles like autonomy and justice with an essentially communicative or "procedural" ethic. . . . The value of a communicative ethic is to find commonly agreed upon ways of negotiating our differences when we fail to agree in binding principles or rules. Institutions that promote communication and dialogue increase the likelihood of a "wise" outcome. (Moody, 1991, p. 13)

Professional protocols do not provide plans for action. Such plans come from the communicative encounter among professionals and clients in the practice setting. Protocols are the safety nets that protect older adults from mistreatment, but we must look to ethical practice to implement policies prescribed in protocols. Consequently, when we talk about "doing ethics," we are referring to the process we use when we encounter each patient, client, and colleague. This process includes gathering information, deliberation over differences, and negotiation that works toward consensus.

ETHICAL PRACTICE IN MULTIDISCIPLINARY GROUPS

Implicit in the discussion of ethical practice above is the potential for a number of groups to be involved in decision-making. The first group is made up of the professional and the client or clients. Other groups may be involved in the practice process, depending on the nature and scope of mistreatment. Some communities around the country have formed elder serving multidisciplinary teams to help victims of abuse and neglect. Hwalek et al. (1991) discuss four types: hospital-based, family practice, consortiums, and community-based. The goal for these teams is to pool professional resources and provide greater objectivity in decision-making. The greater the number of professionals who comprise these teams, the more complex the task of approaching consensus.

Ethical practice, as defined in the preceding section, presumes that, in a sense, the professional and client make up the first multidisciplinary team.

This does not mean that the professional must compromise social distance or objectivity. Professional and client "roles" need to remain intact. However, if practitioners are to engage in ethical practice, they must give the ethical starting points of their clients as much credence as their own. To that end, professionals must also be prepared to clearly distinguish their own and their clients' ethical protocols, as well as their clients' private ethical standards.

For example, it may be important to know that the client is an Asian, never-married, Buddhist, disabled female or one's clients are a homosexual male couple, one of whom is a Christian Scientist and the other is a Catholic, and both of whom are on welfare. Each of these pieces of information carries with it its own ethics history. In addition, their private ethics may require absolute loyalty to the mistreater, no matter how dangerous the situation. Their position could be based on their feeling that they have the right to be abused or neglected. Deciding what is ethical for them along with what the professional thinks should be ethical conduct is the practitioner's central objective.

Ethical practice presumes that the clients' protocols are on an equal footing with that of the professionals.' Their ethics are just as valued and valid as those of the professional. Therefore, practitioners and their clients form the first multidisciplinary team in ethical decision-making. Although ethical decision-making takes time, the benefit is, as Moody proposes, a "wise" outcome, an outcome that has the potential for resolving the mistreatment. The professional who enters the life of a client must also enter into a relationship. Anthony Cortese observes:

> Relationships, not reason nor justice, are the essence of life and morality. . . . We are very much aware of the political, scientific, theological and metaphysical doctrines to which we ourselves subscribe. But we are scarcely conscious of the parallel tenets held by persons of other ethnic, racial, cultural and religious groups. (1990, p. 158)

He goes on to say that we can be conscious of the other ethics when we participate in a "relationship."

The relationships between professionals and clients also imply interdependence. This is true of any encounter, no matter how objective. The client's success is the professional's success as well. Once they have joined together in a relationship, they are "in it together." Whatever the outcome, some level of joint action has taken place. Another feature of the relationship is power. According to Knud Logstrup, power is a very important part of that relationship. "We may very much dislike the idea of having another person's life in our hands. . . . Nevertheless, this is wishful thinking which has nothing to do with reality. For in reality . . . eventually we will have someone's entire destiny in our power" (Logstrup, 1971 p. 56). Because elder serving professionals often find themselves in this situation, willingly or unwillingly, they must do all they can to protect their client from exploitation. This can only be accomplished by mutual participation which implies mutual cooperation.

In the words of a colleague, Paul G. Blanton, to whom this volume is dedicated, who modelled professional ethics so beautifully until his untimely death in an automobile accident shortly after he wrote these words:

> No thing exists except as a part of this ongoing, creating and procreating, and interdependent process. . . . What this has to do with elder abuse is that each participant in an adult protective case is related. An older man—bedfast and alone, lying in his own feces and urine, dying of a malignancy, without food or medicine—is you. This awareness is fundamental—not whether he is eligible for Medicaid, not if he is mean and deserves his misfortune, not if he has the mental capacity to make sound decisions, and not whether we should label his case "abuse" or "neglect." His need for help, first of all is our need. (Blanton, 1989, p. 31).

Once again we observe union between the practitioner and the client. They become connected in the moment the practitioner offers assistance.

When several professionals are helping one's client or clients, their ethical standards may not be uniform. Therefore, they offer a greater challenge to consensus in decision-making. It is probably more often the case than not that several different professionals are involved in resolving the individuals' elder mistreatment. There may be a protective services social worker, an ombudsman, a lawyer, a social worker from an area agency on aging or similar group, a clergy person, a physician, and a mental health professional. Each of these public agents arrives with the backdrop of his/her respective ethics protocols. These protocols range from rules established by the federal, state, and local governments to the governing bodies of the various professions, to agency or workplace policies, to specific professions' codes of ethics for their practitioners.

Given this diversity of starting points for ethical protocols, including the spectrum of ethical concerns takes time. One way to economize on time is to limit the number of protocols the professional must address. For example, one might wish to discourage the clients from articulating their ethical starting points or those of the mistreater. Professionals may feel they can take some shortcuts because of their expertise and experience in similar cases. Since they are empowered to act in the client's best interest anyway, they may not believe they need to identify their client's ethical standards. Or, the practitioner might choose to limit the number of other professionals involved, thus limiting the ethical agendas that professionals would need to confront. Another way to save time might be to solicit colleague input from those whose protocols are the same, especially if they should happen to represent other disciplines. Clearly, these approaches would aid the practitioner in promoting uniformity in ethical decision-making. However, one cannot call any of these detours true ethical decision-making. Negotiation imposes the obligation to hear the starting points of all parties involved. To do otherwise is to be unethical. The question one must ask is "If you do not identify all of the ethical issues and dilemmas operating in a given situation, and do not complete the process of information, deliberation, and negotiation, can you make an ethical decision?" Based on the usage of the terms developed in this chapter, the answer is no.

Finally, professionals must not co-opt power from other professionals who may play a role in the case. Outcomes based on multidisciplinary professional decision-making using information, deliberation, and negotiation are the best protection against such exploitation. It is critical that everyone on the multidisciplinary team have equal authority in the decision-making process. Sometimes members come to the team with greatly differing statuses which would seem to confound democratic communication. Participating in the ethical decision-making process does not compromise one's status. Rather, it suspends it in the decision-making setting in order to establish the best plan of care. Doing ethics is not about status; it is about providing the best ethical decision the group can fashion. It is hammering out ways to fulfill and enforce decisions. This cannot take place if members of the group exercise superiority in status. Doing ethics requires openness, being able to listen and to learn from one another, skill that can only work if members of the group act as partners. John Kultgen considers these encounters partnerships beginning with the client.

> Professionals compose partnerships with their clients and with their employers in which all parties must make ethical decisions. . . . Medical ethics is not identical with physicians' ethics, as often assumed. It comprises principles that are valid for medical decisions whoever makes them and in the formulation of which all parties should have a share. The same applies to the ethical principles of law, engineering, and other professions. . . . Everyone, therefore, should have a say in the content of professionals' ethics. (1988, p. 6)

Ethical decisions are like fitting pieces together into a picture puzzle that all parties have had a hand creating. The fact that all parties contribute with equal participation helps assure that the final picture will be the best one possible because all participated in its development.

DECISIONS AND RESOLUTION

The last terms that need some explanation are decisions and resolutions. Ethical decisions are not synonymous with resolutions. Decisions are proposals for resolution, but they are far from resolution. Only the passage of time and the eventual enactment of the proposals can lead to resolving dilemmas. Logstrup defines these distinctions. "The life blood of resolution is discernment, which in due time will bring it to a state of maturity. . . . The decision should have had time to mature in order that there might be greater discernment and certainty" (Logstrup, 1971: p. 157). Therefore, when the multidisciplinary team is in the negotiating phase of deliberations, it is only making decisions. In effect, it is only the beginning of the long journey to resolving the dilemmas, not the end. Further, the process from decision to resolution will likely involve a group other than the multidisciplinary team. Membership should be made up of all who will be expected to play a role in the resolution process at the time the multidisciplinary team made its decision. All the multidisciplinary team may be expected to do is prepare a plan of action. How that action is carried out and its degree of success will come about some time in the future after the decision is implemented.

CONCLUSION

What we end with is what we all knew from the start. Ethics is a complicated subject, but it need not be an esoteric pastime for a few theorists. As we move toward a greater awareness of how some older adults live the last years of their lives and a realization that we as practitioners may hold their future in our hands, ethical practice has taken on a special importance in the work of elder-serving professionals. We need to make ethics an important part of our professional work for the welfare and well-being of our clients. Ethical protocols offer the foundation for this practice. However, each professional must interpret his/her protocols anew with every new case. Informed by our various ethical protocols, ethical practice creates the possibilities for realizing the values embedded in those protocols to protect the rights of older adults so that they may live a life free from unnecessary suffering.

Ethical practice includes information, discovering all of the protocols operating in a particular situation, but being aware that not every situation has its roots in ethics. There may be issues such as routine behaviors in daily living or personal preferences in elder mistreatment cases that are non-ethical in nature. Therefore, practitioners need to separate these orientations from those that are truly ethical. The second step is the deliberation in which all parties listen to one another, discuss, and debate differences. The third and final step is the movement toward the negotiation of differing ethical realities when we are aware that there may be several operating. Ethical protocols are static and ongoing, but ethical practice requires continual interpretation in an ever-changing environment.

Ethical practice leads to decisions about managing issues and dilemmas. Effective decision-making must include all parties involved in those issues and dilemmas. Therefore, decision-making will very likely involve a number of multidisciplinary teams. The first team is comprised of the client and the professional. Unless the professional is able to understand the client's ethical starting point, it is not possible to come to a meaningful ethical decision (given the model of information, deliberation, and negotiation). Several other multidisciplinary teams are likely to form, depending on the case. If there are a number of professionals, ethical practice for decision-making will include many levels of participation. Regardless of the number, all parties are expected to give and take with equanimity. While they may not be equals in professional status, they must be equal with regard to decision-making in order to develop the best plan of care for the older adult. Ethical decision-making can only function effectively through negotiating realities for all of the participants, clients and professionals. All must work together as partners.

Once the multidisciplinary teams have made ethical decisions, this does not automatically mean that the case will be successfully concluded. A decision is just a proposal for a plan of action. After decisions are reached, the final step is to advocate for, adapt to, and support implementation by appropriate parties of the decisions so that the resolution will be congruent with the decision.

The terms which have been defined in this chapter will guide the reader in the discussion of ethical issues, dilemmas, and decisions in the chapters that follow. The next chapter will present three cases of potential or actual mistreatment. Those that follow have been written by elder serving practitioners, physical and mental health providers, social workers, lawyers, and clergy. Each professional discusses these cases from an ethical practice perspective so that we might see how various disciplines approach the same ethical issues and dilemmas. The final chapter will pull together the discussion in the previous chapters and propose concrete ways to integrate ethical practice into the multidisciplinary context.

> The need for protection from harm is the single, universal factor in all protective cases. Without this need, there is no protective case. Everything else varies from case to case. To know that we are part of the suffering and dying life of the old man is necessary if we are to understand and carry out responsibilities properly. It makes no difference if we are attorneys, administrators, researchers, caseworkers, judges, or sheriffs; this fact alone is primary. All that follows from this perception is different because of this perception.
>
> –Blanton, 1989, p. 31

REFERENCES

Blanton, P. G. (1989). Zen and the art of adult protective services: In search of a unified view. *Journal of Elder Abuse & Neglect*, 1(1), 27-34.

Callahan, J. C. (1988). *Ethical issues in professional life*. New York, NY: Oxford University Press.

Cortese, A. (1990). *Ethnic ethics. The restructuring of moral theory*. Albany, NY: State University of New York Press.

Cortese, A. (1990). *Ethical issues in professional life*. New York, NY: State University of New York Press.

Habermas, J. (1990). *Moral consciousness and communicative action*. (trans. Christian Lenhardt and Shierry Weber Nicholsen.) Cambridge, MA: MIT Press.

Hospers, J. (1961). *Human conduct: An introduction to the problems of ethics*. New York, NY: Harcourt, Brace and World, Inc.

Hwalek, M., Williamson, D. & Stahl, C. (1991). Community-based M-team roles: A job analysis. *Journal of Elder Abuse & Neglect* 3(3), 45-71.

Johnson, T. F. (1981). *Elder mistreatment: Deciding who is at risk*. Westport, CT: Greenwood Publishing Group.

Kultgen, J. (1988). *Ethics and professionalism*. Philadelphia, PA: University of Pennsylvania Press.

Logstrup, K. E. (1971). *The ethical demand*. Philadelphia, PA: Fortress Press.

McCarthy, T. (1978). *The critical theory of Jurgen Habermas*. Cambridge, MA: MIT Press.

May, K. & Sharratt, S. C. (1994). *Applied ethics: A multicultural approach*. Englewood Cliffs, NJ: Prentice Hall.

Moody, H. R. (1992). *Ethics in an aging society*. Baltimore, MD: The Johns Hopkins University Press.

Saveman, B. (1994). *Formal carers in health care and the social services: Witnessing abuse of the elderly in their homes*. Umea, Sweden: Umea University Medical Dissertation.

Chapter Two

Three Case Studies of Elder Mistreatment: Identifying Ethical Issues

Vicki Kryk, MSW

SUMMARY. Three case studies involving ethical issues in elder mistreatment are presented. They were created from a variety of actual situations to illustrate the range and complexity of ethical issues that professionals encounter in elder mistreatment and to serve as the basis for discussion of ethical issues by professionals from a variety of disciplines in subsequent chapters of the publication.

Problems of physical and mental disability, relational loss, and mistreatment in institutional settings are illustrated. Elements of self neglect as well as neglect and abuse by others are contained in the cases, and intentional and unintentional mistreatment are portrayed. The author highlights some of the ethical dilemmas presented by each of the three cases. *[Article copies available from The Haworth Document Delivery Service: 1-800-342-9678.]*

The three cases of mistreatment presented in this chapter are the basis for the discussion of ethical issues in the chapters that follow. Professionals from a variety of disciplines will bring to the discussion perspectives rooted in the ethical standards of their professions. The situations pre-

Vicki Kryk is Program Manager, Adult Protective Services and Guardianship Unit, Adult and Family Services Section, North Carolina Division of Social Services, Raleigh, NC 27603-5905.

[Haworth co-indexing entry note]: "Three Case Studies of Elder Mistreatment: Identifying Ethical Issues." Kryk, Vicki. Co-published simultaneously in *Journal of Elder Abuse & Neglect* (The Haworth Press, Inc.) Vol. 7, No. 2/3, 1995, pp. 19-30; and: *Elder Mistreatment: Ethical Issues, Dilemmas, and Decisions* (ed: Tanya Fusco Johnson) The Haworth Press, Inc., 1995, pp. 19-30. [Single or multiple copies of this article are available from The Haworth Document Delivery Service: 1-800-342-9678, 9:00 a.m. - 5:00 p.m. (EST)].

sented in these cases do not represent any one particular client or case. They are composites, crafted from cases shared by the other contributing authors and from personal experience in the field of Adult Protective Services (APS). These cases were purposefully designed to illustrate a wide variety of issues to give the authors a basis for discussion of their professional ethics as applied to each of these cases. The fact that these cases may look very "real" to the reader is a testimony to the complex nature of many of the situations involving mistreatment that practitioners encounter in their practices.

The three cases illustrate both potential and actual elder mistreatment. They represent problems of disability, relational loss, and institutional abuse. There are elements of self neglect and abuse as well as neglect or abuse by caregivers. Instances of intentional and unintentional mistreatment as well as situations of victims and mistreaters reversing roles are portrayed. These cases are intended to represent the broad range of clients, living arrangements, and types of mistreatment that elder-serving professionals encounter as they provide services.

CASE ONE

Mary and Martha

Mary is 70 years old, widowed, and lives in a rural area with her sister Martha. She received an in-home psychiatric consultation to evaluate her competence to live independently with her sister, who is 76 years old. Mary was referred to a case manager in the agency on aging by an anonymous phone caller who complained that she was dumping garbage around her property. An initial social service evaluation disclosed that there was refuse outside the kitchen door and window, but the client claimed that it was her sons who discarded the garbage this way. Her bills and other mail were stacked carelessly in one place where, she said, her sons could find them when they came on their monthly visit to help her. She said that if she had better vision she would be able to pay her bills herself. Her sons had taken care of her bills on their last visit, she said; but, in fact, the statements from the utility companies showed that her payments were overdue. There was little food in the house (her sons brought food each month, she said), and what was available was mostly spoiled. Meals-on-Wheels was making deliveries on a regular basis; however, Mary and her sister appeared malnourished, leading the case manager to suspect that the women were not eating the meals that were delivered.

Mary had always been a tidy housekeeper, managed the household budget even when her husband was still alive, and took pride in being able to help others. She has been a member of her church for 62 years and regularly attended worship service as well as being active in the women's groups, until the care of her sister required her to stay home more often. Church members frequently visit Mary and her sister and provide the only social contacts other than Mary's sons.

She acknowledged difficulties with her memory, but not more than "anyone else my age would have." Her mental examination revealed evidence of moderately severe dementia. As is characteristic of many patients with Alzheimer's type disease, her social graces were maintained and, in fact, she had the demeanor of someone who took pride in herself despite her disheveled appearance. Neither she nor her sister had bathed recently. She insisted, however, that her sister was well cared for and that her sons were always willing to help out. She became defensive and visibly annoyed when questions implied that she was not able to adequately take care of herself or her sister. In some ways her sister, who had suffered a stroke, was of greater concern since she was unable to communicate her needs. Mary was responsible for administering her sister's blood pressure medication, but it had not been given on a regular basis over the past year. Mary agreed to have a visiting nurse check her sister's blood pressure which was elevated. She also consented to a physical exam for herself which revealed bruises on her right hip and right arm. She attributed these to a fall a few days earlier. She described the fall vaguely and defensively, leaving little doubt that her memory precluded an accurate retelling of the circumstances surrounding the fall.

Several visits over the period of a month revealed that the sister's health was stabilizing, probably due to the intervention by the visiting nurse. Mary insisted that she could take care of herself and her sister and, therefore, refused homemaker services or offers of assistance for her sister's hygiene.

The sons were reached by telephone and were able to arrange to meet with the caseworker. Their homes were in the city about 30 miles away. They brought food when they came. They appeared to the case manager to be minimally supportive of their mother and aunt. They insisted that when their current business obligations were concluded over the next couple of months, they were going to make another attempt to move them both to their neighborhood in the city. There was a senior high rise there where a friend had situated his mother. If their business arrangements fell into place, they hoped to have some money to contribute to the move. Mary, of course, felt this would not be feasible for them, however. "They really can't afford it," she insisted; "the business is shaky; it's hard for them to admit it." Additionally, she didn't feel comfortable living in a big city; she would lose the contact with and support of her church. She was also concerned about moving her sister to a high rise where people lived "on top" of each other.

Ethical Issues

The ethical issues raised by this situation include the values of self-determination, society's responsibility to protect its citizens, a family's responsibility to protect its members, and the principle of nonmaleficence or doing no harm. The dilemmas created by conflicting or competing values pose an additional problem for professionals in resolving the dilemmas and particular circumstances of the case. The question of Mary's competence may create such a dilemma. Her level of impaired competence and inability to care for herself and her sister versus the desire of the two women to remain independent and in their home creates a dilemma between the need to protect those who cannot protect themselves and the right of self-determination. The circumstances of this case may require a definitive answer to the question of Mary's competence and may subject her to the stress of an incompetence hearing. If a hearing were held, the dilemma would still not be resolved. If Mary were found to be competent, the question might be raised of how much monitoring by agencies, friends, and family would be needed and appropriate. Mary obviously has some mental impairment and may not be able to safely care for herself and Martha, even if she were found to be legally competent. If she were to be found incompetent, a dilemma might still exist in deciding how much decision-making power Mary should retain since she does have some ability to make choices and state preferences.

The dilemma of Mary and Martha's right to self-determination and society's role to protect them is perhaps the most frequently encountered conflict for professionals working with elder mistreatment cases. Elderly victims may make a choice to remain at home before experiencing a decline in their physical or mental health. Even when such a decision had been reached, professionals often find the need to question what is best for the elderly victim after that person suffers a severe decline in health. A related ethics issue raised by the case of Mary and Martha is whether society's role changes when elderly adults experience such a high degree of functional loss that their lives are endangered.

The broader role of society to protect all of its citizens also plays a part in this case. The neighbors have a right to be protected from any health hazards created by the garbage being thrown into the yard. A conflict may exist between Mary's rights and those of the neighbors that would require drawing professionals into a decision-making role. At what point does the garbage become a health hazard? When should health authorities be notified, and who should be responsible for this?

Mary is very committed to being her sister's caregiver, even if it means giving up church attendance. Another conflict of values may be Martha's right to adequate care versus Mary's right to be the caregiver. When Mary's care for her sister becomes inadequate, even though this decline in care is unintentional, should Martha be provided with a different caregiver? The issue of nonmaleficence arises here. More harm may be done by professionals interfering with this relationship and taking away from Mary a role that she believes is hers. On the other hand, serious harm may result if there is no intervention.

The sons have a need to run their business and make a living to support themselves and their families. They cannot devote as much time and financial resources to their mother and aunt as are needed. On the other hand, they may be expected to protect their mother and aunt. This expectation may create another dilemma. For the sons this may become the question of how much time they devote to their families and business versus the amount of time they spend in the country with their mother and aunt. A solution for them is to move the women into the senior high rise in the city. The resulting dilemma for the two women would then be the desire to stay in their home and the pressure to move to the city.

CASE TWO

John and Manny

John, age 82, had operated a small business for 60 years in the community where he lived. He had reluctantly sold the business at his wife's urging so that they could travel in their retirement. John had always hoped that Manny, their only son, would return home to run the family business. Shortly after he retired, John suffered a stroke that left him partially paralyzed. This delayed the plans he and his wife had for travel. Six months later, John's wife had a heart attack and died. When his wife died, John was the sole inheritor of their estate–a fact that Manny never accepted. Manny had recently returned from abroad where his employment with an oil company had abruptly ended. He offered to move into the home and help his father. After moving in, he had the telephone disconnected so John would not be "bothered" by friends and neighbors calling to see how he was doing. He installed a new phone, with an unlisted number, in his room which he kept locked when he was away. He would not allow John to use the phone when he was home.

Although John was alert, lucid, and mentally capable of handling his affairs, Manny began to lay the groundwork for John's supposed mental incapacity. When family, friends, and neighbors dropped by, he told them that John was not receiving visitors because his health was poor. He told John, however, that his friends told him that they thought John was losing his mind. Manny boxed up John's favorite books and fishing equipment and donated them to the Salvation Army, telling John that he would never be healthy enough again to use them. However, Manny told his father's friends he had destroyed his possessions "in a fit of anger." Manny also mentioned to others that he might have to go to court to become John's guardian so he could more effectively take care of his father and the estate. Under the pretense of "cleaning out the junk," Manny began removing valuable antiques. He shifted money from his father's bank account to his own and had his name put on the title to the house, convincing his father this was best.

Manny told John that in his present mental and physical condition he was lucky to have anybody to help him at all. Believing that his friends had abandoned him, John was persuaded to change his will so that Manny would inherit everything. Manny began to yell at his father and on several occasions pushed him and treated him roughly when John would not do what Manny asked. People who saw Manny in town began to be concerned and talked about how odd he was behaving. While everyone recognized that he was intelligent and articulate, they thought that things he said about the government, television news, and spy satellites were bizarre. People were also concerned that John, who had been active and visible in the community for so many years, did not go out of the house.

Concerned about John's withdrawn behavior and Manny's excuses for why the family could not see John, John's sister called Adult Protective Services. Manny did not want to let the social worker in the house, but he did so when told the social worker had a legal responsibility to see John and could return with a court order. John was frail, appeared malnourished, and had bruises on his face which he said were the result of a fall. The social worker wanted a second opinion from a mental health professional before making a decision about John's mental capacity and planned to come back with another social worker. The social worker suspected that John was being abused and neglected by Manny and offered services to John, but he refused.

Before the social worker could return to the home, the hospital called reporting that John had been admitted with another stroke. John admitted to the hospital social worker that Manny had started hitting him. He defended Manny, though, saying he was under a lot of stress. John said he felt bad about not seeing his friends or family and wished they would visit. He also felt badly about the responsibilities his son was having to take for his care and said it was not right for a child to have to take care of a grown man. He thought that if he could still be the provider and father figure that Manny would not be having the problems he was having. John was a faithful church goer and took his family care obligations seriously. His religious conviction emphasized parental responsibility. Therefore, John believed that his role as a father took precedence over concerns for his own personal safety.

While in the hospital, a psychiatric evaluation was done revealing that John had the mental capacity to understand the situation he was in; he was mildly, but not clinically, depressed and did not require treatment; and he was able to make informed choices about what he wanted. Both the APS social worker and the hospital social worker tried to persuade John to go to a nursing home from the hospital so he could recover in a safe environment while legal action was taken to get Manny out of the house. However, when John was discharged from the hospital he decided to return home.

Two more hospitalizations followed over the next eight months with signs of physical abuse evident each time he was admitted, and with John lamenting what had become of his life. On the second admission, it was determined that John's mental capacity had declined and that he no longer had the capacity to understand his situation. The hospital filed a petition for guardianship and a public guardian was appointed. It was determined, as part of the court proceedings, that Manny was suffering from a mental illness which was the reason he had suddenly lost his job, so he was not suitable as his father's guardian.

Ethical Issues

The case of John and Manny is not atypical. Often victims of elder abuse choose to stay in an abusive environment, even when options are offered for improvement. The ethical issues in this case include John's right to self-determination and to make bad choices (his right to folly), Manny's right to treatment, and the responsibility of others to intercede on John's behalf.

When victims of elder abuse exercise their right to self-determination in a way that seems reasonable to others, their choices are seldom questioned. It is usually when the victim makes what are considered by others to be bad choices, as in John's case, that the ethical dilemma of the individual's right to choice versus society's obligation to protect is raised.

As with the case of Mary and Martha, this dilemma is complicated by the question of the elderly person's mental capacity to make informed choices.

Related to the issue of self-determination is the conflict between a victim's happiness and safety. John expresses the desire to return home as part of a familial responsibility even though he has admitted being abused by Manny. It is not uncommon for victims of elder mistreatment to refuse intervention. The "sixty-four thousand dollar question" for professionals in weighing the conflicting values of happiness or freedom for the victim and safety may lie in the determination of the victim's mental capacity to reasonably make such a choice. When a victim's personal values system holds strongly a concept such as familial responsibility, the issue of non-maleficence may be raised. Would more harm be done to John by finding him incompetent and placing him in a nursing home against his wishes or by letting him return home to an abusive son?

The right of those with mental illness to be free from involuntary confinement or medications has long been debated. An ethical dilemma raised by this case, however, may be Manny's right to autonomy versus John's right to be free from mistreatment. This situation may well illustrate unintentional mistreatment since it is not clear if Manny can be held responsible for his actions. Regardless of intent, mistreatment is taking place and those professionals working with John may question the need to restrict Manny's rights as they struggle to keep John from further harm.

Another issue raised by this case is the responsibility of others, especially professionals, to recognize and intercede on behalf of those who are victims of mistreatment or illness who cannot help themselves. The principles of justice and beneficence raise other issues in the case of John and Manny. Limited resources may place professionals in a position of not taking immediate or appropriate action or in limiting the scope of options that they can offer a victim. The desire to provide services which will be most beneficial for both John and Manny is then limited by what is actually available in the way of services instead of what would be most helpful.

CASE THREE

Bonnie

Bonnie is a 60 year old woman who is small, frail, and appears much younger than her age. She has a history of cerebral palsy. Sadly, she had some renown for her progress as a child, but she has degenerated physically in adulthood and now resides in a nursing home. She is highly intelligent, has an MA in psychology, is separated from her husband, and has one son. She now requires nearly total care. She is non-ambulatory and cannot move from her bed to her wheelchair. She can eat (with difficulty), can use the phone (with difficulty), has poor hearing (usually does not wear her hearing aid), and has severely impaired speech. When she entered the nursing home, she was addicted to valium and meprobamate which were allegedly used for muscle spasms. Her attending physician says Bonnie did not need these medications for the degree of spasms she had on admission. It is suspected that she was "doctor shopping" prior to admission because she had had several physicians prescribing medications for her. She has been diagnosed with a personality disorder, and she exhibits manipulative behavior and very poor judgment. She is unrealistic regarding her ability for self-care. She uses frailty and diminutiveness to seduce people into looking after her. For example, she gets other patients who are ambulatory to wheel her outside on the porch or get her a soda. When she does not get what she wants, she can become verbally abusive. She accuses staff and other patients of stealing. She refuses to admit she had a drug addiction problem but claims she knows how and where to get valium if the nursing home staff will not give it to her. Her son seldom visits and appears impatient with his mother when he does see her. Her husband, Pete, from whom she separated shortly before admission to the nursing home, does visit regularly.

On several occasions, staff in the facility have noticed that Bonnie seems more lethargic and withdrawn after her husband's visits. A few times they thought they overheard shouting in the room when Bonnie's roommate was gone and her husband was visiting. Once Bonnie told an aide that her husband had taken her spending money. No one thought much about this behavior because Bonnie was so manipulative and had accused just about everyone of stealing at some point in time. None of these observations of shouting or theft were recorded in her chart.

One weekend when Bonnie's husband was visiting, an aide saw him give something to Bonnie which looked like a pill. She swallowed it before the aide could tell what kind of pill it was. The aide reported this to the nurse in charge of that shift and was told not to worry about it. Sometimes on the day after her husband's visits, the staff noticed bruises on Bonnie's arms, chest, and shoulders. Documentation of the bruises was made in her chart, but no further examination was done; and neither Bonnie nor her husband were confronted.

This nursing home was part of a national chain and had been experiencing difficulties keeping beds filled and staff employed in key positions. While Bonnie was there, 10% of the beds were vacant and several of the head nurses were hired through a temporary service. The staff did not want to "rock the boat" because they already knew that if more vacancies occurred headquarters would close the facility.

When Bonnie's husband arrived on his next visit, her roommate was in the room. The roommate did not like Bonnie's husband and usually left the room when he came for visits. He seemed particularly agitated on this occasion. Bonnie's roommate wanted to gather a book and some other things before she left the room, and as she was doing so Bonnie and her husband began to fight. They were shouting at each other and her husband pushed Bonnie's wheelchair up against the wall. The roommate left immediately and reported what she saw to the head nurse.

This time the nurse did go to the room. She thought she heard noises that sounded like someone was being struck as she neared. When she got to Bonnie's room, Bonnie was in her wheelchair against the wall where her husband had pushed her, and he was sitting on Bonnie's bed. The nurse questioned them both about the shouting and noises she had heard. Both Bonnie and her husband denied any beating, but the nurse was able to convince Bonnie's husband to end his visit for the day and leave the facility. She recorded the incident to Bonnie's chart, but no physical exam was done.

Later that evening an aide noticed that Bonnie was having difficulty breathing and was in pain. The nurse in charge of that shift was notified and she contacted the physician who requested Bonnie be brought to the hospital. Upon examination, it was discovered that Bonnie had severe bruising and two fractured ribs. When the lab work was completed, it revealed she also had elevated blood levels of what appeared to be valium. Bonnie was admitted to the hospital. Social work services were requested for Bonnie, and the social worker learned from the son that there had been a long history of mutual physical and emotional abuse in his parents' marriage; both had abused drugs as well. He thought the nursing home knew this and should have taken better measures to limit or supervise the visits by Bonnie's husband. He said his mother separated from his father because the physical abuse was becoming more violent during the time period before she entered the nursing home.

Ethical Issues

The ethical issues presented by this case include not just the rights of Bonnie and her husband. They are complicated by factors such as the responsibility of the facility to provide care to and treatment for Bonnie as well as the other patients and the rights of other patients to receive a fair share of staff time and attention as well as a safe and stress free environment in which to live.

Bonnie's right to have visits with her husband must be weighed against her right, or need, to be protected. Whether staff in the facility have an obligation to recognize and address the warning signs of abuse or at what point they could reasonably be expected to recognize these signs is another issue. It would be reasonable to assume that Bonnie and her husband should be allowed a degree of privacy for their visits. At what point do facility staff have a responsibility to intervene with this couple's privacy and observe, supervise, or restrict visits? The principles of beneficence and nonmaleficence may be applied here. Will greater harm be done to Bonnie if her visits with her husband are restricted? What is the right course of action to take to benefit Bonnie, her husband, the facility staff, and the other patients, and can all parties win in a case such as this?

What ethical responsibilities do others have? The son is aware of a past history that he does not bring to the attention of the facility until he learns his mother has been admitted to the hospital with broken ribs. Is there an obligation for family members to be sure that service providers have all the relevant information about an individual, even when the victim is competent? Other patients in the facility, including Bonnie's roommate, may have seen or suspected something. Do they have a responsibility to intervene, to tell someone on staff what they saw or suspect, or should they respect Bonnie's privacy?

A situation such as Bonnie's poses the problem of dual directional abuse between Bonnie and her husband and between Bonnie and the facility. The issue of whose rights take precedence often arises in this type of situation. If it is believed that the rights of the victim are the most important, then professionals may focus on deciding who is the victim. Since the victim changes depending on the circumstances, this type of effort may not be productive. In the case of Bonnie and her husband, they appear to verbally abuse each other. Bonnie's husband is also physically abusive towards her. The facility staff mistreat Bonnie through neglect, and she has been verbally abusive with both staff and patients in the facility. Should Bonnie's need to be protected from her husband and the right of other patients to be free from the stress of domestic violence in the facility be valued over Bonnie's right to have visitors? Does her husband continue to have a right to visit if he is abusive during these visits? Does Bonnie precipitate the abuse by her husband in some way that is not observed by anyone in the facility, and does he have rights as a victim?

CONCLUSION

Professionals working with elders who have been mistreated face the problems of multiple and often conflicting ethical issues in addition to the specific service or treatment needs of the elderly person. The case of Mary and Martha, for example, does not simply involve the need to offer supportive services to these women but necessitates consideration of their individual rights to make choices, the neighbors' right to live in a safe environment, and the sons' right to their own pursuits. The presence of mistreatment in the case of John and Manny changes this situation from one of professionals offering supportive services after John's stroke to questioning his ability to make reasonable decisions. Spouse abuse, institutional abuse, and self abuse present in Bonnie's case make decisions of whose rights take precedence a challenging dilemma from an ethical perspective especially given the commitment to provide services.

These three cases illustrate types of ethical issues presented by elder mistreatment cases. In the chapters that follow, professionals from a variety of disciplines will grapple with issues raised in these cases from the ethical frameworks of their individual professions.

Chapter Three

A Medical Perspective

Terrie T. Wetle, PhD
Terry T. Fulmer, RN, PhD, FAAN

SUMMARY. Elder mistreatment is explored from the perspective of the health care professional, beginning with a brief review of relevant values and ethical concepts. These include beneficence, nonmaleficence, autonomy, confidentiality, paternalism, filial piety, and justice. The chapter then raises several ethical dilemmas faced by health care professionals in evaluating, reporting, and caring for cases of elder mistreatment. These include the difficulty in balancing patient autonomy with the obligation to protect them from harm, the problem of confidentiality and reporting requirements, the impact of reporting on relationships with patients and other professionals, and the problems in working with patients and their families. Approaches to developing appropriate institutional responses are suggested. The chapter concludes with a discussion of the three cases. *[Article copies available from The Haworth Document Delivery Service: 1-800-342-9678.]*

INTRODUCTION

The prevention, identification, and resolution of elder mistreatment raise a variety of ethical issues, questions, and dilemmas for health care

Terrie T. Wetle is Deputy Director, National Institute on Aging, National Institutes of Health, Building 31, Room 5C35, 31 Center Drive MSC 2292, Bethesda, MD 20892-2292. Terry T. Fulmer is Director, Geriatrics Education Center, Columbia University, Geriatrics, 100 Haven Avenue, Tower III, 29-F, New York, NY 10032.

[Haworth co-indexing entry note]: "A Medical Perspective." Wetle, Terrie T., and Terry T. Fulmer. Co-published simultaneously in *Journal of Elder Abuse & Neglect* (The Haworth Press, Inc.) Vol. 7, No. 2/3, 1995, pp. 31-48; and: *Elder Mistreatment: Ethical Issues, Dilemmas, and Decisions* (ed: Tanya Fusco Johnson) The Haworth Press, Inc., 1995, pp. 31-48. [Single or multiple copies of this article are available from The Haworth Document Delivery Service: 1-800-342-9678, 9:00 a.m. - 5:00 p.m. (EST)].

professionals. The intent of this chapter is to briefly outline relevant ethical concepts and values, as well as relevant professional codes of conduct, and then to apply these to the three cases that provide the unifying concept of this book.

Elder mistreatment requires a complex ethical calculus, involving competing values, ambiguous symptoms, confusing obligations, as well as regulations and laws that may complicate professional judgments and ethical analysis. It is our hope that clarification of issues, explication of values, and suggested strategies for resolution of conflicts will assist the health professional in approaching such cases and in improving care and the quality of life for older persons.

ETHICAL CONCEPTS AND VALUES RELEVANT TO MEDICAL CARE

Codes of professional ethics and societal values identify ethical concepts of relevance to the health professional's approach to elder mistreatment (see Appendix for summaries of relevant professional codes). These concepts are described briefly below and include: non-maleficence, beneficence, individual autonomy, paternalism, confidentiality, justice, and filial piety or respect for family rights. (For a more detailed discussion of these concepts, see for example, Beauchamp & Childress, 1989.)

Non-maleficence. Societal values, professional ethics, and criminal and civil law place strong proscriptions against doing harm to others, referred to as non-maleficence. This principle, expressed in the Hippocratic Oath for physicians as "first, do no harm," reverberates in the professional ethical codes of physicians, nurses, and social workers. For example, the American Nurses Association (ANA) Code for Nurses (1976) states that "the nurse's primary commitment is to the client's care and safety" (Section 3.1).

The relevance of this concept to elder mistreatment is, at least, twofold. First, and most obvious, health professionals are obligated not to harm patients. Thus, incidents of deliberate abuse of patients by health care workers are of special concern. Karl Pillemer (1989), in a survey of more than 500 nurses and nurse aides found that psychological abuse had been observed by 81% of respondents and physical abuse, by 36%. In many states, the first "elder abuse" laws were focused on abuse occurring in health care institutions, such as nursing homes. The second application of this concept may be somewhat less obvious, and that is the obligation of health professionals to consider indirect or "secondary" harms that may evolve from actions taken with the intention of helping a patient. By way of example, a report of suspected abuse and subsequent investigation could in turn trigger yet further abuse in retaliation. Similarly, elders may be reluctant to report abuse for fear of losing valued family contact or support. Systems designed to respond to reports of elder abuse must be sensitive to these issues and provide reasonable protections for patients or clients.

Beneficence. This principle, simply put, is doing good for others or generally promoting their welfare. This principle forms the bed-rock of medical and nursing practice and is also embodied in the ethical codes of medicine, nursing, and social work. For example, the National Association of Social Workers (NASW) Code of Ethics (1990) pledges social workers to promote "client best interest." The concept of "best interest" is closely tied to beneficence and refers to balancing the benefits and costs or risks of specific actions to determine the action most likely to benefit (or least likely to harm) the patient. It is not uncommon, particularly with elderly patients, that health care decisions involve such a balancing of intended benefits (protecting the patient from further harm, for example) against potential costs (damaging frail family relationships or removing the patient from a familiar home setting). It should also be recognized that individual health professionals may have very different perceptions regarding just which actions are in the best interest of a particular patient.

Individual autonomy provides fundamental underpinning of societal values in Western thinking. Autonomy refers to the right of an individual to make decisions for oneself that are voluntary and intentional and not the result of coercion, duress, or undue influence. The concept of autonomy has received growing emphasis in the past several decades as illustrated by enactment of related laws and regulations, decisions in case law, adoption of relevant agency procedures and policies, and increased attention to processes in health care such as provision of informed consent or execution of advance directives. The social and political ideal of autonomy, as expressed in the rights of the individual, is so pervasive that many fail to realize that the concept and its expression in everyday life are both time- and culture-bound. This is of particular relevance for individuals who are elderly or from another ethnic or cultural experience and who may not expect a physician or other professional to ask their opinion or otherwise encourage expression of individual autonomy.

Autonomy has been conceptually divided into two levels: *agency*, the freedom to decide among options; and *action*, the freedom to carry out the course of action chosen (Gadow, 1980). Collopy (1988) suggests a more complex model, distinguishing among five types of autonomy. *Direct vs.*

delegated autonomy refers to decisions and actions made by the individual versus the delegation of those decisions and activities to another person. Elder patients frequently "delegate" decision-making to family members or, in some cases, to health professionals (Wetle et al., 1988). *Competent vs. incapacitated autonomy* focuses on the decisional capacity of the individual. *Authentic vs. inauthentic autonomy* moves beyond patient competency to an examination of whether the choice is in keeping with the individual's personal history and values. The simple expression of a choice by a patient is not sufficient to determine authenticity of autonomy. *Immediate vs. long term autonomy* recognizes that choices made now may interfere with autonomous action in the future. Interventions that override the immediate wishes of an individual (for example the wish that abuse or neglect not be reported) are frequently justified by the goal of enhancing long term autonomy (freedom from coercion and abuse). *Autonomy as a negative right vs. a positive right* expands the concept of autonomy beyond the opportunity to say no or to refuse a service. Much of recent emphasis and advocacy surrounds the rights of individuals to refuse treatment (e.g., informed consent and advance directives). Collopy (1988) argues that autonomy as a positive right requires that we support and enhance choice.

Confidentiality refers to the right of the individual to control information regarding her/himself. This right is based on respect for autonomy that entails the freedom to determine how information about oneself is used. Moreover, it is argued that some degree of privacy would be required for autonomous decision-making (Beauchamp & Childress, 1989; Walters, 1991; Kane, 1993). The ethical codes of most health professionals also include confidentiality provisions based both on autonomy arguments and, to some degree, self protection for the professionals themselves (Kane, 1993). Elder abuse reporting laws preempt this duty of confidentiality in patient-health professional relationships.

Paternalism. The making of decisions for another is referred to as paternalism. Two forms of paternalism are defined: "weak" paternalism refers to making decisions for another who is unable to decide for him/herself and is morally justified by principles of beneficence and justice; "strong" paternalism refers to the making of decisions for another who is capable of decision-making for him/herself. The role of health professionals frequently involves "weak" paternalism in that some older patients are impaired in decision-making capacity. However, because of widely held societal values and stereotypes, there is substantial risk of "strong" paternalism with older patients (Wetle, 1988). Collopy (1993) discusses "intrusive beneficence," where the individual may be denied autonomy in the name of her own well being as defined by others. He cautions that social aberrations may accordingly be misconstrued as mental aberrations, physical frailty may be mistaken as indicative of cognitive frailty, and periodic lapses of judgment as proof of permanent incapacity (Collopy, 1993; McCullough, 1984). This is directly relevant to elder mistreatment cases, where there is considerable debate as to the appropriate role of health professionals when a competent client refuses assistance, services, or a care plan developed in response to suspected or confirmed abuse. Collopy also raises concern about beneficence as a means of community control (1993). Under these circumstances, decisions are inappropriately made for an individual who is competent but whose behavior or life style is considered to be eccentric, unusual, or disturbing to others. This issue is of particular concern in evaluation of "self-neglect."

Filial piety/Family obligations. Although there is lack of agreement regarding the exact responsibilities of family members in providing care, there is a general societal agreement, supported by common law, that families do have special rights and responsibilities in the care of frail elders and in making health care decisions. Moreover, because many elders are dependent on care provided by a family member to avoid institutional placement, the dynamics of family relationships are of central importance. Similarly, because of the intimate involvement of family members in providing informal care and the stresses related to providing such care, it is often those closest to the elders who are most likely to be abusive or neglectful.

Justice. One concept of justice is concerned with the fair distribution of benefits (or cost and harms) among individuals. Rawls (1971) argues that liberty should be distributed in such a way as to maximize liberty among all individuals and that public goods should be distributed so that the least advantaged benefit most. Although a primary role of health care providers involves advocacy for a *specific* patient, both individual professionals and the organizations in which they work also have responsibilities for *populations* of patients. It is not uncommon that the interests of a single patient are weighed against the interests of other patients or groups of patients. This may involve, for example, decisions regarding the amount of time spent with an individual patient conducting an assessment, gathering data, providing information, or doing family counseling.

ETHICAL DILEMMAS
RELATED TO HEALTH PROFESSIONALS AND PATIENTS

The application of these values and ethical concepts to specific cases of elder mistreatment often engenders ethical dilemmas involving conflict among two or more values or concepts. Several such dilemmas are outlined below including the balancing of individual autonomy with beneficence and paternalism, concerns of confidentiality and legal reporting requirements, the impact of reporting on patient and professional relationships, and the issue of respect for autonomy for patients with diminishing cognitive capacity.

Balancing Patient Autonomy and the Best Interests of Patients

Perhaps the most difficult ethical dilemma for health professionals is the effort to respect the expressed wishes of the patient (autonomy) while protecting the patient from harm (beneficence) (Wetle et al., 1991). It is not uncommon for individuals to behave in ways that place themselves at risk or are personally injurious, or to choose to remain in risky or abusive circumstances. Respecting the autonomous wishes of such an individual may be in direct conflict with the professional's judgment of what is in the patient's best interest. On the one hand, the principle of respect for the autonomy of an individual would prevent the health professional from intervening with a service or action that is in opposition to the expressed wishes of a competent patient. On the other hand, health professionals are required, by law, to report cases of suspected elder mistreatment. Moreover, there is also an obligation to determine that the patient's refusal of assistance is an autonomous decision, free of coercion or undue duress. These cases are often complicated by questionable decisional capacity or cognitive impairment of the elder patient. Disagreement with a health professional's judgment or advice is not sufficient evidence to make a determination of decisional incapacity. Certainly we have moral obligations to protect incompetent elders from incapacitated decision-making, but we are also obligated to determine if they are truly incapacitated before intervening against their wishes. Such a determination requires a formal evaluation of decisional capacity. If the patient is determined to be competent, even if suspected mistreatment is confirmed, the competent patient has the right to refuse interventions.

Confidentiality and reporting requirements. Another aspect of patient autonomy is respect for confidentiality. Once again, the elder abuse reporting laws override the obligation for confidentiality under very specific circumstances. Nonetheless, this is not a blanket override, in that such reported information must be handled with extreme care, and information identified in subsequent investigations should be shared only on a "need to know" basis.

Impact of reporting on patient/professional relationship. Many professionals express justified concern that an elder abuse report and the subsequent investigation will have deleterious effects on their relationships with patients (and patients' families). Much progress has been made in improving the response system and investigative approaches used to determine whether or not mistreatment has occurred and in planning appropriate interventions. Nonetheless, even the most skilled response to such a report may damage the relationship between professional and patient. Several steps can be taken to reduce negative impacts, including informing the patient that such a report is to be made, describing the process, identifying potential positive outcomes of the process and suggested interventions, working with the family as a unit if possible, and recognizing the needs and concerns of all involved.

Ethical Issues Related to Families and Health Professionals

Family members are often intimately involved in the care of frail elders. Several ethical issues and conflicts relevant to elder mistreatment are faced as health professionals care for the individual patient in the context of family caregiving. These issues include questions regarding just who is the patient, caregiver burden and inadequate family supports, changing dependency relationships and longstanding patterns of family interaction, and ethical approaches to families. Many of these issues are discussed elsewhere in this volume in substantial detail, but are briefly discussed here from the perspective of the health professional.

Who is the patient? It is not uncommon for health professionals to become involved in the treatment of the family as a unit, as well as in care of an individual patient. The burden of caregiving can be substantial, and some cases of elder mistreatment occur when a well-intentioned primary caregiver becomes overwhelmed by caregiving tasks. The health professional faces a particularly thorny dilemma when treating two members of a family as patients and encounters evidence of mistreatment of one by the other (Fulmer, 1991). This raises the question of just who is the primary patient, and how are the professional's obligations to be balanced among various members of the family. Certainly, there is a first level responsibility to the patient who appears to have been mistreated but successful approaches include offering information and services to all involved parties.

Dependency relationships in families change as one member becomes increasingly dependent on the family for care. The health professional may be unaware of long standing patterns of interaction among family members. The stresses of family caregiving may exacerbate a relationship that has always been characterized by verbal and physical abuse. In some cases, changing dependency relationships may turn the tables, and the previously abused may become the abuser. Being aware of these patterns and the specific relationship history of caregiver and care receiver may help explain observed dynamics and provide crucial information for developing effective intervention strategies.

Caregiver burden and spousal and intergenerational responsibilities involve differing personal and societal expectations. Society remains unclear as to the reasonable level of caregiving to be expected from a spouse or adult child. It is not unusual for family caregivers to drain all physical and emotional resources before accepting help or assistance. One responsibility of health professionals is to assist caregivers in recognizing the limits of their own health and to promote their well-being by identifying supportive services and encouraging their use and by assisting in balancing caregiving among all available family members. This may in fact have a double protective effect. First, it may prevent the elder abuse or neglect that might have been triggered by caregiver over-burden and stress. Second, such interventions may protect the caregiver from the overburdening that also could be considered a form of "caregiver mistreatment" or abuse.

Ethical Issues Between Health Professionals, Institutions, and Agencies

Increasingly, health professionals work with other professionals in the context of multiple agencies, institutions, and regulatory bodies. The complexity of such relationships contributes to ethical concerns and value conflicts relevant to elder abuse and mistreatment.

Mistreatment occurring in institutional settings raises certain issues that are different from a community-based case. When mistreatment occurs in the health professional's home institution, the required report often results in an investigation of the professional's own peers and colleagues. Similarly, when the abuse or mistreatment occurs in another institution, the health professional or his/her parent institution may have important business and patient care relationships with that outside institution. Such circumstances carry a strong potential to damage trust and other aspects of professional relationships. On the other hand, with careful attention to how the report and subsequent investigation and interventions are handled, such reports can be used as learning opportunities that actually strengthen professional and interagency relationships. Without such attention, reports can result in actions that are painful and destructive.

Different professionals or professional disciplines may have conflicting views on appropriate responsibilities for reporting and strategies of response. Because many symptoms of mistreatment are ambiguous and potentially attributable to other illnesses, conditions, or accidents, individual professionals may disagree as to whether or not a specific case ought to be reported (Fulmer & Wetle, 1986). Moreover, separate professional disciplines may hold different views as to the most appropriate response to such ambiguous symptoms, or to which profession is responsible for various actions. Identification of specific resources and procedures within institutions as well as agreed upon strategies for individual professionals go a long way in addressing these concerns.

Raising institutional awareness and coordination of response is likely to improve recognition of symptoms of abuse and improve reporting responses. In recognition of some of the institutional barriers and concerns outlined above, some institutions have developed special elder abuse assessment teams (see, for example, Beth Israel Hospital Elder Assessment Team, 1986). These teams are designed to encourage recognition and internal reporting of symptoms of elder mistreatment by convening an interdisciplinary team to provide educational services, conduct timely assessments, and suggest appropriate actions. For example, the Beth Israel Elder Assessment Team addressed the reluctance of professionals to report such suspicions of abuse and reduced the fear of being perceived as "overreacting." It also helped to coordinate the institutional response by reducing multiple reports for the same incident, but ensuring that at least one report would be made when appropriate. Encouraging institutions to have agreed-upon procedures and support for staff as they consider such reports is crucial to appropriate and timely recognition and reporting of elder mistreatment (Fulmer & O'Malley, 1987).

THE THREE CASES

Mary and Martha

Mary lives with and cares for her sister Martha in a state of disarray and apparent malnourishment. This case raises a variety of ethical issues and value conflicts from the perspective of the health professional. The first moral obligation grows out of duties of non-maleficence and beneficence, that is first and foremost–do no harm. The initial visit to the home provides strong indication that sister Martha is not being adequately cared for (evidence of malnourishment and failure to regularly be given medication). Moreover, there is evidence of self-neglect on the part of Mary. The case provides evidence of substantial risk given their physical, mental, and financial status. Upon this initial evaluation, the health professional identifies several needs and the next step is to determine the wishes and preferences of Mary and Martha.

Respect for individual autonomy requires that Mary (and her sister as well) be informed of the purpose and findings of an assessment, be provided information regarding alternatives for interventions, and be presented with the likely benefits and costs of each intervention (including the choice of doing nothing or refusing care). Autonomous decision-making requires, however, that the individual be competent to participate in such decisions. For adults, the health professional should assume competence, until there is evidence to suggest otherwise. In this case, Mary's lack of insight, as well as observed problems with judgment and memory, would raise suspicions of cognitive impairment and necessitate a formal evaluation of decisional capacity.

Another aspect of the assessment is a determination of whether or not the current conditions and lifestyle are a recent aberration or symbolic of life-long preferences and practices. In the case of Mary, there is strong evidence to suggest that the current state of her house and personal care represents a new development and is in contradiction to her previous practices. This is further evidence suggestive of cognitive decline. Nonetheless, if determined to be competent, Mary's right to refuse services would remain.

Yet another consideration for the health professional is the caregiver burden Mary is experiencing as her sister's needs become more intense and Mary's abilities more limited. It appears that Martha's care needs are overwhelming Mary's capacity to provide care and, in addition, have substantially restricted Mary's opportunities for outings and socialization. Thus, the health care professional is faced with balancing the competing needs of two persons.

There is some evidence of self-neglect by Mary and neglect of Martha as well. An important task for the health professional is determination of the underlying causes for the physical and cognitive declines observed in each of the patients. For example, it may be that Mary's change in cognitive status is secondary to medications or an undetected illness such as pneumonia or depression. Successful treatment of such conditions could return Mary to previous levels of function, improve her ability to make decisions and exercise good judgment, and, indeed, improve her capacity to care for Martha.

Mary's acceptance of a home health nurse to provide care to Martha not only supplements Martha's care, but also provides an opportunity to observe improvements or deterioration in health and function. This is particularly useful for elders whose cognitive function has begun to decline and for whom decisional capacity is fluctuating or deteriorating. At each junction, it is important for the health care team to converse with the patient and family members at regular intervals to determine whether or not the goals of the care plan are being met, are in concordance with client goals, and are ensuring the safety of the elder. In this case, it appears that the home heath nurse made a positive difference in stabilizing Martha's health. However, in the absence of regular professional visits, it is likely that circumstances will revert to the previous dangerous situation.

The involvement of Mary's sons also raises issues and concerns. Their involvement in care appears to be ineffective and sporadic. Although they expressed a plan to move Mary to a highrise apartment building, there were serious questions as to their ability to carry out the plan as stated. It is quite possible that Mary's judgment that the sons would not be able to implement the plan was quite accurate. This, added to her reluctance to leave modest remaining contacts with her church as well as unwillingness to move her sister, makes this plan undesirable. An important role for the health professional is facilitating communication among family members, clarifying preferences and wishes, testing the feasibility of family plans of action, and suggesting viable and desirable alternatives.

John and Manny

The case of John, an elderly gentleman who, after the death of his wife, is socially isolated by his adult son raises somewhat different questions. From the facts of the case as presented, it appears that the son is financially, psychologically, and physically abusing his father. The primary ethical dilemma presented in this case is to balance John's autonomous wish to continue to be a "father figure" and remain with his son against the health care provider's moral obligation to protect John from harm. Once John has been assessed for cognitive impairment and found to be able to make informed choices, the course open to the health care professional is, with John's permission, to monitor his well-being and cognitive status on subsequent contacts and hospital admissions. When

John was determined to no longer be able to make decisions for himself, the hospital appropriately files for a guardianship determination. As difficult as it may be to observe circumstances such as these, respect for individual autonomy requires that we abide by the wishes of competent adults, even when we disagree with such wishes. Certainly, every effort should be made to "keep the door open," to continue to communicate and to offer options, including evaluation and services for the troubled son.

Bonnie

The case of Bonnie is particularly interesting and raises a variety of issues of direct relevance to health professionals. While we may have special obligations to protect persons who live in health care facilities such as nursing homes, we must also recognize that nursing home residents retain rights of personal autonomy. Therefore, the evaluation of this case should proceed, as do mistreatment cases occurring in the community, from the perspective of first determining Bonnie's decisional capacity. From the facts of the case, although Bonnie may have exercised poor judgment, she appears to be competent from a legal perspective and have decisional capacity from an ethics perspective. Therefore, the health professional would need to move very carefully in considering restrictions on her freedoms to have visitors or to engage in private activities with those visitors.

The nature and extent of behavioral restrictions that can be imposed on competent residents of nursing homes is a timely issue. This is, after all, their home, and although health conditions may necessitate substantial care, their quality of life is dependent upon identifying as much freedom of choice as possible (Kane & Caplan, 1990). For example, a facility does not have the right to restrict visitors desired by a competent patient, as long as the facility's rules of visitation are followed. Thus in Bonnie's case, even though her son has asked that Bonnie's visits with her husband be restricted or terminated, it is Bonnie's decision with whom she visits and under what circumstances. Certainly, health professionals ought to make every effort to provide family counseling and other supports to Bonnie and her family, but not override Bonnie's expressed wishes.

The question of medication abuse raises yet another set of concerns. First, the facility has a right to enforce its own appropriately promulgated rules and regulations regarding medications and their use in the facility. Bonnie (and her husband) should have been properly informed about the facility's rules and the sanctions imposed if rules are broken at the time of admission–and reminded of those rules at regular intervals. If found to have broken the rules, Bonnie should suffer whatever sanctions are indicated in facility policy. The health care professional should recognize, however, that abuse of medications is an illness for which there are appropriate treatments, and Bonnie should be offered such care.

The evidence of physical and emotional mistreatment should be discussed directly with Bonnie and her husband, and a care plan offered to them to address family conflicts, medication abuse, and other concerns. Given the description of this case, it is quite likely that many interventions will be refused and that even if improvements are made, behavioral relapses will occur. Continued efforts are appropriate, even if difficult. Manipulative patients such as Bonnie are particularly difficult for staff, yet it is just such patients that test our mettle and our commitment as health professionals to respect the individual patient and that patient's quality of life.

CONCLUSION

Health care professionals face a spectrum of ethical concerns and value dilemmas in addressing cases of suspected mistreatment. Optimal patient care requires that the individual practitioner develop a systematic approach to such patients, including careful attention to relevant values and ethical concepts, an effort to balance expected benefits with potential harms, maintenance of up-to-date knowledge of relevant reporting laws and regulations, and access to current information regarding service resources and efficient access to those services. The institutions in which health professionals work should also develop and promulgate clear and comprehensive policies and procedures to support staff as they evaluate patients and address elder mistreatment.

REFERENCES

Beauchamp, T.L. & Childress, J.F. (1989). *Principles of biomedical ethics* (3rd edition). New York: Oxford University Press.

Collopy, B.J. (1988). Autonomy in long term care: Some crucial distinctions. *The Gerontologist, 28*(Special Supplement), 10-17.

Collopy, B.J. (1993). The burden of beneficence. In R.A. Kane & A.L. Caplan (Eds.), *Ethical conflicts in the management of home care.* New York: Springer.

Fulmer, T. (1991). Elder mistreatment: Progress in community detection and intervention. *Family and Community Health, 2,* 26-34.

Fulmer, T. (1986). The nurse practitioner approach to elder abuse screening and intervention. *Nurse Practitioner, 11*, 33-38.

Fulmer, T. & O'Malley, T. (1987). *Inadequate care of the elderly: A health care perspective on abuse and neglect*. New York: Springer.

Gadow, S. (1980). Medicine, ethics and the elderly. *Gerontologist, 20*(6), 680.

Kane, R.A. (1993). Uses and abuses of confidentiality. In R.A. Kane & A.L. Caplan (Eds.), *Ethical conflicts in the management of home care*. New York: Springer, 147-158.

Kane, R.A. & Caplan, A.L. (Eds.). (1990). *Everyday ethics: Resolving dilemmas in nursing home life*. New York: Springer.

McCullough, L.B. (1984). Medical care for elderly patients of diminished competence: An ethical analysis. *Journal of the American Geriatrics Society, 32*, 150.

National Association of Social Workers. (1990). *NASW Code of Ethics, Professional Standards*, Silver Springs, Maryland.

Pillemer, K. & Moore, D. (1989). Abuse of patients in nursing homes: Findings from a survey of staff. *Gerontologist, 29*(3), 314-320.

Rawls, J. (1971). *A theory of justice*. Cambridge, MA: Harvard University Press.

The American Nurses Association. (1987). *Standards for gerontological nursing practices*. Kansas City, MO: The American Nurses Association.

Walters, L. (1991). The principle of medical confidentiality. In T.A. Mappes & J.S. Zembaty (Eds.), *Biomedical ethics*. New York: McGraw-Hill.

Wetle, T. (1988). Ethical Issues. In J. Rowe & R. Besdine (Eds.), *Geriatric Medicine*. Boston: Little-Brown & Co., 75-88.

Wetle, T., Crabtree, B., Clemens, E., Dubitzky, D., Eslami, M. & Kerr, M. (1991). Balancing safety and autonomy: Defining and living with acceptable risk. *Gerontologist, 31*(11), 237.

Wetle, T., Levkoff, S., Cwikel, J., & Rosen, A. (1988). Nursing home resident participation in medical decisions: Perceptions and preferences. *Gerontologist, 28*, 32-38.

APPENDIX

TABLE I. American Medical Association, Principles of Medical Ethics

Section I

A physician shall be dedicated to providing competent medical service with compassion and respect for human dignity.

Section II

A physician shall deal honestly with patients and colleagues, and strive to expose those physicians deficient in character or competence, or who engage in fraud or deception.

Section III

A physician shall respect the law and also recognize a responsibility to seek changes in those requirements which are contrary to the best interests of the patient.

Section IV

A physician shall respect the rights of patients, of colleagues, and of other health professionals, and shall safeguard patient confidences within the constraints of the law.

Section V

A physician shall continue to study, apply and advance scientific knowledge, make relevant information available to patients, colleagues, and the public, obtain consultation, and use the talents of other health professionals when indicated.

Section VI

A physician shall, in the provision of appropriate patient care, except in emergencies, be free to choose whom to serve, with whom to associate, and the environment in which to provide medical services.

Section VII

A physician shall recognize a responsibility to participate in activities contributing to an improved community.

Source: *Code of Medical Ethics: Current Opinions with Annotations*, American Medical Association, ©1994.

APPENDIX (continued)
TABLE II. American Nurses Association Code for Nurses

Statement I

The nurse provides services with respect for human dignity and the uniqueness of the client unrestricted by considerations of social or economic status, personal attributes, or the nature of health problems.

Statement II

The nurse safeguards the client's right to privacy by judiciously protecting information of confidential nature.

Statement III

The nurse acts to safeguard the client and the public when health care and safety are affected by the incompetent, unethical, or illegal practice of any person.

Statement IV

The nurse assumes responsibility and accountability for individual nursing judgements and actions.

Statement V

The nurse maintains competence in nursing.

Statement VI

The nurse exercises informed judgment and uses individual competence and qualifications as criteria in seeking consultation, accepting responsibilities, and delegating nursing activities to others.

Statement VII

The nurse participates in activities that contribute to the ongoing development of the profession's body of knowledge.

Statement VIII

The nurse participates in the profession's efforts to implement and improve standards of nursing.

Statement IX

The nurse participates in the profession's efforts to establish and maintain conditions of employment conducive to high-quality nursing care.

Statement X

The nurse participates in the profession's efforts to protect the public from misinformation and misrepresentation and to maintain the integrity of nursing.

Statement XI

The nurse collaborates with members of the health professions and other citizens in promoting community and national efforts to meet the health needs of the public.

TABLE III. Standards for Gerontological Nursing Practice

Standard I

All gerontological nursing services are planned, organized and directed by a nurse executive with a Bachelors or Masters preparation and experience in gerontological nursing.

Standard II

The nurse participates in the generation and testing of theory as a basis for clinical decisions and uses theoretical concepts to guide effective practice.

Standard III

The health status of the older person is regularly assessed in a comprehensible, accurate, and systematic manner. The information obtained during the health assessment is accessible and shared with appropriate team members of the interdisciplinary health care team including the person in their family.

Standard IV

The nurse uses health assessment data to determine nursing diagnoses.

Standard V

The nurse develops the plan of care in conjunction with the older person and appropriate others. Mutual goals and priorities are set and measures in the care plan address the therapeutic, preventative, restorative, and rehabilitative needs of the older person. The care plan helps the older person obtain and maintain the highest level of health, well-being, and quality of life achievable as well as a peaceful death. The plan of care facilitates continuity of care over time as the client moves to various care settings and is revised as necessary.

Standard VI

The nurse guided by the plan of care intervenes to provide care, to restore the older person's functional capabilities, and to prevent complications in excess disability. Nursing interventions are derived from nursing diagnoses and based on gerontological nursing theory.

Standard VII

The nurse continually evaluates the client and family's responses through intervention in order to determine progress toward goal obtainment and to revise the database nursing diagnoses, and plan of care.

Standard VIII

The nurse collaborates with other members of the health care team in the various settings in which care is given to the older person. The team meets regularly to evaluate the effectiveness of the care plan of the client and family to adjust the care plan to accommodate changing needs.

APPENDIX (continued)

TABLE III (continued)

Standard X

The nurse uses the code of ethics for nurses established by the American Nurses Association as a guide to ethical decision making in practice.

Standard XI

The nurse assumes responsibility for professional development and contributes to the professional growth of the interdiciplinary team members. The nurse participates in the peer review and other means of evaluation to insure quality of nursing practice (1987).

Reprinted with permission from *Standards and Scope of Gerontological Nursing Practice,* ©1987, American Nurses Association, Washington, DC.

Chapter Four

A Mental Health Perspective

Robert S. Marin, MD
Bridget K. Booth, MSN
Charles W. Lidz, PhD
Richard K. Morycz, PhD
Robert M. Wettstein, MD

SUMMARY. Mental health professionals contribute in important ways to both the clinical and ethical issues raised by cases of elder mistreatment. Their clinical competencies contribute to improving quality of life by diminishing psychological suffering and the symptoms of mental illness. They are also used for managing the ethical issues raised by these cases. The ethics of mental health care are based on the values of beneficence, nonmaleficence, autonomy, and justice. The value of autonomy in mental health care gives priority to an individual's long-term ability to act as independently, rationally, and fully in all aspects of life as possible. The concepts of legal and clinical competence also aid in managing the ethical problems presented by cases of elder mistreatment. The ethical protocols of mental health professionals may be distinguished from some other disciplines by the premium given to long-term autonomy and by the aim

---

Robert S. Marin, Bridget K. Booth, Charles W. Lidz, Richard K. Morycz, and Robert M. Wettstein are affiliated with the Department of Psychiatry, University of Pittsburgh School of Medicine.

Address correspondence to: Robert S. Marin, MD, Western Psychiatric Institute and Clinic, 3811 O'Hara Street, Pittsburgh, PA 15213.

The authors thank Ms. Barbara Medfisch who provided valuable assistance in preparing the manuscript.

[Haworth co-indexing entry note]: "A Mental Health Perspective." Marin, Robert S. et al. Co-published simultaneously in *Journal of Elder Abuse & Neglect* (The Haworth Press, Inc.) Vol. 7, No. 2/3, 1995, pp. 49-68; and: *Elder Mistreatment: Ethical Issues, Dilemmas, and Decisions* (ed: Tanya Fusco Johnson) The Haworth Press, Inc., 1995, pp. 49-68. [Single or multiple copies of this article are available from The Haworth Document Delivery Service: 1-800-342-9678, 9:00 a.m. - 5:00 p.m. (EST)].

49

of insuring treatment for all persons involved in cases of elder mistreatment, rather than limiting treatment responsibilities to the victim. *[Article copies available from The Haworth Document Delivery Service: 1-800-342-9678.]*

INTRODUCTION

Mental health professionals have an important role to play in managing cases of elder abuse and neglect. Alleviating psychological suffering and the symptoms of mental illness may contribute directly to the clinical care of victims, as well as others, involved in these cases. But mental health professionals are also called on to help manage the ethical questions that such cases present. When should victims of elder abuse be forced to accept clinical interventions? Under what circumstances should neglected elders be permitted to remain at home when this endangers their safety or health? Although clinicians usually think of their clinical competencies in strictly clinical terms, mental health care also offers a valuable and powerful perspective for approaching the ethical problems presented by cases of elder abuse and neglect.

To illustrate how mental health professionals approach such ethical problems we will first discuss the professional ethics of the mental health disciplines. We will then describe the broader ethical framework of health care professionals. Since the treatment ethic of health care professionals entails integrating ethical principles with the clinical process, we will summarize briefly the major elements of assessment and treatment in mental health care. Also by way of introduction to the case discussions, we will offer a brief discussion of the concept of competence whose evaluation is often integral to clinical intervention.

ETHICS OF THE MENTAL HEALTH DISCIPLINES

Mental health care is not the province of any one discipline. Mental health professionals may be trained within the fields of nursing, social work, psychology, psychiatry, and others. Since the social work and nursing viewpoints are presented in other chapters, we focus here on psychology and psychiatry. Actually, the ethics of psychiatric social workers and psychiatric nurses may have as much in common with other mental health professionals as they do with their larger professions. Most of the principles we discuss probably would be agreed to by each of these disciplines, although differences are undoubtedly present.

Formal guidance on the ethics of mental health professionals is found in the ethical codes of the American Psychiatric and American Psychological Associations (American Psychiatric Association, 1993; Directory of the American Psychological Association, 1993). Both offer important statements of the values, aims, and obligations of mental health professionals. Both codes emphasize competence and its elements, e.g., acquiring and applying knowledge to patient care; consulting with others as indicated; using the talents of other health professionals and insuring that collaborative or multidisciplinary efforts yield care of high quality; recognizing the limits of one's competence; and practicing with integrity, honesty, fairness, and respect for others. The code of the American Psychological Association urges psychologists to be "aware of their own belief systems, values, needs, and limitations and the effect of these on their work . . . to accord appropriate respect to the fundamental rights, dignity, and worth of all people . . . [and] to respect the rights of individuals to privacy, confidentiality, self-determination, and autonomy, mindful that legal and other obligations may lead to inconsistency and conflict with the exercise of these rights." It goes on to say that such judgments must be informed by awareness of individual, role, and cultural influences on personal and social values. A final section, "Resolving Ethical Issues," notes that there may be conflicts between the ethical codes of psychologists and other professions. Such conflicts are to be clarified and resolved in a manner that permits the most complete adherence to the ethical code.

These professional codes are important. However, the ethical concerns of mental health professionals are addressed more fully in the literature of medical ethics. Medical ethicists have tried to develop coherent frameworks for guiding reasoning and actions about ethical questions. Ideally, the rules and principles that make up such "action guides" (Beauchamp & Childress, 1994) would be deducible from ethical theories. In reality, theorists and practitioners move freely between theory, principles, rules, and actual cases in attempting to develop an approach (or protocol) to the ethical questions arising in providing health care. In other words, ethical questions about clinical care are not answered by appealing directly or unambiguously to some theory or principle. Rather, knowledge of ethical theory and principles is considered in evaluating the persons and circumstances of a particular case or situation.

Four values frame the dominant biomedical approach to ethical decision-making. Autonomy, the first of these values, is concerned with respecting and promoting self-determination. Autonomy involves both the "freedom to" act and acting with "freedom from" external sanctions. The second value is nonmaleficence which holds that decisions or actions should be guided by the obligation not to inflict harm. The principle of nonmaleficence applies both to clients and professionals involved in elder abuse cases. As an ethical guide for health professionals, nonmaleficence constrains the types of treatment that are acceptable in a particular situation, for example, by limiting the risks patients are subjected to by a treatment. The third value, beneficence, articulates our obligation to perform acts that will benefit others, including those positive acts taken to prevent harm being done, although the latter also might be construed as illustrating nonmaleficence. Clearly, many of the most difficult dilemmas faced in managing cases of elder mistreatment have to do with competing claims of autonomy and beneficence. Justice, the fourth value, is concerned with the fair and equitable distribution of benefits and burdens. Justice applies to cases of elder mistreatment when professionals need to apportion their efforts because of limited funding for services or personnel. For example, issues of justice influence health service providers who tolerate milder forms of elder mistreatment because they do not have the resources to provide services to the less needy among their caseloads.

Of these four values the dominant trend in American medical ethics, which is shared by many mental health professionals, is to give priority to the principle of autonomy as a guiding principle for evaluating the process of decision-making about health care (Murray et al., 1994). However, the literature of general medical ethics has focused on autonomy as applied to patient decision-making per se, so-called decision-making autonomy. Patient decision-making is certainly important to mental health professionals; mental health professionals are often involved in preserving the opportunity and right of patients to make autonomous choices. However, mental health patients are often compromised in their general or day-to-day, functional autonomy as well as their capacity for making independent, rational decisions. As a consequence, mental health professionals have a broader or more fundamental concern with what may be called long-term autonomy or autonomous living. (This is related to the distinction between immediate and long-term autonomy discussed in Chapter Three.) By this we mean that when conflicts arise, mental health professionals often place a premium on promoting the individual's long-term ability to act as independently, rationally, and fully in all aspects of life as possible. In other words, the central value is on a long-term and comprehensive concept of autonomy, rather than the circumstances surrounding the freedom of choice exercised around a treatment decision, i.e., decision-making autonomy. As a corollary, mental health professionals tend to focus on the underlying problems that interfere with long-term autonomy. When there is a conflict between decision-making autonomy and long-term autonomy, mental health professionals are often willing to compromise decision-making autonomy to the minimal extent necessary to support long-term autonomy (Lidz, 1983; Lidz & Arnold, 1993).

This view of autonomy derives primarily from the fact that some recipients of mental health care have diminished functional capacity, even when they are legally competent. They suffer from disabilities that preclude or at least substantially compromise their capacity for making sensible and autonomous decisions regarding their own welfare. Individuals suffering from serious mental illnesses often do not have the self-control, judgment, or understanding necessary to make decisions that fulfill their goals. Focusing on such disabilities and their long-term consequences leads mental health professionals to urge others–patients, families, legal systems–to accept short term or limited intrusions upon decision-making autonomy to invest in treatment resources that in the long term will restore ability or at least minimize disability.

These values can be used to characterize many of the ethical dilemmas posed in the cases we are discussing. For example, in Case One, attending to Mary's well being entails a conflict between respecting her decision-making autonomy (e.g., her preference to refuse care or remain at home) and the beneficent intent of health care providers to support the health and long-term autonomy of Mary and her sister. In Case Two, it may be desirable to respect John's decision-making autonomy by permitting him to remain at home, but choosing to do so obviously places him at continued risk of being neglected and abused by his son (a problem of nonmaleficence). In Case Three, the administrator of the nursing home may find a conflict among the values of beneficence and justice: Beneficence dictates preventing Bonnie from being mistreated by her husband; but if disciplinary action is taken against neglectful staff, the beneficent mission of the nursing home may be compromised by society's failure to provide adequate training and staff to run the nursing home acceptably, which is an issue of justice.

The foregoing are not the only values in the protocols of health professionals. Two additional values are of particular importance in understanding how the foregoing values are integrated into clinical practice. The first, already mentioned, is the obligation to perform work competently. It is by providing competent (skillful, knowledgeable, judicious, experienced) care that the mental health professional implements ethical protocols. The second is that mental health care, along with other health care fields, is guided by a treatment ethic. By this we mean that a fundamental aim of mental health professionals is to take clinical actions that will ameliorate psychological suffering and enhance psychological well being; the social and functional concomitants of psychological impairment are addressed in the process. Thus the treatment ethic provides the rationale for many of the actions that the mental health professional takes to manage or resolve the ethical dilemmas presented by cases of elder abuse and neglect. To understand how competence and the treatment ethic function within the mental health protocol, it will be helpful to briefly describe the clinical aspects of mental health care.

CLINICAL ASPECTS OF THE MENTAL HEALTH PROTOCOL

Broadly speaking, the mental health approach to clinical care operates within a medical model. A person's problems are characterized in terms of symptoms that warrant comprehensive assessment. This assessment requires examining the biological, psychological, social, and environmental structure of the person's life and functioning. The multidisciplinary comprehensive assessment integrates these several domains of information into a diagnostic formulation of the patient's symptoms. A treatment plan is then developed based on the patient's diagnosis and the biopsychosocial context of the patient's current life. Personal and cultural values, family and community resources, legal precedents and restrictions, and a host of other variables are considered as part of this process.

The treatment ethic in mental health care is realized through three forms of treatment: biomedical interventions such as psychotropic medications and electroconvulsive therapy; interpersonal and other psychological interventions such as individual or family therapy; and socioenvironmental interventions such as arranging for in-home services, protective service evaluations, legal consultation, or transportation. Treatment is provided with knowledge of legal constraints and resources, particularly those based on the patient's legal and clinical competence, which will be addressed shortly. The outcome of this treatment oriented mental health protocol is that biological and interpersonal interventions, operating within the social and legal context of a particular case, provide an effective means for resolving or integrating the competing ethical concerns that must inform competent mental health care.

The treatment ethic of mental health care leads to obvious, but easily neglected, ways to resolve some of the dilemmas faced in cases of elder mistreatment. For example, without a treatment ethic, a self-neglecting psychotic older adult living in a trailer might be placed involuntarily in a personal care home or long-term care facility on the grounds of incompetence and endangerment. However, from a mental health vantage, this would be premature and potentially inappropriate. If this person's psychosis is due to hypothyroidism or schizophrenia, diagnosing and treating these conditions would offer a reasonable possibility that the patient could continue to live at home. In fact, such treatment might even be accomplished without hospitalization. Offering an older adult these options is of obvious value in resolving dilemmas between the principles of autonomy and beneficence or between long-term autonomy and decision-making autonomy. Educating patients about such options provides a useful means of approaching their reluctance to collaborate with health care professionals. Such psychoeducational approaches, coupled with effective communication and alliance building, may suffice to persuade an older adult at risk for abuse or neglect to accept a treatment or safeguard that would otherwise be rejected because it was perceived as an infringement on autonomy. Similar possibilities are central to the clinical and ethical management of Mary and Martha, John and Manny, and Bonnie and her husband. In each case, there are diagnosable conditions whose treatment may lead to crisply different determinations of "the right" thing to do. Our discussion of the three cases will illustrate these possibilities.

LEGAL ASPECTS OF THE MENTAL HEALTH PROTOCOLS: THE CONCEPTS OF LEGAL AND CLINICAL COMPETENCE

There are many aspects to the interface of mental health and the law. Of particular relevance for these cases is the mental health perspective on the concept of competence. Mental health practitioners follow broadly the approach to competence used in the medical setting (Weiner & Wettstein, 1993). We distinguish between two forms of competence: legal competence and clinical competence. Competence generally refers to the individual's ability to perform a task. An adult is presumed to be legally competent, and remains so, unless and until declared incompetent by a court of law. Legal competence is a dichotomous concept. One either is or is not legally incompetent. An individual can be adjudicated incompetent to function in all or only one or more specific areas.

Depending upon applicable state law, individuals may be adjudicated incompetent based upon a variety of conditions, all of which are relevant to the setting of elder mistreatment. These conditions include mental disorders (of any etiology, including substance abuse), mental retardation, physical handicap, medical disorder, and sometimes old age. The presence of such conditions, of course, is not sufficient to be adjudicated incompetent. In fact, few individuals with mental illness are ever found legally incompetent. Most psychiatric patients, whether symptomatic or not, are capable of making and communicating appropriate decisions regarding their welfare. In particular, hospitalization per se does not imply that an individual is legally incompetent, not even if the person has been involuntarily hospitalized.

Clinical competence, usually referred to as "capacity," is task-specific in that the issue is whether the individual is able to perform a particular act, whether making a decision about one's health care or completing a particular task (Weiner & Wettstein, 1993). Clinical capacity is also time-specific in that a person's capacity can vary over a period of time, even a few hours. A patient's changing clinical status means that the person's capacities will correspondingly be altered. Clinical capacities are not dichotomously present or absent but vary in degree.

Criteria or standards for competence, whether clinical or legal, vary among jurisdictions and with the particular issue, e.g., competence to execute an advance directive or to refuse treatment. Typically, to be competent the person must be able to understand, if not appreciate, the current situation or problem, the nature of the proposed action, including its risks and benefits, and must be able to communicate this understanding to others. The individual may also be required to make and communicate a decision that is rational based upon the available information (Appelbaum & Grisso, 1988; Roth, Meisel, & Lidz, 1977). Many authors speak of a "sliding scale" of clinical competence based on the balance between the functional capacity of the individual and the risk/benefit ratio of the particular task or procedure that must be decided (Weiner & Wettstein, 1993). Specifically, the greater the potential harm or the smaller the potential benefit of a proposed intervention, the higher the level of competence required of the consenting individual. Thus, Mary (Case One) would be considered competent to consent to a hospitalization to evaluate her for potentially reversible causes of dementia, but she might not be considered competent to consent to a less useful intervention. Correspondingly, she may be considered competent to refuse a risky intervention, such as experimental surgery, but may not be considered competent to refuse a highly beneficial and low risk intervention, such as homecare services. Making judgments of clinical competence "risk-specific" in this way may lead to the paradoxical situation that a patient might be considered competent to consent to a highly beneficial and minimal risk procedure but incompetent to refuse it.

Decisions about an individual's competence are value-laden, which in part may explain differing opinions between disciplines about an individual's competence. Further, it is difficult if not impossible to opine about an individual's capacity without knowledge of that person's previously expressed attitudes, opinions, values, and decisions, and whether a currently expressed preference or decision is concordant with earlier ones, i.e., "authenticity" (Baumgarten, 1980; Faden & Beauchamp, 1986).

THE THREE CASES

Mary and Martha

There are three parts to the mental health approach in this case: obtaining appropriate clinical assessments of Mary and Martha; circumventing Mary's resistance to intervention using clinical and interpersonal strategies; and organizing community and legal resources to safeguard both of them. The clinical assessment component is based on the knowledge that the mental status symptoms of patients like Mary and her sister may be caused or aggravated by medical, neurological, or psychiatric disorders that are treatable. Progressive dementia in this setting is most often due to irreversible neurological disease, especially Alzheimer's disease and vascular dementia (American Psychiatric Association, 1994). But there are many causes of dementia that are themselves reversible. Examples include hyperthyroidism, hypoparathyroidism, vitamin B12 deficiency, normal pressure hydrocephalus, and subdural hematoma. Furthermore, even if an irreversible dementia is a correct diagnosis, it may be complicated by delirium, depression, psychosis, irritability, apathy, or other behavioral abnormalities that constitute important reversible factors (Marin et al., 1995: Schneider et al., 1994; Trzepacz, 1994). Evaluating these possibilities requires competent, comprehensive neuropsychiatric and medical evaluation. Arranging for such an evaluation is required to meet the standard of care of the mental health professional or other health care clinician.

Finding such reversible behavioral problems might contribute directly to resolving some of the ethical problems in the case. A reversible factor in Mary's dementia or in the condition of her sister Martha might lead to improvement in self-care behavior or judgment. This would decrease the risk of continued in-home living, provide an opportunity for strengthening relationships between Mary and the service providers, and offer the possibility of a change in judgment that would eventually lead to Mary's accepting alternative living arrangements when clinically warranted.

This assessment is an integral part of the second step, finding ways to circumvent Mary's resistance to accepting care. It is a clinical axiom that the approach we take to presenting information influences the responses we obtain. As an illustration, consider the attempts made to inform or educate Mary about her current situation. What were the circumstances under which it was determined that Mary was not going to accept care or help from anyone? Was the question asked on her doorstep in the last 10 minutes of a hurried evaluation? Or were these questions raised after a lengthy and perhaps extended evaluation–one lasting perhaps an hour or two, or extended over a period of two or three meetings? Were attempts made to involve the sons in getting Mary to accept evaluation and treatment? It is also important to consider that Mary may misunderstand the rationale she has been given for the recommended interventions. If not, it may help to reframe the rationale so that the link is clearly made to the way Mary understands her problems. Patients with Alzheimer's disease frequently deny the severity of their problems and many will resist intervention to help them with their memory problems. However, given a trusting relationship, it is common for them to accept assistance for some other purpose. Anxiety or fear, depression or despair, worries about money or mobility, are just some of the problems that can be used by clinicians to develop an alliance out of which agreements can be developed. In Mary's case, we are told that she agreed to a physical examination that revealed bruises on her hip and arm. She attributed them to a fall a few days earlier. Mary may be closed to the idea of a "psychiatric examination to rule out Alzheimer's disease," but she might be amenable to seeing her family doctor to check if she is having neurological problems whose treatment would improve her balance, keep her from falling, or make it easier for her to take care of Martha.

If we fail to secure Mary's cooperation in safeguarding her and her sister, the competency laws of most states would enable mental health clinicians to seek determinations of legal incompetence for Mary and Martha. These determinations would be made independently and the guardians would then make the necessary decisions on their behalf. But what decisions would be the appropriate ones to make? Mary may wish to remain her sister's caregiver, but our willingness to respect that wish, assuming Mary is not legally incompetent, hinges on her clinical competence to do so. Mary's clinical competence would be evaluated based on her capacities *and* on Martha's needs. If Martha simply needs antihypertensive medications, and if a visiting nurse can elicit Mary's cooperation in setting up a medication box that would insure this outcome, then Mary can continue to function as "the caregiver," although, in fact, she is now sharing these responsibilities with the visiting nurse. On the other hand, if Mary cannot meet Martha's elementary hygiene, medical, or safety needs, she will not be able to continue in this role at all. Thus, evaluating Mary's clinical competence entails determining Martha's needs, the risks if these are not being met, and the probabilities that Mary can meet some or all of these needs. This information is then evaluated in light of Mary *and* Martha's values and the availability of the necessary resources within the household, the family, or the community. This approach provides a useful way of answering the question, "Should Mary be permitted to remain Martha's caregiver?" Rather than answer the question in purely ethical terms or in all-or-none fashion, we would analyze the many aspects of the problem in practical and specific terms, guiding ourselves by the knowledge of the sisters' values.

Determining the rights and obligations of Mary's sons and church visitors entails similar ambiguities and limitations. Although some would argue that adult children have an obligation to provide care for their elderly and disabled parents, this is controversial (Gilliland, 1986). In the United States many families agree that children have a responsibility for the care of their elderly and disabled parents. This is borne out, on first glance, by the fact that many homebound elderly are indeed cared for by their children (U.S. Select Committee on Aging, 1987). However, the individuals who agree in principle that children bear such a responsibility also may claim that such responsibility should not require them to use or sacrifice their own resources for this purpose. In the United States when parents' resources have been expended, the government becomes the preferred source of financial and residential support (Gillaland, 1986). This is a culture specific value system, however. In the People's Republic of China children offer their financial support as well as their homes to their aging parents (Sung, 1990).

The clinician's task is to appraise the values of the children, determine whether they are consistent with the clients' values and, if so, facilitate the children's finding ways to take actions that express their own beneficent obligations toward their parents. Given the range of individual values and circumstances involved in such situations, a mental health professional attempting to insist that a child accept a beneficent role vis-à-vis a parent would be ethically problematic and, likely, counterproductive. To the extent that value conflicts exist among the children's, the clients,' and the professional's ethics, these differences need to be made explicit and negotiated. When mutually agreeable values and goals are present, the mental health professional would develop a plan to identify and overcome obstacles that exist to realizing these goals. This may mean that the clinician will work with the children to help obtain or identify the information, resources, support, advice, or treatment that will make it possible for them to meet their responsibilities more fully.

If faced with a surfeit of available, competent, and appropriate caregivers, legal and mental health convention would give priority to Mary's sons as potential care providers. This does not eliminate ethical conflicts and ambiguities, however. If, as the case suggests, the sons will be remotely involved, their potential role would be diminished. The same would be the case if their involvement would prove unacceptably disruptive to Mary and Martha. But here again the principle of clinical competence needs to be invoked. Who should determine whether a move to another community is too disruptive? In principle, a patient with moderate cognitive impairment may be unable to refuse neuropsychiatric evaluation, but she may be competent to choose to live with her sons even if it entails giving up her home. If her care is placed in the hands of a guardian, however, it is the guardian who will make the decision, albeit with appropriate consideration of Mary's and Martha's values or preferences.

If the sons are not able to serve as guardians, other potential caregivers may be considered. If the church visitors and sons did not offer the necessary resources for Mary and Martha, the institution providing the multidisciplinary assessment and its case manager would assume responsibility for the needs and care of Mary and Martha.

John and Manny

The outlines of the mental health approach to managing this case are similar to that of the previous one. The ethical dilemmas in this case would be approached as part of a comprehensive, biopsychosocial evaluation. After evaluating John's medical and psychosocial status, we would introduce clinical, interpersonal, legal, financial, and community interventions aimed at terminating or reducing the risk of further abuse.

As with Mary there are numerous clinical conditions, both medical and psychiatric, that may be contributing to John's and Manny's behavior. A few questions of diagnosis and treatment deserve emphasis. First, the case history mistakenly indicates that John does not need treatment because he suffers only from a minor depression. The fact that he is mildly depressed *may* mean that he does not require medication as part of his treatment. But it certainly does not mean that he does not require treatment. Ongoing mistreatment with or without depression is an indication for mental health evaluation (Ammerman & Hersen, 1990). Perhaps John tolerates Manny's abuse because of his own personality or interpersonal difficulties or perhaps it is part of longstanding adaptation that he (and his wife) made to Manny's serious mental illness throughout their lifetime. Either of these would be indications for a psychoeducational and counseling approach to working with John and, if his psychosis were properly treated, Manny also (Marin & Morycz, 1990; Quinn & Tomita, 1986). Furthermore, a growing literature highlights that patients with mild or so-called subsyndromal depression are diagnostically related to those with major depression and responsive to similar treatment (Schneider et al., 1994). Thus, medications as well as psychosocial interventions may be helpful even if John suffers "only" from a minor depression.

Second is that a mental health assessment would focus on the possibility that John may be suffering from an unrecognized serious mental illness, including depression. The fact that he is lucid and able to manage his own affairs does not exclude the possibility of serious impairment in judgment due to neuropsychiatric illness. Diseases affecting frontal lobe function or other so-called executive functions can be detected by simple clinical assessments (Royall, 1994). However, they may go undetected by what are now conventional screening devices, such as the mini-mental state examination (Folstein et al., 1975; Royall, 1994). Actually, the symptoms of executive function or frontal lobe disease include many features that are important in this case: passivity, withdrawal, lack of initiative, lack of reactivity, perseveration, inability to make use of new information, environmental dependency, lack of drive, impairment of insight, impulsivity, and poor judgment.

The issue of poor judgment is of particular relevance to this and other cases of elder mistreatment. Abused elders may rationalize tolerating others mistreating them by citing their parental obligations or religious beliefs, but this does not explain their poor judgment. The vast majority of responsible and religious-minded people probably would not permit themselves to be mistreated. Therefore, John's judgment requires careful evaluation. From a clinical standpoint the presence of depression or executive dysfunction are examples of useful clinical explanations for John's passivity and related features.

Assessment of John's judgment is also important from the standpoint of the ethical issues in the case. Under some circumstances, John certainly would have the right to place his parental responsibility above his personal safety. However, this is a qualified right. Respecting John's preferences will depend on the assessment of his competence prior to his discharge from the hospital. This competence evaluation would benefit from the general clinical assessment already discussed. As implied in the earlier discussion of clinical competence, John's returning home would require a high level of capacity on his part since the level of risk for him is high. As the foregoing discussion of neuropsychiatric assessment makes clear, a great deal more clinical information would be necessary before the mental health staff and the hospital evaluated the appropriateness of John's returning home. Equally important in evaluating John's competence and, thereby, our obligation to support his wish to return home, would be an understanding of John's values, his personality, his understanding of Manny's actions and motivation, the history of their relationship before and after his wife's death, and so on.

John legally retains the right to return home until he is adjudicated incompetent. However, there is opportunity to intervene even if John is not legally incompetent. If, as is likely, John's decision-making capacity is to some degree diminished, the mental health professional should attempt to negotiate with John a treatment plan that would permit him to return home (thus respecting his decision-making autonomy) in exchange for John's accepting some combination of services that would safeguard him and his interests (thus respecting John's long-term autonomy). This plan would include involving Adult Protective Services staff or other professionals who can monitor the ongoing nature or risks of further mistreatment. At this juncture in the case the responsibility for John's welfare is shared by John and his treatment team. His sister's capacity to assume responsibility for his care, either formally through guardianship or informally through supporting the outpatient care plan, would be evaluated as part of the ongoing assessment.

In concluding, it is important to emphasize that the mental health professional's approach to this case would be guided throughout by a treatment ethic. The clinical and competence assessments are of direct clinical use. They serve other purposes simultaneously. First, carrying them out will begin the process of developing a treatment alliance with John. John needs to be actively and positively engaged in his own treatment. Obstacles to the treatment alliance need to be identified and treated. Second, health care providers have a duty to inform their clients or patients about their evaluations and recommendations. If the facts of the abuse are at odds with John's understanding, the professional should explain them clearly to John. The mental health professional will provide John with a reasonable understanding of the potential interventions, including their rationale, risks, and potential benefits. Third, the exchange of information involved in the clinical and competence assessments serves a therapeutic purpose. Providing information and educating John permits accurate labeling of the nature and circumstances of the abuse. This will help develop a shared understanding of the problem that will provide a foundation for actions John (or the health care professional) may eventually take to terminate or prevent further abuse.

Treatment per se entails developing interventions to terminate or prevent ongoing mistreatment. The interpersonal precipitants of abuse need to be identified and concrete suggestions offered that may reduce the risk of their recurring. In longer term interventions the aims of prevention might be furthered by psychotherapeutic interventions (Marin & Morycz, 1990) that would address the ways in which John's attitudes and values, his lifelong relationship with his son, his attitude toward his son, the loss of his wife, and the meaning of his own aging may be contributing to his tolerating mistreatment. Our discussion has focussed on John, but the mental health professional also would attempt to arrange treatment for Manny, albeit with different providers so that a conflict of interest would be avoided. Arranging treatment for Manny would be of direct value to Manny and his long-term autonomy, although in the short run his autonomy might have to be compromised in order to assure his treatment. Given Manny's mental state and the injurious actions he has taken he would likely be found committable to a psychiatric hospital. The treatment ethic would lead us to arrange treatment for Manny, both for his own sake and as an integral part of helping John. Of course, fulfilling an obligation to provide treatment to Manny does not mean that his needs are the same as John's. Clearly, safeguarding John takes priority over respecting Manny's right to pursue his own (psychotic or antisocial) interests. However, from a mental health vantage managing the ethical dilemmas involved in safeguarding John are compatible with the aim of supporting Manny's long-term autonomy as well. Both Manny and John deserve competent mental health care.

Bonnie

Alliance building, multidisciplinary assessment, and comprehensive treatment planning are the mainstays in approaching the ethical problems posed by this case as well. The behavioral problems are complex. However, their management from a mental health standpoint is eased, in principle, by the fact that Bonnie resides in a health care facility that has responsibility for her treatment. In this context, a mental health perspective provides useful interventions for preventing or minimizing many of the symptomatic disturbances described, including the emotional and physical abuse.

The case summary offers ample information regarding the main problems requiring treatment. Bonnie suffers from multiple, severe impairments that have led to her residing in a nursing home where she can receive the care she needs to deal with her disabilities. We assume for the sake of discussion that the nursing home is appropriate for managing a patient like this.

Bonnie's nursing home care must take into consideration three interacting psychiatric issues: her drug dependence, her personality disorder, and her marital problems. Of the three, the drug dependence is most important, partly because it is likely to have such a large impact on the other two. It is also important because there is no ambiguity for the nursing home in specifying the expected behavior: use of illicit drugs in the nursing home is not acceptable. By contrast, there may be disagreements about the acceptability of some manifestations of Bonnie's personality disorder and her marital problems. At least in the initial stages of treatment, interventions focussed on her drug dependence will provide the most effective ways of diminishing the manifestations of Bonnie's marital conflicts and personality disorder.

As presented there is strong evidence that Bonnie's drug dependence is highly symptomatic. The evidence includes: excessive doses of drugs, use of more than one sedative hypnotic agent, history of doctor shopping, and her access to multiple physicians to obtain drugs. In the nursing home Bonnie's unexplained lethargy and withdrawal should serve as warning signs that clinical investigation is indicated. The fact that these symptoms coincide with conflictual visits from the husband should be documented *and* reported to the nursing home administrator. Given the severity of these problems, the nursing home should request a psychiatric consultation.

As was the case for Manny, carrying out a full history and assessment would help engage Bonnie constructively in her own treatment. It would also provide a means for beginning to identify and confront Bonnie with the nature of the problem behaviors. Appropriate staff need to identify themselves to Bonnie as her clinician(s). The staff will explain that they intend to help Bonnie have a healthy, constructive life in the nursing home. Bonnie needs to understand that she, as well as the nursing home staff, have responsibilities for making this possible. The nursing home's resources and limitations must be described to Bonnie. The conditions for her remaining in the nursing home need to be made explicit.

Focussing on Bonnie's drug dependence and disruptive behavior leads to a variety of interventions that can be undertaken to prevent or minimize the risks of further incidents. At an early point in this assessment and contracting process, the nursing home, via the treating clinicians or consultant team, will inform Bonnie of staff concern that she is abusing medications with her husband's complicity. Bonnie would have the opportunity to voice her concerns, questions, and complaints as well. The nursing home has no need to negotiate regarding the issues of drug use, physical and psychological abuse, or Bonnie's mistreatment of other patients. However, given the severity of her personality disorder, the nursing home probably will have to anticipate a lot of negotiating regarding more subtle instances of interpersonal conflict.

Faced with firm limits regarding her drug dependence, Bonnie may prefer to leave the nursing home. Given her disabilities, this decision is unlikely. If she did express a desire to leave the nursing home, her competence would have to be evaluated with this option in mind. Preventing further abuse in Bonnie's marriage would be difficult if she and her husband had contact with each other outside of the nursing home. Under that circumstance, a question could be raised regarding her right to submit herself to the ongoing risk of abuse. Evaluating her competence would be a critical and complex issue under such circumstances. However, within the nursing home environment the situation is quite different. Bonnie may claim that she has a right to let herself be abused. However, the nursing home has the prior right and obligation to prevent Bonnie from letting herself be abused by her husband or herself. The nursing home is responsible for insuring the safety of its staff and patients; when visiting, it also must safeguard visitors as well.

In developing a treatment plan that will safeguard Bonnie, the nursing home needs to stipulate the conditions for her husband's visiting. Bonnie can be informed that her husband has a right to visit if: Bonnie agrees; he agrees not to bring in drugs and is willing to be searched to insure compliance; and he agrees to appropriate interventions to prevent further conflict with Bonnie. At a minimum the latter entails supporting Bonnie's treatment. Under some circumstances this would include his participating in couple's counseling. Bonnie's husband deserves treatment as well; this should be recommended as part of Bonnie's treatment. He may choose not to comply with these recommendations. However, the nursing home retains the responsibility and the prerogative to set limits on his visits or the kinds of behavior which will be tolerated. For example, the nursing home staff should prevent visiting whenever the husband is intoxicated.

From a mental health or medical standpoint, detecting and reporting physical or psychological abuse is as much a responsibility of the nursing home staff, either the paraprofessional staff or the professional staff, as detecting shortness of breath, inadequate food intake, or chest pain. The discovery of bruises should have been ample cause to prompt definitive investigation by the nursing home. Even in the absence of Bonnie's personality disorder and drug addiction, a psychiatric and medical assessment would be called for. Failure to act appropriately once such information is identified is certainly clinically neglectful and might provide grounds for legal action by the son, for example, if he felt his father's actions were predictable and preventable.

As suggested already, the physical and psychological abuse in this relationship would be managed in the larger context of Bonnie's drug dependence and her personality disorder. This larger context, however, does not overshadow the focus that needs to be given to safeguarding Bonnie from herself and her husband. There is no dilemma from a mental health treatment standpoint in deciding whether Bonnie's right to have visitors deserves priority over her need to be safeguarded. With or without the addiction dimension of this case, Bonnie's husband should be prevented from visiting unless adequate safeguards are obtained. To do this her husband should be brought into the treatment process if possible. The nursing home's assessment of his role would be presented and the conditions for future visiting specified. These might include limiting the couple's visiting time, supervising them, or restricting them to public parts of the facility. If these measures were not successful, the nursing home, as a private institution, could prohibit the husband from visiting. If the husband fails to comply with the nursing home's restrictions, legal action could be taken against him. Despite the longstanding nature of abuse in the marriage and the possibility that Bonnie is also a perpetrator, Bonnie has the option to file criminal charges against her husband. The nursing home may be able to empower and safeguard Bonnie by counseling her accordingly.

CONCLUSIONS

The ethics of mental health professionals are guided by the values of beneficence, nonmaleficence, autonomy, and justice. Mental health care integrates these values into the process of assessment and management because it is based on the treatment ethic: the aim of mental health care is to alleviate psychological suffering and to provide relief from the symptoms and consequences of mental illness. Thus, the clinical and ethical aims of mental health care are interwoven. By providing relief from suffering, mental health professionals contribute to the beneficent aims of health care. The skills and knowledge of mental health professionals also provide valuable and powerful means for managing the ethical problems presented by cases of elder mistreatment. Alliance building and interpersonal skills may allow clients to accept interventions that would otherwise have seemed objectionable. Treatments that yield symptomatic improvement may alter either the judgment or capacities of clients so that ethical dilemmas are diminished or resolved. The treatment ethic also calls on mental health professionals to provide the greatest possible support to clients' autonomy, especially their long-term autonomy. Perhaps more than case managers and protective service professionals, mental health professionals are obliged to offer treatment to the perpetrators or precipitators of abuse. This serves a humane and beneficent aim. It also serves the immediate aims of preventing future abuse and neglect.

REFERENCES

American Psychiatric Association. (1993). *The principles of medical ethics with annotations especially applicable to psychiatry.*

American Psychiatric Association. (1994). *Diagnostic and statistical manual of mental disorders fourth addition.*

Ammerman, R.T. & Hersen, M. (1990). *Treatment of Family Violence.* John Wiley & Sons, Inc.

Applebaum, P.S. & Grisso, T. (1988). *Assessing patients' capacities to consent to treatment. New England Journal of Medicine, 319,* 1635-1638.

Baumgarten, E. (1980). The concept of competence in medical ethics. *Journal of Medical Ethics, 6,*180-184.

Directory of the American Psychological Association. (1993 edition). *Ethical principles of psychologists and code of conduct,* pp. XXVIII-XLI.

Faden, R.R. & Beauchamp, T.L. (1986). *A history and theory of informed consent.* NY: Oxford University Press.

Folstein, M.F., Folstein, S.E. & McHugh, P.R. (1975). Mini mental state: A practical method for grading the cognitive state of patients for the Clinician. *Journal of Psychiatric Research, 12,* 189-198.

Gilliland, N. (1986). Mandating Family Responsibility for Elderly Members: Costs and Benefits. *The Journal of Applied Gerontology, 5,* 26-36.

Lidz, C.W. (1983). Informed consent in mental health treatment: A sociological perspective. *Behavioral Sciences and the Law, 1,* 21-28.

Lidz, C.W. & Arnold, R.M. (1993). Rethinking autonomy in long term care. *University of Miami Law Review, 47,* 603-623.

Marin, R.S. & Morycz, R. (1990). Victims of elder abuse. In R.T. Ammerman and M. Hersen (eds.), *Treatment of Family Violence,* pp. 136-164.

Marin, R.S., Fogel, B.S., Hawkins, J., Duffy, D. & Krupp, B. (1995). Apathy: A treatable syndrome. *Journal of Neuropsychiatry and Clinical Neurosciences, 7,* 23-30.

Murray, T. H., Sagoff M., Childress, J.F. & Fletcher, J.C. (1994). Individualism and community: The contested terrain of autonomy. *Hastings Center Report, 23,* 32-35.

Quinn, M., & Tomita, S. (1986). *Elder abuse and neglect: Causes, diagnosis, and intervention strategies.* New York: Springer.

Roth, L., Meisel, Lidz, C. (1977). Tests of competency to consent to treatment. *Journal of the American Psychiatric Association, 134,* 279-284.

Royall, D.R. (1994). Precis of executive dyscontrol as a cause of problem behavior in dementia. *Experimental Aging Research, 20,* 73-94.

Schneider, L.S., Reynolds, C.F., III, Lebowitz, B.D. & Friedhoff, A.J. (1994). *Diagnosis and treatment of depression in late life: Results of the NIH consensus development conference.* Washington, DC: American Psychiatric Press.

Sung, K.T. (1990). A new look at filial piety. *Gerontologist, 3,* 610-617.

Trzepacz, P.T. (1994). The neuropathogenesis of delirium, a need to focus our research. *Psychosomatics, 35,* 374-391.

U.S. Select Committee on Aging, House of Representatives, 100th Congress. (1987). Exploding the myths: Caregiving in America–A study by the subcommittee on human services. Washington, D.C.: U.S. Government Printing Office.

Weiner, B.A. & Wettstein, R.M. (1993). *Legal issues in mental health care.* New York: Plenum Press.

Chapter Five

An Adult Protective Services Perspective

Paula M. Mixson, LMSW-AP

SUMMARY. This chapter briefly discusses the development of Adult Protective Services (APS) programs in the United States in relation to federal law and policy, depicting the variety in such programs among the states. The chapter then describes ethical values and protocols as well as systemic constraints in public agency practice. These concepts and issues are applied to the three case examples, illustrating the need for multidisciplinary cooperation and coordination to gather the information and resources necessary to resolve the presenting problems. *[Article copies available from The Haworth Document Delivery Service: 1-800-342-9678.]*

INTRODUCTION

In this chapter the term "Adult Protective Services," or APS, refers to publicly funded programs that investigate and intervene in reports of abuse, neglect, and exploitation of adults who are physically or mentally impaired and unable to protect themselves from harm. Although this de-

---

Paula M. Mixson is Assistant to the Deputy Director, Office of Adult Protective Services, Texas Department of Protective and Regulatory Services, P. O. Box 149030, Agency Mail Code E-561, Austin, TX 78714-9030.

The author gratefully acknowledges Nicolo Festa and Tanya Fusco Johnson for their thoughtful review of the draft manuscript.

[Haworth co-indexing entry note]: "An Adult Protective Services Perspective." Mixson, Paula M. Co-published simultaneously in *Journal of Elder Abuse & Neglect* (The Haworth Press, Inc.) Vol. 7, No. 2/3, 1995, pp. 69-87; and: *Elder Mistreatment: Ethical Issues, Dilemmas, and Decisions* (ed: Tanya Fusco Johnson) The Haworth Press, Inc., 1995, pp. 69-87. [Single or multiple copies of this article are available from The Haworth Document Delivery Service: 1-800-342-9678, 9:00 a.m. - 5:00 p.m. (EST)].

scription seems relatively straightforward, understanding how APS workers might approach the three case examples in this volume is more complex. APS programs now exist in every state but practices may vary greatly according to specific law and policy of the particular jurisdiction responsible for the program. This phenomenon perhaps can be attributed to the fact that APS has developed relatively free from the constraining or unifying influences of federal regulation.

Origins of APS

APS in the United States appears to have originated in 1958 when the National Council of Aging created an *ac hoc* committee of social workers to "discuss the potential nationwide need for some type of protective service for elderly persons" (U.S. Department of Health, Education and Welfare [DHEW], 1971, p. 3). Concerned about the growing numbers of incapacitated and isolated older persons at risk due to lack of appropriate caregivers, the committee made recommendations which precipitated "a number of studies, conferences, and research projects and demonstrations" (DHEW, 1971, p. 4). By 1968, although the federal government had funded six protective service programs for the elderly in the interim, a U.S. Senate special committee identified fewer than twenty community protective services programs (Dunn, unpublished, citing pg. 17 of the U.S. Senate Special Committee on Aging's *Protective Services for the Elderly: A Working Paper*, July 1977, U.S. Government Printing Office).

Federal Involvement

The next milestone in the development of APS occurred in 1975, when Congress enacted Title XX of the Social Security Act to strengthen the delivery of social services in the states. To receive Title XX funds, states were required to provide protective services to children, elderly people, and adults with disabilities who were reported to be abused, neglected, or exploited. The enactment of Title XX marked a change in focus, as prior to that time, the little public policy that existed concentrated on "the seriously mentally and physically impaired older person" (Burr, 1982, p. 79), rather than on adults with mental and physical incapacities.

Anticipating further federal involvement in funding and regulation (as had happened with child protective services), states began to enact laws establishing their authority and responsibility to provide protective services for adults and/or older persons. The passage and refinement of these laws at the state level has continued until the present, with little or no federal influence other than financing the resulting programs with Title XX and its successor, social service block grants.

Federal Elder Abuse Legislation

The federal support anticipated after the passage of Title XX did not materialize until late in the following decade. After the 1984 amendments to the Older Americans Act mentioned the need for a national study of elder abuse, the 1987 amendments authorized a $5 million appropriation for an elder abuse prevention program. Congress, however, did not appropriate funds for the prevention of elder abuse, neglect, and exploitation until 1991 and thereafter through the 1992 reauthorization of the Older Americans Act, when Title VII, Chapter 3 was added. The federal funding stream of $2.9 million, minuscule in comparison to what the states already were dedicating to adult protection/elder abuse, flowed through the state units on aging (SUA).

Shortly before Title VII was funded, research conducted by the National Aging Research Center on Elder Abuse (NARCEA) found that all states and US territories had established some type of APS or elder abuse program, with the majority of such programs existing organizationally in various configurations within state human services agencies. For example, in thirty-four states the APS program functioned as part of the state human services agency, independent of the SUA. In another twenty states the APS program was located or joined with the SUA *within* the state human services agency. In only three states was the APS program located within a SUA *outside* the human services agency (Tatara, 1990).

Significantly under-financed as well as overdue, Title VII was designed to coordinate with existing APS programs rather than attempt to replace or significantly revise them. Title VII is meant to "foster activities to assist vulnerable older people to exercise their rights; to secure the benefits to which they are entitled; and to be protected from abuse, neglect, and exploitation" (*Federal Register*, p. 59056).

APS IN THE PUBLIC AGENCY

Variety Among Programs

The absence of a "formally endorsed Federal model" (DHEW, 1971, p. 3) during the early decades of the development of APS systems undoubtedly has contributed to distinct differences in the scope and nature of the states' programs (Wolf, 1988). As early as 1982, federal policymakers recognized this fact and also noted variations among the states in the quality of protective services, attributing the diversity to differing levels of staff expertise, the scope of programs, the populations targeted, the types of services provided, and the amount of state funding appropriated (Burr, 1982). Not surprisingly then, discussion and understanding of elder abuse and APS is marked with definitional debates and complicated by the varied structures of service delivery around the nation. Perhaps recognizing this variety, Gordon and Tomita (1990, p. 137) state:

> The term *adult protective services* does not refer to one agency. It is a generic term that describes a mixture of legal, medical, and social services which permits the broadest array of interventions. Many practitioners in different fields provide protective services in the normal course of their work while public agency adult protective services social workers, known as APS workers, are mandated by state law to accept and investigate reports of suspected elder abuse and neglect on a full-time basis.

In the 1966 DHEW request to state departments of public welfare for applications to carry out a national adult protective services demonstration project, the letter defined both "social" and "legal" protective services and acknowledged that protective programs had both components (DHEW, 1971, p. 8). Now, almost thirty years later, these elements appear in a variety of configurations among the states' laws and social services systems. For example, states may encompass adult protection within social services, or they may have an adult protective program in lieu of other adult social services. They may have entirely separate programs for elder abuse and adult protection. The state approach may be legalistic and closely allied with law enforcement or may follow a social work or case management model. Some adult protective programs include investigations of abuse and neglect in institutions, as well as in the community in private settings. Protective services may be provided by state or county employees or via contract with private non-profit agencies. Eligibility for protection may be based on age (e.g., 55, 60, or 65), may require age plus some incapacity, or may be based solely on the incapacity or vulnerability of the adult, regardless of age. APS or elder abuse programs may or may not address situations of neglect in which there is no perpetrator (commonly referred to as "self-neglect"). Domestic violence services usually exist within a separate, non- or quasi-governmental structure, but also may be found within public agency programs.

One must realize, therefore, that the adult protective services role in each of the case examples will be largely contingent upon the law and social service structure of the particular state in which the cases are found. Depending upon the values and constraints of the particular agency environment, the protocols of the protective entity may differ. For example, protective services programs closely allied to law enforcement may not intervene unless there is evidence of the violation of a criminal statute, an alleged perpetrator, and a party willing to press charges. Programs based on social work values, on the other hand, tend to focus on the individual's need for protection and attempt to solve the presenting problem and prevent its recurrence, rather than placing emphasis on affixing blame and collecting a chain of evidence.

Practice Guidelines

Generally speaking from the vantage point of the public agency APS worker, however, ethical practice is guided by values commonly accepted in the profession of social work (Texas APS program briefing material, unpublished):

- Practice is to be client-focused, individualized, and based on a social work model of problem-solving as opposed to a prosecutorial or purely psychological approach.
- The vulnerable adult is the primary client rather than the community or the family.
- The client is presumed to be mentally competent and in control of decision-making until facts prove otherwise.
- The client actively participates in defining the problem and deciding the most appropriate course of action to resolve it.
- The client exercises freedom of choice and the right to refuse services as long as the individual has the capacity to understand the consequences of his or her actions.
- The service alternatives that are pursued are the least restrictive possible; more intrusive remedies, such as guardianship or institutionalization, are undertaken as a last resort.
- When legal remedies are unavoidable, the client has a right to an attorney *ad litem* to represent his or her interests in court.

Systemic Constraints on Ethical Practice in the Public Agency

Although these principles are relatively easy to state, putting them into practice is more difficult, given the psychosocial, cultural, economic, and other factors that may influence client/practitioner interaction. Regrettably, truly ethical and humanistic practice in APS too often is constrained by the limits of the system in which the caseworker functions. For example, resources usually are scarce, and community expectations for assistance often exceed what is possible with available funding. APS rarely receives a high priority in state appropriations, leading to chronic understaffing. As a result, caseloads are too large, which restricts worker time for rapport building, thorough assessment, and adequate follow-through with clients. Finding adequate legal assistance is a frequent problem. Dealing thoughtfully and carefully with conflicting values and needs becomes even more difficult when workers have no choice but to triage incoming cases. These high caseloads and chronic crisis modes drain caseworker energies and dull their effectiveness.

To make the challenge even greater, the requirements for ethical APS casework are complex. The body of knowledge necessary to accurately assess the physical and mental status of an incapacitated adult in a protective situation is formidable. Even though caseworkers are expected to draw on the expertise of other professionals–as this volume is attempting to demonstrate–first they must be able to recognize when such assistance is advisable, which presupposes a general familiarity with those disciplines. Knowing the basic language, functions, and biases of other professional groups is fundamental to ethical APS practice.

The expectation of professional collaboration also presupposes that multidisciplinary teams are functioning, either formally or informally, in the particular worker's social service environment, which unfortunately, may not always be the case. If the only way caseworkers can access multidisciplinary teams (to assist in dealing with ethical dilemmas and other practice issues) is to form them themselves, who minds their caseloads while they take the time to develop the teams? On the other hand, if workers sacrifice personal time for the sake of community development (not only of multidisciplinary teams, but of other needed resources), they run the risk of depleting the emotional and physical reserves they need to stave off burn-out.

For those in the trenches of APS casework, therefore, discussing these case examples in terms of ethical practice requires demonstrating sensitivity to workload and other time constraints and recognizing their very real effect on casework decisions. What *should* be done and what *can* be done in a particular case or community all too often are drastically different realities. It is not to say that ethical practice in APS is impossible or irrelevant but to point out the complexity of the task, which argues all the more for continued attention to the subject not only in the literature but through supportive management practices, appropriate curriculum development, and advocacy for human rights.

Competing Values in APS Practice

Many clients have capacities so diminished that giving informed consent is problematic, if not impossible. Adhering to the principles of presumed competence, freedom of choice, and right to refuse services presents enormous challenges for the practitioner when the client's capacity is questionable and some degree of danger exists in the situation. The practitioner is operating under dual and potentially contradictory mandates to protect the person's safety while preserving the individual's freedom of choice (Abramson, 1991). This, perhaps, is the most basic ethical dilemma that an APS practitioner faces.

As Fins (1994) says about guardians, and contrary to what is commonly understood, adult protective practitioners are expected to exercise substituted judgment as well as to determine what action is in the client's best interest. In applying substituted judgment, the surrogate makes the decision the individual would have made, regardless of the individual's lack of capacity or the apparent foolishness of the decision. For example, when a cognitively impaired client is making a choice that appears to be contrary to the client's welfare (such as refusing medical treatment), but the decision appears to be consistent with the person's history prior to the incapacity, then the duty of the APS worker may be just as much to honor the client's right to refuse treatment as it may be to act in the client's best interest by protecting the person from the danger the refusal presents. However, supporting the client's right to self-determination in these cases also may place the worker in another ethical dilemma by opposing the wishes of the family or community, whose concerns may be rooted in the desire for the person's safety rather than the value of his or her personal liberty.

Balancing Autonomy and Protection

Drawing on H.R. Moody's (1988) explication of negotiated consent, we can construct a model for understanding APS practice: Visualize a scale, a horizontal line with "capacity" at the left end and "incapacity" at the right. Imagine that this scale is suspended over a background of danger. When capacity or incapacity is clear, so are the choices. Capacity, even in the face of danger, equals autonomy, as long as this stance does not endanger the community. Incapacity plus danger most likely will equal surrogate decision-making at some level. The greater the incapacity and the greater the danger to self or others, the more comprehensive the loss of autonomy may be.

The area between each pole represents the "gray area" in which capacity is questionable, and negotiating this territory is the heart and soul of APS practice. Moody (1988) specifies advocacy, empowerment, and persuasion as techniques for navigating the gray zone, and places "non-intervention" and "making decisions on behalf of the patient" (p. 66) at the opposite ends of the continuum. Undoubtedly, achieving advocacy, empowerment, and persuasion require consummate personal and professional skills. Patience, the ability to build trust and rapport, respect, sensitivity, persistence, compassion, and a comprehensive knowledge of the conditions causing incapacity as well as resources for treatment are among the qualities that enable practitioners to elicit from clients and families the information and cooperation necessary to arrive at ethical solutions. These ethical solutions either will balance freedom and protection or support resolutions at the appropriate point on the scale.

Noting that "the ultimate purpose of the relationship in adult protective services work with clients who do not want services is to influence the client to change," Abramson (1991, p. 126) analyzes APS worker/client interactions and finds "five categories of influence" (ibid) used by workers when attempting to balance the competing values of autonomy and beneficence in case situations. She describes these strategies as "use of the relationship, positive inducement, coercion, persuasion, and manipulation" (ibid). Although the workers were able to justify their actions on various grounds, Abrahamson remarks that others could argue that the workers were taking advantage of power imbalances and rationalizing that the ends (i.e., compliance, protection) justified the means (i.e., type of influence) used to gain them. Abrahamson does not attempt to reconcile these viewpoints, but makes the case for a closer connection between core social work values and actual practice interventions and the development of "new conceptual paradigms . . . to help practitioners to make these hard decisions in as much ethical comfort as possible" (p. 135).

THE THREE CASES

Mary and Martha

The case of Mary and Martha illustrates a conflict between autonomy and beneficence in circumstances that pose a threat to the well-being of physically and cognitively impaired older persons. Mary is cognitively impaired and appears to be expressing her autonomy in her denial that anything is wrong and her subsequent refusal of assistance. Martha is physically incapacitated, unable to communicate, and dependent largely upon Mary for her care. Those who wish to see conditions improved for the couple are acting out of beneficence and most likely will attempt a variety of strategies to bring about change. In many locales, given the absence of other adult services or case management programs, both Mary and Martha could be considered APS cases on the basis of neglect.

At the point the reader is introduced to the scenario, the first task of the caseworker would be to get more information. Exactly what is Martha's physical and mental status? Martha may be unable to speak, but is her cognitive function intact? Have alternative methods of communication been attempted? What is the prognosis for rehabilitation? What does *she* want in terms of her treatment and environment? If she can not tell us now, what can we find out about the preferences she may have articulated earlier?

We are told that Mary has been given a mental examination and that she has moderately severe dementia, but the APS worker still must not discount her description of the facts without checking further. For example, are the bills unpaid because the sons are using the money for themselves? Has the trash service been canceled for lack of payment, or is someone who is expected to pick up the garbage failing to do so for some other reason? Are the sons—or other persons—dumping trash in the sisters' yard? If further investigation rules out Mary's explanations of the circumstances, then the worker has more reason to question Mary's cognitive functioning.

Realizing that the scope of a mental status examination will vary according to the physician's practice setting, experience, and skill, the worker needs specific information about the examination given Mary. For example, in order to assess mental status properly, the physician must also evaluate the client for physical problems that might be manifesting as mental illness or dementia. We do not know if this was done, and it is possible that there are physical causes for Mary's confusion. She says that her vision is poor; she admits that she has been falling; she appears to be malnourished. Does she take any medicine? Could her dementia be reversible with proper nourishment and/or treatment of a hitherto undiagnosed illness?

Obviously, the APS worker needs the assistance of medical professionals to assess these factors. Equally obvious, their respective opinions may not always agree. When the physician's conclusions about the client's condition and capacity differ from the worker's professional judgment, the worker must attempt to determine the extent and quality of the assessment. If the physician's decision appears to be based on limited information, ethical protocol in APS calls for the worker to seek either a broader assessment, a change in physicians, or both. On the other hand, if the medical assessment appears to have been extensive and thorough, then the worker's deference to the physician's diagnosis is appropriate. The recommended treatment, however, and the patient's autonomy still may conflict, and when the patient's capacity is questionable, resolution by a multidisciplinary team may be very appropriate. If the individual has the capacity to understand the situation and its consequences, then autonomy prevails, regardless of the danger this may present to the client.

Assuming that Martha is the more vulnerable sibling and is in the most danger, the first duty of the APS worker would be to protect her, ideally with the goal of doing so in a manner that (1) suits Martha and (2) is acceptable to Mary. The siblings' social resources may be the key to achieving this balance. In addition to trying to find out the root causes of the problems that the sisters are experiencing, the worker will need more facts about the church friend and the sons. Are the church members willing to become more involved in ways that would help Mary to remain in her home? Would Mary accept assistance from them? If so, the worker can attempt to engage the social resources represented by Mary's church to upgrade the level of care given to both sisters. Can Mary's strengths, her social graces and prideful demeanor, be built upon with techniques such as those in Naomi Feil's Validation Therapy®?

Feil (1993) posits that normal human development includes four stages at the end of life that have not been recognized heretofore because people did not live as long. She describes these states as (1) malorientation, (2) time confusion, (3) repetitive motion, and (4) vegetation. Mary may fit the profile of an individual experiencing time confusion. Feil teaches that these persons respond better to active listening, which acknowledges and reflects the emotional tones of what the older person is expressing, rather than to reality orientation. For example, if the older person were to address a daughter as if the daughter were the older person's sister, reality orientation requires that the older person be corrected with the actual facts, such as, "I'm not your sister; I'm your daughter. Aunt Jane died thirty years ago." A person using Validation® techniques, on the other hand, would not correct the facts, but would allow the older individual to talk about her sister, reminisce, and express feelings. The daughter might say instead, "You and Aunt Jane were really close, weren't you? I'll bet you really miss her. Tell me about the time . . . " According to Feil, this type of empathetic communication enhances the dignity and self-esteem of the older person and is more likely to improve orientation than more confrontational attempts to ground the individual in concrete reality. Conducting familiar rituals, such as preparing refreshments for guests or folding napkins or wash cloths, also may help to orient persons who are experiencing confusion. Therefore, finding activities that reinforce Mary's social graces might be attempted here as a method of helping her deal more accurately with reality.

Assuming that the sisters' acceptance eventually can be gained, the APS worker will attempt to connect them with whatever the community can offer in the way of in-home services, as well. However, Martha's needs for care and protection, as she apparently is more physically incapacitated than Mary, will override Mary's desire for independence. On the other hand, we do not know Martha's mental status, and if she is not cognitively impaired and does not want services, then Martha's right to self-determination (i.e., to refuse services) must be honored. The challenge then for the APS worker will be to find some solution or solutions that will be acceptable to the sisters, even if the starting point is nothing more than their allowing the worker to visit again, and thereby giving the worker time to try to develop trust and rapport. At this point, the size and complexity of the worker's caseload becomes a critical factor, because those planned friendly visits may be sidetracked quickly when more urgent cases come in.

Although it appears that the sons are not contributing significantly to their care at present, the sons might prove to be additional resources for the sisters. The APS worker could attempt to raise the sons' sensitivity to Mary's and Martha's needs and rights and involve them in their care. However, without acquiescence from Mary and Martha, the worker probably would not support the sons' plan to move the sisters to the city. As an APS worker remarked about Mary when reviewing this case scenario, "you'd be committing murder if you moved her to the city." Well-intentioned as such a move may be, experienced caseworkers can relate story after story in which an incapacitated older person is removed involuntarily from an environment far below community standards, only to die six months later in nice, clean surroundings while receiving adequate care. For many people, residing in familiar surroundings, no matter how dirty, hazardous, or unacceptable to others, is an essential ingredient in quality of life. This preference for the familiar is likely to become even more pronounced as persons age and sensory perceptions dim. So if the sons have been thinking in terms of their paying for an apartment in a senior high-rise, perhaps they could be persuaded to contribute an equivalent amount toward caregiving that would help the sisters stay at home. Even if moving to the city is really important (for example, to obtain appropriate medical care), this alternative still should not be forced upon the sisters, but presented as an option, debated, and negotiated.

Unfortunately, if the brothers decide to take action unilaterally and move the sisters against their will, APS has little authority to intervene. Unless the sisters have the wherewithal to take the matter to court (in a civil lawsuit), their rights may be violated. If the APS worker thinks that the sisters are incapacitated, he or she might precipitate a guardianship hearing, but one of the sons, as next-of-kin, would be the primary candidate to serve as guardian. The APS worker and/or the *ad litem* would need to prove that the sons were unfit in order for the judge to consider an alternate choice. What happens if none is available?

Finally, recognizing the community's right to a sanitary environment, the APS worker would seek to have the garbage cleared away, even if this were contrary to Mary's wishes. Again, most of this plan is contingent upon Mary's accepting it, and her denial of the need for help is the crux of the presenting problem. If Mary's continuing refusal is placing Martha in greater danger and Martha cannot give informed consent, then the likelihood of involuntary action to protect Martha is much greater. If Martha is capable of consent, then her autonomy must be respected, and she may or may not want changes. Practically speaking, if Mary is not capable of informed consent, then her refusal does not have sufficient validity to overcome the danger present. Nevertheless, before considering involuntary measures, ethical practice in APS would demand that every attempt be made to gain Mary's acceptance of the services that would remove the danger.

The multidisciplinary team that helps the APS worker to resolve this case situation might include the sisters' physicians, the visiting nurse, a psychologist or psychiatrist, church members, the sons or other family members if applicable, and the person who delivers meals. Other resources might be the city sanitation department for the garbage problem, law enforcement (if exploitation is confirmed), an attorney, a bank trust department or other financial management service if appropriate, and an Alzheimer's support group for the sons. The medical professionals can conduct the mental and physical examinations necessary to assess competence and diagnose mental and physical conditions that may affect the sisters' ability to live independently. Getting this information is basic to making ethical decisions about the sisters' care. The visiting nurse can provide useful information about the sisters' daily behavior as well as help develop and carry out the service plan (and physician's orders are necessary to authorize the nurse's visits unless the sisters can pay privately). The person who delivers meals can observe and report conditions in the home, as can church members, who also can support Mary socially (perhaps by having meals with her, which might encourage her to eat). Because she knows and trusts them, Mary may be more likely to accept other kinds of assistance, such as help with chores, from the church members as well. If Mary allows this, then getting her to accept the services of a home health agency might become feasible. The Alzheimer's support group should help the sons learn about dementia and appropriate care and treatment. If the sisters are to remain at home, as Mary clearly wishes, this type of multi-faceted approach is essential, with APS or another type of case management professional coordinating the effort.

John and Manny

In the second case example, that of John and Manny, we are presented with an elderly man who is being forced into isolation, confined to his house, exploited, and verbally and physically abused by an adult son who is mentally ill and financially dependent upon the father. John has experienced many losses: he retired reluctantly, his health has failed, his wife has died, and his son was unable or unwilling to take over the family business and help fulfill John's lifelong dream. Deeply religious, John blames himself for Manny's dysfunctional behavior and is unwilling to try to make changes or accept assistance from APS or others. In the scenario he is deemed capable of informed consent, and no intervention is provided until his capacity declines sufficiently to justify involuntary measures.

In cases such as John's, when client autonomy overrides what the APS worker thinks is in the client's best interest, the duty of the worker is to explore every opportunity that might increase the potential for voluntary acceptance of alternatives that will protect the client and secondarily, the alleged perpetrator, who in this situation might also become an APS client due to his untreated mental illness. When such attempts have been made the APS worker can accept with equanimity an unsuccessful intervention, that is, failing to protect the client. This failure is made tolerable by understanding that the client's rights have been protected foremost. Unfortunately for John, this is not how the scenario played out.

Although John's autonomy has been honored in this case, the only measure attempted by the APS worker was to persuade him to enter a nursing home, an attempt that failed and left John in danger, as subsequent hospitalizations proved. Best practice in APS would have sought permission from John for continued contact with the caseworker, which would have provided the worker an opportunity for building trust, rapport, and a better relationship, as well as observing what was happening in the household. The worker might have attempted to provide John with alternatives for long-term care other than nursing home placement, with choices that could have kept APS and/or his friends and family and other professionals in frequent contact. These choices might have included in-home services to relieve Manny of his caregiving role, a function with which John was profoundly uncomfortable. Outside contact most likely would have revealed Manny's illness sooner, which in turn might have provided a means for his removal from the household (as a threat to himself or others for mental health treatment or via an action such as a warrantless arrest for domestic violence), regardless of John's consent. Had John understood that Manny was mentally ill before he (John) lost capacity, John might have been convinced that his parental responsibility obligated him to get Manny into treatment. Perhaps not, if John persisted in blaming himself, but at least the possibility could have been explored.

If John had consented to continued contact from APS, despite his refusal of other interventions, the worker could have kept the case open and thereby increased the likelihood of a multidisciplinary approach to his protection. The team might have included family and friends, a psychiatrist, psychological and/or domestic violence counselor, and police social services. With APS present to protect John's rights to have visitors in his own home, his family and friends could have visited him again, which might have alleviated some of his depression. The presence of others in the household would have increased the chances that Manny's dysfunction would have been observed much earlier and an intervention attempted. A second opinion as to the level of John's depression would have been appropriate, in case medication or other therapy were advisable. Counseling also might have helped John to realize that Manny needed professional help. Law enforcement might have prosecuted Manny without John's cooperation, an intervention that is recommended by professionals in the domestic violence field.

However, because the APS worker did not appear to try to gain trust and rapport with John, the worker lost the opportunity to try to find out about the beliefs and motivations that fed his victimization and then search for means to change them. We do not know if John knew about the in-home services that might have relieved Manny of round-the-clock care-giving and John of some of his guilt. We are told that John had the capacity to make informed choices, but not that anyone helped him to fully explore what those choices might have been. He "lamented what had become of his life" during his hospitalizations; surely he would have talked to the APS worker or a counselor? Chances are, all the person had to do was listen, and John would have allowed him or her into his home. That one listener, having gained John's trust, might have been the catalyst for change that could have saved both John and Manny from themselves.

Bonnie

Case three is equally difficult, if not more so, because it appears that Bonnie needs protecting from herself as much as from other parties. Reportedly addicted to valium, Bonnie denies this, and her physical incapacities prevent those around her from allowing her to face the consequences of her addiction (and other anti-social behavior). Allegedly separated from her husband, Bonnie continues to receive visits from him, apparently willing to endure physical and verbal abuse in exchange for drugs.

In its role as paid professional caregiver, the nursing home has an obligation to protect Bonnie from harm, but its staff make several glaring omissions in handling this case. They do not obtain a social history on Bonnie; they repeatedly fail to chart her behavior; they do not investigate for abuse (or report it elsewhere for investigation) after finding bruises on Bonnie's body, and they do not conduct a physical examination to rule out injury after hearing what sounds like a fight in her room. Bonnie does not get the attention of a social worker until she is hospitalized for injuries apparently sustained in the altercation, and at this point the scenario ends.

What can or should happen next to protect Bonnie? The scenario states that Bonnie entered the nursing facility addicted to valium and meprobamate, but we are not told if or how she was withdrawn from these substances. Is there a possibility that some of her inappropriate behavior is related to substance abuse or withdrawal? Clearly, the drug addiction should be addressed, but there is no indication that Bonnie sees this as a problem and is willing to stop. Even if an involuntary commitment for substance abuse treatment were to be possible, are not the chances high that Bonnie will return to drug abuse if she is not emotionally and intellectually committed to sobriety? Moreover, access to involuntary treatment may depend upon a number of factors. Someone has to bring the matter to the attention of the proper authorities (that is, to file the necessary paperwork for the mental health order). APS and the nursing home's ability to file will depend upon state or local protocols, and there may not be a family member or friend available or willing to do so. The extent of Bonnie's health insurance coverage also will be a factor, as will the availability of publicly funded substance-abuse treatment if Bonnie has insufficient coverage.

Bonnie is highly dependent on others for her care, and allowing her to face the consequences of her actions (as advocated by treatment programs such as Alcoholics Anonymous [AA] and Al-Anon, a similar program for families and friends of alcoholics), would be problematic. Al-Anon teaches the significant others of chemically dependent persons not to rescue their loved ones, because the act of rescuing, or enabling, permits the person to continue the destructive behavior, which is felt to eventually result in the person's "hitting bottom" and facing the addiction. However, leaving Bonnie to face the consequences of her actions may mean that she is discharged from the nursing home without having an acceptable alternative living arrangement. Often in cases such as Bonnie's, the nursing home is the last resort after the person's behavior has caused those alternatives to fail. Public housing and the home health care agency may refuse to take her as a resident or client, for example. Bonnie would therefore become a homeless person with a severe and very visible disability, a threat to the nursing home's public image and a repeat case for APS when someone in the community reports the case.

On the other hand, allowing Bonnie full autonomy while protecting her from facing its consequences would mean the facility's condoning illegal drug use, tolerating her anti-social behavior, and permitting further physical abuse from the husband, all of which could put the nursing home's licensure or certification in jeopardy if reported to the authorities and confirmed. The nursing home has an obligation to meet standards that include protecting all the residents from harm, and allowing this situation to continue unchecked will violate those standards. Discharging Bonnie or refusing to re-admit her after hospitalization will be an option for the facility, but federal regulations do not allow such action without due process and the decision of the hearings officer will prevail, so the outcome will not be assured. Bonnie's incapacities will not necessarily protect her from discharge if her behavior is illegal or jeopardizes other residents of the home, and these conditions, combined with her history, are likely to make finding another placement very difficult.

In addition to substance abuse treatment, the protective worker in this case will need to address the problem of domestic violence, first by exploring Bonnie's relationship with her husband. Bonnie's entering a nursing home to escape the husband's abuse is hardly consistent with allowing the husband to visit and continue the abusive behavior. But perhaps Bonnie's withdrawal symptoms are so acute that enduring the mistreatment is a small price to pay to get more drugs. If Bonnie is not willing to seek a protective order to keep the husband away, perhaps the nursing home could do this. In many localities warrantless arrests are possible, regardless of the victim's willingness to press charges. Surely the facility has the right (because of the risk to its licensure or certification status) to prohibit Bonnie from having private visits with her husband. In addition to domestic violence interventions, drug charges may be possible.

If we assume that Bonnie has maladaptive personality traits, the experienced practitioner knows that coping with it will require close communication and a unified approach among nursing home staff and other residents in order to try to prevent or at least limit her manipulation and mistreatment of others. Professionals dealing with clients such as Bonnie have been known to say that if these individuals were not so physically impaired, "they'd already be in jail if somebody hadn't killed them first." These cases are extremely frustrating for all involved. In the face of such a client's continuing non-compliance with treatment, abuse of others, irresponsibility, poor judgment, lack of cooperation, and participation in illegal activity, her caregivers and others affected by her behavior may be driven to consider some form of coercion, such as guardianship, medication, or imprisonment, in order to protect society from Bonnie, rather than vice versa. Even so, this would be only a partial solution, because a guardian, for example, would not be able to control Bonnie's behavior. Chemical restraints or criminal prosecution may be tempting solutions for those dealing with her, but are not likely to be realistic given Bonnie's functional limitations. These same limitations keep Bonnie from freely exercising her preferred lifestyle, which must be terribly frustrating for her and probably contributing to her anti-social behavior.

The treatment team, likely composed of nursing home staff, her physician, family members, a domestic violence counselor, a substance abuse counselor, and a social worker (who may or may not be an employee of the APS agency, depending on the jurisdiction) must assess Bonnie comprehensively and pool available resources to address her multiple problems. A pharmacist and someone representing law enforcement also might be included, if not as regular team members, then as resources to the team. Bonnie's physical conditions need to be differentiated from those caused by substance abuse and medications. Her cognitive ability and emotional status should be assessed, as well. Her relationships with her family need to be ascertained, along with Bonnie's financial resources. If Bonnie is to leave the nursing home, then placement alternatives, including residential treatment for substance abuse, should be explored. The team needs to know what Bonnie wants out of life, and what she is willing to do to reach her goals. After these questions have been answered, the team will have a better idea how to approach Bonnie.

CONCLUSION

Although these cases are hypothetical, they in no way exaggerate the complexity of typical APS situations and the difficulties of resolving them. This assessment of the values, issues, and ethical dilemmas in each of the cases is constrained by the facts given in the case descriptions and by the assessor's knowledge and experience. The same is true in most social work cases, and for that reason we call upon our colleagues in other fields in hopes that together we can arrive at the best course of action (or inaction, as the case may be) for ethical practice.

Richard C. Ladd, former Commissioner of the Texas Health and Human Services Commission, when speaking about the regulation of long-term care, once remarked, "Government has followed the wishes we have for our loved ones, rather than the wishes we have for ourselves" (personal communication, 10/22/92). He went on to stress that the goal of policy and practice should be to give impaired adults the freedom we would want for ourselves rather than the safety we want for them because we love them. Adult protective practitioners, duly charged with an authority to protect that carries with it a frightening potential for causing inadvertent harm, bear an equally great responsibility to foster the autonomy, respect the privacy, and preserve the human dignity and freedom of the persons we attempt to safeguard. This enormous power is best not exercised or undertaken alone, a fact that underscores the value of multidisciplinary teams to APS practice.

REFERENCES

Abramson, M. (1989, February). Autonomy vs. paternalistic beneficence: Practice strategies. *Social Casework: The Journal of Contemporary Social Work, 70,* 101-105.

Abramson, M. (1991). Ethical assessment of the use of influence in adult protective services. *Journal of Gerontological Social Work, 16* (1/2) 125-135.

Burr, J.J. (1982, Spring). Protective service for adults: a guide to exemplary practice in states providing protective services to adults in OHDS programs [Monograph]. Administration on Aging, Office of Human Development Services (DHHS Publication No. OHDS 82-20505).

Department of Health and Human Services, Administration on Aging. Grants for state and community programs on aging; grants for vulnerable elder rights protection activities. *Federal Register* (1994, November 15). *59* (219), 59056.

Dunn, P.F. (unpublished). Rediscovering the vulnerable elderly in the United States. Charles Sturt University, Wagga Wagga, NSW, Australia.

Feil, N. (1993). *The validation breakthrough.* Baltimore, MD: Health Professions Press, Inc.

Fins, D. L. (1994). Health care decision-making for incapacitated elders: An innovative social service agency model. *Journal of Elder Abuse & Neglect, 6* (2), 39-51.

Gordon, R. M. & Tomita, S. (1990). The reporting of elder abuse and neglect:

mandatory or voluntary? In Dutton, D.G. and Sacco, V.F. (eds.), *Family violence: Perspectives on treatment, research, and policy* (135-150). Barnaby, British Columbia: B.C. Institute on Family Violence.

Moody, H.R. (1988). From informed consent to negotiated consent. *The Gerontologist, 28* (Suppl.), 64-74.

Tatara, T. (1990, November). Elder abuse: An issue paper, prepared for the Administration on Aging, the Department of Health and Human Services by the National Aging Resource Center on Elder Abuse, Washington, DC.

U.S. Department of Health, Education, and Welfare, Social and Rehabilitation Service, Community Services Administration, *Report of the national protective services project for older adults,* 1971 (DHEW Publication No. (SRS) 72-23008).

U.S. Senate Special Committee on Aging. (1977). *Protective services for the elderly.* Washington, DC: U.S. Government Printing Office.

Wolf, R. (1988, Spring). The evolution of policy: A ten-year perspective. *Public Welfare, 46* (2), 7-13.

Chapter Six

An Ombudsman Perspective

Jo Ellen Skelley-Walley

SUMMARY. The role and scope of authority of the Office of the Long-Term Care Ombudsman is explored in relation to three case examples. The ombudsman's primary responsibility to the client is compared to the need for productive working relationships with other disciplines to effect client goals in a manner which is responsive to ethical decision-making. *[Article copies available from The Haworth Document Delivery Service: 1-800-342-9678.]*

The Office of the Long-Term Care Ombudsman is a federally mandated program of the Older Americans Act, Public Law 89-73. The scope of authority and responsibility of the Office is described in Title VII, Chapter 2 of the Older Americans Act of 1965 as amended. Among the requirements of the Act are provisions regarding infrastructure of the program, conflicts of interest, reporting, training of representatives of the Office, access requirements, legal counsel, liability, and noninterference. These provisions are very important to the mission and operation of the Office. However, most significant to this discussion are the functions of the program found in Section 712(a)(3). The primary function of the program is to:

> . . . identify, investigate, and resolve complaints that: (i) are made by or on behalf of residents; and (ii) relate to action, inaction, or decisions

Jo Ellen Skelley-Walley is Certified Ombudsman Program Director, Ohio Office, Long-Term Care Ombudsman, Associate State Long-Term Care Ombudsman, Ohio Department of Aging, 50 West Broad Street, Columbus, OH 43215.

[Haworth co-indexing entry note]: "An Ombudsman Perspective." Skelley-Walley, Jo Ellen. Co-published simultaneously in *Journal of Elder Abuse & Neglect* (The Haworth Press, Inc.) Vol. 7, No. 2/3, 1995, pp. 89-113; and: *Elder Mistreatment: Ethical Issues, Dilemmas, and Decisions* (ed: Tanya Fusco Johnson) The Haworth Press, Inc., 1995, pp. 89-113. [Single or multiple copies of this article are available from The Haworth Document Delivery Service: 1-800-342-9678, 9:00 a.m. - 5:00 p.m. (EST)].

89

that may adversely affect the health, safety, welfare, or rights of the residents (including the welfare and rights of the residents with respect to the appointment and activities of guardians and representative payees), of: (I) providers, or representatives of providers of long-term care services; (II) public agencies; or (III) health and social service agencies . . .

The functions of the Office also include informing residents about means of obtaining services provided by the providers or agencies described above (OAA Sec. 712(a)(3)(C)); and representing the interests of the residents before governmental agencies including seeking administrative, legal, and other remedies (OAA Sec. 712(a)(3)(E)).

The Office provides these services to residents of long-term care facilities. The Act defines a long-term care facility as:

(A) any skilled nursing facility, as defined in section 1819(a) of the Social Security Act (42 U.S.C. 1935 i-3(a)); (B) any nursing facility, as defined in section 1919(a) of the Social Security Act (42 U.S.C. 1396 r(a)); (C) . . . a board and care facility; and (D) any other adult care home similar to a facility or institution described in subparagraphs (A) through (C). (OAA Sec. 102(34)).

While the OAA limits the Ombudsman mandate to long-term care facilities, many states have expanded the ombudsman mandate to include provision of the above functions to consumers of home and community based long-term care services.

The classic definition of an ombudsman is generally accepted to describe a neutral party who investigates and makes reports regarding grievances. The long-term care ombudsman is directed to serve as a resident or consumer advocate, representing the resident or consumer, to resolve a grievance. This requires the ombudsman to be free of conflicts of interest, to represent client interests, and to work under the direction of the client taking only those actions the client empowers the ombudsman to take. Even though the long-term care ombudsman, like the classical ombudsman, has no enforcement powers, the Office and its representatives are not without power. The ombudsman advocates for the client, using various strategies to obtain the client's goal. The scope of these strategies may range from conciliatory to coercive actions, including education, coordination with other service agencies, win/win negotiations, pursuing the involvement of regulatory agencies, administrative and civil or criminal legal actions, or public disclosure activities such as using the media.

The ombudsman receives complaints from a wide variety of sources. Complainants may be residents/consumers, family members or friends, attorneys-in-fact, government or social services agencies or their staff, or service providers or their staff. To assure that the resident/consumer interests are represented, ombudsmen make a distinction between "clients," persons who are receiving services, and "complainants," persons other than those receiving service who report a concern or grievance to the ombudsman. (This distinction should not be construed to indicate that the person receiving services may not make a complaint on their own behalf.) The following example demonstrates the importance of this distinction.

> The ombudsman received a complaint from the daughter of a recently institutionalized, widowed man. Things had gone well the first few months, she reported. Recently, when she visited her father on her lunch hour, she found him unbathed, unshaven, generally unkempt, and still in his pajamas. The daughter felt the nursing home was failing to meet her father's needs. The ombudsman agreed to visit the facility to observe the situation and to talk with the resident about his satisfaction with the services of the nursing home. The ombudsman asked the resident if he had a concern about the issue and if he wished to have the assistance of the ombudsman in addressing the problem. The ombudsman received an emphatic "No!" It had taken him three months to convince the facility that he wished to sleep late and have "lazy" mornings, attending to dressing and grooming later in the day. The ombudsman assured the resident no action would be taken and explained to the complainant that the facility was honoring her father's choice to direct his daily schedule and personal care, a choice he had the right to make.

This example shows the importance of the ombudsman making a distinction between a client and a complainant in determining a course of action.

Not all cases are so clear cut, and identifying the client and determining his or her interests is frequently more difficult. A number of factors can contribute to the need for careful evaluation of client interests. As we will see in the following case studies, there may be more than one client involved and the clients may have competing interests. The client's capacity for decision-making may be limited, questionable, or lacking entirely. In some situations an attorney-in-fact, such as a health care power of attorney or guardian, may have been appointed to act on behalf of the client, and the client and attorney-in-fact disagree on the course of action to be pursued. Or, as is often the case, the client lacks decision-making capacity and there is not a legally appointed attorney-in-fact. The ombudsman must work through each of these situations to determine a course of action that most accurately represents the client's wishes.

The right of autonomy, or self-rule, is a primary value in the ombudsman program. In support of autonomy and right to choice, the ombudsman recognizes the responsibility to provide, or assure the provision of, the scope of information necessary for the client to make an informed decision and thereby exercise choice. Autonomy can be viewed in two sub-categories: decisional autonomy, the ability and freedom to make decisions without external coercion or restraint, and autonomy of execution, the ability and freedom to act on this decisional autonomy, to carry out and implement personal choices (Collopy, 1988; Hunt, 1989). When working with a frail or impaired population, recognition of this distinction is important to ensure autonomy. This right to choice and exercise of autonomy sometimes results in people making choices that have negative consequences for their well-being as perceived by society. It is the ombudsman's role to support the right of the individual to make such choices by advocating on the client's behalf.

The ability to make informed decisions is based upon capacity. Capacity for decision-making is often situational. For example, a client who can make health care decisions may not be able to handle his or her finances; or a client who cannot make health care decisions may be able to make decisions about which visitors he or she wants to see. Assessing a client's areas of capacity helps the ombudsman work with the client to establish a course of action and to represent the client's interests. Within this context the ombudsman may act to effect the choices of a client even in situations where the individual has been adjudicated and a guardian has been appointed.

The ombudsman uses three principles of decision-making to be supportive of client choice. These include informed consent, best interest, and substituted judgment, the use of which depends upon a client's decision-making capacity. To the extent the client can evidence capacity and choice, the ombudsman pursues the client's goals. Where capacity is lacking, the ombudsman attempts to discover information regarding what kind of choice the client would have made were he or she able to do so (Caplan, 1985). This information might include advance directives; social or values history documents or other records; past conversations with family, friends, and professionals; and accounts of previous lifestyle. It supports decisions and choices consistent with those the client would make if he or she were able. This method represents the substituted judgment principle of decision-making. When a client is incapable of making a decision or contributing to decision-making and there is no information to establish what choice the client would make, the principle of best interest is used. Regardless of the style of decision-making that is used, professionals are generally most comfortable when the decision results in a choice that supports the welfare of the client. It is when client choice varies from that of caregivers and other professionals or societal norms that conflict may develop. In this circumstance the ombudsman's role is to advocate the client's interests in the resolution. At times it may appear that the ombudsman advocates action or non-action that others may believe is inappropriate or may have negative consequences for the client. However, if this position is consistent with client choice, or documented client values, the ombudsman is acting ethically.

There are, of course, limitations to the ombudsman's advocacy on behalf of a client, and the ombudsman must advise a client of those limitations and seek alternate or creative solutions to meet the client's interests. In some circumstances, the ombudsman cannot advocate a client's choice, and alternate solutions are not satisfactory to the client. The client may inform the ombudsman that he or she no longer represents him. In these situations or when a client does not enlist the representation of the ombudsman as in the example above, the ombudsman's role is at an end. This is ethical behavior for an ombudsman working within a client-directed philosophy.

The primary value of client choice can present a personal burden to the ombudsman who must subvert personal values in pursuing a client's goals. It may also appear to others involved in the case that the ombudsman is advocating inappropriate actions in the face of societal norms or an individual's best interest. In the case examples that follow it will be possible to see how some of these dynamics work.

THE THREE CASES

Mary and Martha

This case example involves two sisters living in a private residence. It is not immediately clear how the ombudsman might become involved unless the ombudsman received the initial call of concern. If so, it is likely that the ombudsman would provide information regarding alternatives and refer the caller to another service such as the adult protective services or a case management assessor. In a limited number of states where the long-term care ombudsman has a state mandate to serve consumers of community based services, and should the ombudsman become involved, his or her role is to represent the interests and rights of the client. It is possible that in this example the ombudsman may be representing both Mary and her sister Martha. This would require that the rights of each sister be represented and that the exercise of these rights be balanced in a manner that did not infringe one upon the other. The most likely actions of the ombudsman, given the case scenario, would involve advocating for Mary to remain in her home and, where a formal care plan is created, to serve Mary in attempting to resolve any problems or concerns she may have regarding the delivery of the services. The ombudsman would also talk with Martha regarding her concerns and interests and support her in taking actions designed to meet her interests. A large part of the ombudsman's work is ensuring that those who provide services perform their work in a manner acceptable to the client.

The facts provided in the case example leave a number of questions from the ombudsman's perspective although there may be no ombudsman activity in this case as explained above.

Rights

The "rights" expressed in this question involve the relationships of family members interacting within a given set of circumstance rather than established rights. Mary's sister, to the extent of her decision-making capacity, has the right to choose or reject care services or a care environment. Notwithstanding any regulatory requirements for the quality of services to be provided, the care Mary's sister may choose is an individual right. In this case example the decisional capacity of Martha is not clearly addressed. An inability to communicate does not in and of itself indicate a lack of mental capacity. This is an assumption that the ombudsman would question. Greater attempts would be required to assess Mary's sister's capacity for decision-making and to learn how she currently feels about her circumstances.

Mary has assumed the role of caregiver for her sister. There is no information within the case summary to indicate what, if any, promises have been exchanged between the sisters that have established a perceived obligation between them nor are any facts provided to clearly indicate a personal or family value system that Mary and her sister share. Mary may feel a moral obligation to care for her sister. Her chosen role may even represent an act of self preservation. Perhaps Mary is living in her sister's home and would be required to move herself if her sister resided elsewhere, or perhaps Mary recognizes that the care of her sister forces or assists her in maintaining her own physical and mental capacities. The "right" of Mary to be a caregiver to her sister does not supersede her sister's right to choice of caregiver. Mary's ability to perform the task is more accurately the question being posed. The answer is found in evaluation and recognizing each woman's decisional capacity, autonomy of execution; and the available, effective, and accepted support services.

The rights of the sons to lead their own lives and care for their families are not in question in the given scenario. More to the point is how the sons choose to exercise these rights in relation to the perceived needs of their mother and aunt. Certain value systems may perceive a moral obligation on the part of the sons to provide, or assure the provision of, appropriate care for Mary and Martha. However, the case facts do not establish a legal obligation, such as guardianship, by the sons/nephews. If a legal obligation existed, the ombudsman would research and address the obligation as a part of the resolution of the situation.

Although the case example relates Mary's comments regarding her sons' role in her support systems, there is not an exploration of the scope of acceptable action on the sons' part according to Mary or Mary's sister. Although there is indication that the sons wish for Mary to move closer to their home, Mary has indicated some reluctance about this idea. Mary's comments about her sons may be more of her actions described as:

> her social graces were maintained, and . . . she had the demeanor of someone who took pride in herself . . . , or, as is often the case, an attempt at preservation of the status quo when faced with a perceived threat of the loss of independence.

The rights of the three parties fit together only as competent adults choose to exercise their individual rights in a mutually acceptable manner. Although there may be a moral perception that family members should care for each other, in particular adult children caring for elder parents, it is not an enforceable role nor is it necessarily a healthy choice in some circumstances. Many care plans within the community setting include the informal care-giving of family members or others as the underpinning for a successful care environment. Many community based medicaid waiver programs that provide care to persons otherwise eligible for nursing home care cannot be cost effective and provide adequate care without the participation of family members or other informal caregivers. In these situations the ombudsman recognizes the importance of the family caregiver relationship as an integral part of maintaining the client's independent environment. In these situations, the informal caregivers must be included in the development of a care plan with their responsibilities clearly outlined. Any arrangements for respite and processes for coverage for the informal caregivers must also be addressed. While this is not the case in the facts presented, it is possible that a similar arrangement might be worked out for Mary and her sister that would include Mary's sons and the local church membership.

Responsibilities

The case scenario presents no facts to indicate Mary has a legal responsibility to be a caregiver of her sister. In the event Mary did have a legal responsibility to care for her sister and in the event Mary was assessed and it was determined there was a verified dementia (with proper nutrition, etc., the apparent confusion may clear up), Mary may be released from or denied further legal responsibility for her sister's care. Mary's own value system and perception of a moral obligation may be discussed with Mary and Martha as needs and abilities change.

The question of legal responsibility of the sons to protect their mother and her sister from unintentional abuse and neglect may vary in accordance with state laws. The sons are not legal guardians; however, proximity to their mother may create a perception of denial of needed goods or services and may be actionable in the civil court system. However, the acceptance of such goods or services by Mary or her sister may not be within the control of the sons.

State laws vary on mandated reporting requirements by non-professional persons of suspected self abuse or neglect. Often individuals report such situations based on the effect on themselves (such as the neighbor who was personally concerned about the sanitary conditions jeopardized by improper disposal of trash) or their personal value system. The values of the church community may direct the action of its members to seek a solution. The meals-on-wheels workers, as representatives of a service provider, have a greater responsibility to recognize changes in clients' well-being over time. Any evidence of meals uneaten on a regular basis, at the least, should raise a question of need for the service or the quality of the service. Recognition of physical decline of the clients combined with failure to consume meals are worth noting and being referred to a supervisor for further action. Delivery persons, even those who are volunteers, can be trained to look for these types of situations and to whom to report these observations.

If the case manager, upon receiving and investigating the complaint, offers a service and it is accepted, then she has an on-going responsibility to review the situation for change, either positive or negative. Adjustment of the service arrangement should be offered on an on-going basis as necessary. This process should take place within the context of discussion with Mary and her sister regarding various options and alternatives and the possible outcomes or consequences of various courses of action that they may choose. Every attempt to meet the needs of the clients, in accordance with decisional capacity, in a manner acceptable to the client should be made prior to engaging services that lead to legal remedies.

The role of public agencies with regard to interceding to protect vulnerable citizens should be directed towards providing service to assist in situations where (1) decisional capacity is present but autonomy of execution is lacking; (2) decisional capacity is lacking, and there is no surrogate decision-maker to arrange service in keeping with the client's values to the extent that these are known; or (3) capacity is lacking, and there is no surrogate decision-maker to provide services or take action in the best interest of the client.

Community members have a legally supported expectation that public health be maintained. Where individual circumstances create a health hazard to other private or community property or persons, action should be taken to maintain public health and safety. However, the solution to such problems should be accomplished with the least restriction or disregard of the rights of the individual who is the catalyst of the concern. In this case example, Mary may be willing to accept the assistance of her church friends or sons more easily than an unknown social service provider. Therefore, the church may be prevailed upon, with Mary's agreement, to make sure Mary's trash is properly disposed of on a weekly basis. It is important that Mary is told and understands why proper trash disposal is important and the consequences to her if this does not happen. The church members should be aware of the consequences to Mary as well and should be provided with a clear explanation of their role and the importance of maintaining any services to which they may commit as discussed above.

Unless adjudicated incompetent by a court of law, Mary retains the right to make final decisions regarding her care. However, those involved in the arrangement for or provision of services may retain responsibility regarding the provision of and quality of care. Those caregivers who are part of a formal care network have the greatest responsibility for ongoing efforts to assure that Mary is making informed decisions, that the services received meet an acceptable level of quality, that ongoing evaluation of care needs is performed, and that ongoing evaluations of Mary's capacity take place. It is also an appropriate role of formal caregivers to provide information to Mary regarding her right to create advanced directives that reflect her values and choices for care should Mary choose to delegate decision-making authority for health care decisions. Informal caregivers such as church members or Mary's sons should be adequately informed of the importance of meeting any responsibility they assume in Mary's care plan and the importance of notifying the case manager regarding any temporary or permanent change in responsibility.

The capacity of Mary's sister is not fully established in the case example. Strong efforts should be made to determine the level of Martha's decision-making capacity to ensure her rights are not abridged. To the extent that Martha has decision-making capacity, authority for decisions and responsibilities of caregivers are the same as in the example above. However, presuming that Martha lacks the capacity to make health care decisions, none of the parties introduced in the case facts has legal authority to make health care decisions.

It is possible that care may proceed without the appointment of a legal guardian. To be successful in this situation generally requires a high degree of agreement among the involved parties regarding the course, level, and means of providing care. Care should be provided, to the extent possible, using a standard of substituted judgment or care decisions consistent with those which Martha would have made or which reflect previously stated preferences or life values. In the event there is not adequate information to direct a substituted judgment decision-making process, a standard of best interest must be employed.

Final responsibility for Mary's welfare may present one of the more difficult questions in this scenario. Given Mary's questionable capacity for decision-making, her well evidenced desire for independence and demonstrated feelings of obligation for her sister's care, it is difficult to determine how Mary would be affected by a change in circumstances. Maintaining Mary's welfare is a delicately balanced task. To the extent that a formal caregiver, such as the case manager, continues to be involved, the greatest responsibility rests with this person to ensure that all facets of the care plan continue in place and are effective.

The welfare of Martha must be viewed in much the same way as that of Mary. However, there is one significant difference to be addressed. Information is provided regarding the importance of the role of caregiver to Mary, but no information is provided regarding Martha's value of Mary's role in the relationship and how it may affect Martha's welfare. Therefore, it is imperative that there is recognition by professionals, Mary, the sons, and others who may become involved, that Mary's welfare cannot be attained at the cost of her sister in the current situation or in the future as circumstances change. While all parties maintain their rights, in a situation where the rights of everyone cannot be met simultaneously, the rights of the most grieved party may be prioritized.

Competency

Competency or incompetency are legal terms. Therefore the authority to make a decision regarding competency is left to a judicial body. The court is generally responsible for evaluation of evidence presented to make such a determination. Evidence to the court often includes evaluations performed by licensed professionals such as physicians, social workers, and mental health professionals. The alleged incompetent has rights of notice of an adjudication action, the right to be present at the hearing, and the right to be represented by counsel, including the provision of legal counsel if the individual cannot afford to retain counsel. The long-term care ombudsman may be called upon in these situations to assist a client in understanding the proceedings, to obtain legal representation, or to testify on behalf of the client. While the client will have the final determination about the ombudsman's involvement, it may be the client, the court, or the care provider or others who are aware of the impending action who call upon the ombudsman to become involved.

Formal caregivers, such as the care manager or an ombudsman who has been asked to represent Mary, should have an assessment of Mary's capacity for decision-making. Capacity is generally situational. Mary may be able to make an informed choice regarding components of her care plan but may be unable to handle financial issues. An assessment of capacity can lead to putting services in place or granting of authority by Mary such as powers of attorney and thereby avoiding the more drastic intervention of adjudication.

John and Manny

Of the three case examples being explored, this case seems the least likely to include the involvement of the long-term care ombudsman as a client advocate, even in those states that provide ombudsman services to consumers of community-based long-term care. It is doubtful that any of the involved parties would make a complaint to the ombudsman program. However, should the concern come to the attention of the ombudsman, the most likely scenario would have the ombudsman educate the complainant regarding the incidence of abuse and the protective and legal options that exist.

In the event that the ombudsman became involved to the point of talking with John regarding the situation, it would be the ombudsman's role to provide him with information about (1) available alternative courses of action, (2) agencies and services that could assist him (and to facilitate that contact if he so wished), (3) services available to help Manny if he recognized Manny's needs, and (4) the ombudsman's role, which in this case is most likely to include acting as a broker, making a referral to other services on John's behalf. John would be offered a choice in how he wished to proceed. Should John inform the ombudsman that he was not interested in having the ombudsman's involvement, the ombudsman must respect that choice, recognizing the potential for harm to John should John choose not to access any type of service or act in any way to defend himself against Manny's actions. Thus, the ombudsman may be faced with a dilemma: John's choice of no action and anonymity versus laws that may subject ombudsmen, or ombudsmen who may hold a professional license, to mandatory reporting requirements. This issue does arise for ombudsmen in the long-term care setting and has resulted in frequent debate regarding conflicting laws, interpretation of laws, and the client-driven philosophy. It is therefore likely that ombudsmen may act differently from one another regarding the facts of a case. The following discussion provides one ombudsman's perspective to the issues raised by this case example.

Autonomy

Autonomy is self-rule. A suggestion to limit decision-making suggests a lack of capacity for reasoned decision-making. It should be noted that there is a difference between reasoned decision-making and what others may perceive as reasonable decisions. An individual's competency or capacity is questioned when the individual makes decisions that may bring harm to himself. In this case example John chooses to follow his life-long value of parental responsibility over his personal welfare. Others may perceive this as a bad choice and therefore question John's decision-making capacity, and they desire to act in a beneficent or paternalistic manner by limiting John's autonomy in decision-making. While professionals have a responsibility to present John with all the alternatives and their benefits and burdens, John, in the long run, has the right to make a decision and act upon it. Individuals have the right to make decisions that may affect them negatively. John's autonomy of decision-making should not be limited when he is capable of making a reasoned decision.

Manny has the right to seek and receive or deny treatment for his mental illness and to be represented by counsel in a court of law should legal action be brought against him. Additionally, Manny may be eligible for a variety of public benefits, including representation by the federally appointed protection and advocacy agency, as well as rights afforded under the Americans with Disabilities Act.

From a legal standpoint, John has the right to file civil and criminal charges against Manny related to trespassing, theft, and assault. A restraining order could also be filed. In accordance with state law, John could request a conservatorship which would assure that his assets were managed with accountability to the court. The legal actions available to John cover punitive measures, recouping losses, and assurances of current and future physical and financial security. These measures exist as a result of our societal values and make it easy to say John "should" take such actions for his own welfare. However, experience shows that older adults are hesitant to take such actions against adult children, behavior that for John has been reinforced through strongly held religious beliefs in parental responsibility. If John (or other older adults) is forced to take legal action against an adult child, for example to become eligible for Medicaid to pay for long-term care, he is faced with an ethical dilemma that he must carry alone regardless of the many arguments that others may make for such action. John might also petition for guardianship of Manny if mental illness may result in harm to others. A guardian would be expected to seek appropriate treatment for Manny and to recompense John.

As a capable adult, John is ultimately responsible for directing his own welfare. Based upon state law requirements, persons with knowledge of John's situation may have mandatory reporting responsibilities. Adult Protective Services (APS), with knowledge of the situation, must take action to ascertain John's wishes and attempt to provide services, and, although John may refuse service initially, they must follow-up on subsequent reports to assure that John is informed of available services and alternative courses of action. Many victims are offered services numerous times before they are ready to accept assistance. John's sister, if she shares John's family values, may also feel an obligation for John's welfare. If John and his sister share this family value, John may be more accepting of her involvement and counsel.

The hospital cannot, ultimately, prevent John's release. However, the hospital has a responsibility to provide John with options and alternatives to his situation including assisting John in making contacts to facilitate alternate arrangements. The American Medical Association has emphasized the role of the medical profession in this area through the release (1992-93) of educational materials and protocols to all physicians as a part of the AMA's growing concern regarding domestic violence and elder abuse.

The suggested protocol includes the recommendations that the hospital staff initiate and participate in team meetings with other appropriate professional disciplines in the community to develop comprehensive action plans with the abuse victims. The action plan may range from detailed plans to eliminate the abusive situation or emergency "safe" plans to developing a future plan for leaving the abusive environment when the victim becomes ready to abandon his/her current situation. If John continues to refuse these alternatives, the hospital may be responsible, in accordance with state law, for reporting suspected abuse to APS and/or other mandated reporting agencies and to alert these agencies of the time that John returns to the threatening environment.

Best interest may be interpreted as what is best for a person's welfare. It would be in John's best interest to pursue a course of action that would provide for his own physical, psycho-social, and financial safety and security in a manner consistent with his family values. This might include John taking a variety of actions to ensure that Manny receives appropriate treatment for his mental illness with John as a temporary surrogate decision-maker.

It would be in Manny's best interest to seek treatment for his mental illness. To the extent that Manny has decisional capacity, he remains responsible for his own welfare. John's feeling of obligation to Manny's welfare is indicative of another family value. In accordance with state law, APS may have a role in offering services. However, where APS does not serve younger adults there may or may not be other organizations that exist to address these types of concerns.

Attempts should be made to pursue equal exercise of rights for both John and Manny. Allowing individuals to exercise their rights of choice may result in actions with negative outcomes to John or Manny, from their own actions or the actions of the other. One individual's rights should not impose on the rights of another when professionals or legal representatives are in a position of exercising decision-making. Where this is the case, generally a best interest standard is applied and attempts are made to balance the rights of the victims.

The dilemma posed between John's parental responsibility and his personal safety is an age-based question. Few people would question the actions of parents who would place themselves in harm's way for a child who is not an adult. In fact there may even be negative public reaction to a parent's failure to act on behalf of a younger or disabled child. When children grow to adulthood, society and the law place less responsibility on parents and, in fact, question the judgment of parents who take actions detrimental to themselves on behalf of their children. However, this choice, as much as any other choice, when made by an individual with decision-making capacity, is the individual's right regardless of the negative consequences.

CASE THREE

Bonnie

Of the three case examples presented, this scenario is the most likely to encounter the participation of a long-term care ombudsman. Responding to complaints and concerns in nursing homes comprises the major work of ombudsmen. Given the facts in this case example, it suggests that staff of the facility may first relate concerns to the ombudsman. Regardless of the source of the complaint, the ombudsman will approach Bonnie to discuss the concern with her, determine what her interests are, describe the role of the ombudsman, and pose various alternatives and strategies for resolving her concerns. Bonnie's interests are likely to be different from those of the facility in some areas, and, perhaps, similar in some areas. Although Bonnie's husband, too, may be considered a victim, he is not a resident of the nursing home, nor is he receiving any long-term care services. Thus, even in those states where the ombudsman serves consumers of long-term community based care, it is unlikely the ombudsman would be involved in his representation.

One of Bonnie's main interests is the availability of valium and/or meprobamate. To that end she is exposing herself to potential physical harm and financial exploitation by her husband, a situation that she previously rejected when she sought admission to the nursing home. However, upon admission, the facility's attending physician determined that these medications were inappropriate and did not prescribe continued use of them. The physician has acted in what he deems Bonnie's best interest. It is not clear that the physician consulted with Bonnie or anyone else in making this determination. It is possible that the nursing staff of the facility may have raised the issue because federal regulations for certification place limitations on the use of chemical restraints in nursing homes. The position of the physician and that of the nursing home not to allow Bonnie these drugs, represent a valid interest in compliance with federal regulations. In making these decisions, the physician and facility are responding, at least in part, according to professional ethical protocols. Granting visits to her husband to gain access to drugs with resulting psychological, physical, and financial abuse is not, however, an acceptable outcome to Bonnie, the physician, or the facility. It is clear that another solution to meeting the interests of the three parties must be found. This is truly a case where meeting needs or interests solves problems. It should be noted, for the purpose of this case example, that the regulation of the nursing home is a significant factor. The nursing home is held responsible for meeting regulations, and, as a part of them, must ensure that physicians act in accordance with the regulations. Through ombudsman experience in similar situations, it is reasonable to assume that the decision made regarding the valium and meprobamate (the nursing home's position) may have no more to do with what is "good" for Bonnie, or what is appropriate to her medical care, than what the nursing home perceives it must do to be in compliance with limitations on the use of chemical and physical restraints (the nursing home's interest).

The ombudsman, as Bonnie's authorized advocate, will approach the facility and the physician to plan a care conference. Prior to the care conference, the ombudsman will review Bonnie's records, discuss significant points with her including the anticipated interests of all of the parties and various solutions to meet the interests of each party, and Bonnie's desired outcomes. A significant point to be covered in discussion with Bonnie will consider her desire for continued visits with her husband, her position, and to determine if the visits are for the singular purpose of obtaining drugs, her interest. A part of this discussion may also explore Bonnie's reasons for choosing a nursing home rather than seeking home care services. A decision will be made regarding Bonnie's participation in the care conference. In this particular case, it is likely that Bonnie will take part in the plan of care conference.

The first order of discussion in the plan of care conference is likely to be the degree of completion and accuracy of the resident assessment that is required upon admission to a nursing home. Federal regulations require nursing facilities to perform a comprehensive evaluation of each resident, to develop a comprehensive plan of care to address all identified needs, and to implement the plan of care. Frequently, these assessments are not fully performed. The ombudsman will point out the areas of the assessment that may require further attention, particularly the social history and the behavioral areas including the Resident Assessment Protocols (RAPs) of the Minimum Data Set (MDS).

The MDS and RAPs are assessment and planning tools required to be used by every nursing home that is reimbursed by the Medicaid or Medicare program. These tools are an excellent resource. Proper use guides the nursing home in meeting resident needs. Information about a resident's past occupation, community involvement, and family life may prove helpful in creating solutions to problems, establishing appropriate social or care goals for the resident, and knowing and respecting the resident as an individual. For example, the "wandering" resident who attempts to leave the facility every morning and becomes combative when denied exit may have been a person who had a decades-long routine of leaving the house each morning for work. A quick walk through the parking lot may give this resident the sense of having met an obligation and relieving the frustration of being kept from his goal. As another example, setting a goal for a resident to fix her hair and put on make-up each morning is inappropriate to the resident who never wore make-up but may be very important to the resident who never faced the day without such grooming.

Through use of these tools the facility may learn new information about Bonnie and may also find potential avenues to solve some of the current problems. These very important documents are a part of professional ethical protocols that are often overlooked. For example, the nursing home's interest in reducing or eliminating the use of chemical restraints and not using a chemical restraint with a resident with no previous mental health background can be addressed through use of the RAPs. Good, detailed care planning addresses all needs of residents and provides documentation of the resident's needs and choices. This documentation justifies surveying agencies regarding the appropriateness of the use of various medications and facility actions in that regard. Clearly these provisions provide the opportunity for the facility to be more responsive to Bonnie's interests while still meeting its own interests. Because of Bonnie's medical and mental health background, it is possible that the valium and meprobamate can be reintroduced as Bonnie's choice. Many professional nursing home staff and physicians recognize that the resident's choices, with informed consent, can be met. Although it may, in some circumstances, present an ethical dilemma for the professional who believes that a certain course of treatment is not in an individual's best interest, within the professional ethical protocols, the resident's choice is allowable and may be enacted by the facility and physician.

If this course is pursued, Bonnie may be more agreeable to solutions that eliminate her husband's visits and the drug trade and abusive behavior that accompany these visits. In addition it may set a positive tone to further interactions between Bonnie and the nursing home. This will be important due to Bonnie's multiple needs of personal, medical, and psychosocial care. Many residents of nursing homes, particularly those who are faced with physical limitations, have a strong need for control that may be expressed in ways that are very frustrating to staff. (The ombudsman finds this to be particularly true of younger residents.) It becomes very important that the facility work with the resident to find ways in which the resident may exercise control in the most positive manner possible. There is no doubt that, as a resident, Bonnie will present many challenges to the nursing home with varying degrees of success. Various issues raised by the case example from the ombudsman's perspective are discussed below.

Personal Safety

The attending physician, presumably the facility medical director since she/he was not the original prescribing physician, has determined valium and meprobamate are not necessary to control muscle spasms related to cerebral palsy or to act as an anti-depressant. Apparently Bonnie has been denied the medications since her arrival at the facility and has therefore been obtaining the drugs from her husband (possibly through a legal prescription which Bonnie was not allowed to bring into the facility with her upon admission). In receiving valium, Bonnie and her husband are engaged in what may be considered illegal drug trade. The nursing home cannot condone any illegal activity and additionally, must be concerned about the drugs as they affect Bonnie's appropriate and adequate medical care. Nursing facilities are required to have specific protocols for the maintenance and administration of all medications. This generally includes over the counter drugs. Any prescribed medication from home generally cannot be brought into the nursing home because it was not prescribed by the attending physician, the facility does not have an order to administer the drug, or the drug may not meet other pharmacy protocols of the state regulatory body and the facility.

The facility has a responsibility to perform a full multidisciplinary assessment of each resident. The facts given in the case example do not indicate that adequate assessment and care planning have taken place. The MDS and RAPs assessment protocol includes a psychological component. Use of this section is clearly appropriate to Bonnie's past history. In Bonnie's case, assurance should be sought regarding the purpose of the previously prescribed antidepressant. Continued availability of psychological services should be considered as a part of the plan of care. Bonnie should be fully involved in the plan of care process and may choose to have other persons present to support her or advocate for her, including the ombudsman.

Should there be continued visitation between Bonnie and her husband, measures may be taken by the nursing home to ensure Bonnie's personal safety. Not only does the nursing home have a responsibility as a requirement of licensure or certification for the safety of residents, but Bonnie has also expressed her desire, it may be presumed, to be free of physical abuse by separating from her husband and entering the nursing home. The issue of Bonnie's personal safety during visits with her husband should be discussed with Bonnie to seek possible solutions. However, it is unlikely that a solution satisfactory to all parties will be defined unless the issue of Bonnie's "addiction" to valium and access to it and meprobamate are addressed. Should it be the case that valium and meprobamate are provided Bonnie, she continues to exercise her constitutional right of association, and there is continued physical abuse between the spouses, alternate solutions may be explored. These might include open-door, chaperoned, or otherwise public visits. The ombudsman may face an ethical dilemma if Bonnie continues to insist on private visits and the abuse continues. How does the ombudsman support this choice which results in abusive behavior? Will other residents be affected by its occurrence? Will the ombudsman be asked to represent other residents to address this situation? Balancing the rights of multiple residents can be a difficult situation. The nursing home is facing potential liability and questions from the survey agency of failure to protect a resident and is likely to draw the line on documenting resident choice to allow such a situation to continue. The facility may attempt to negotiate an agreement with Bonnie and/or her husband regarding acceptable behavior in the nursing home. Failing compliance with the agreement, the nursing home may pursue legal remedies such as a restraining order or filing assault charges with the local law enforcement agency. The nursing home may or may not consult the ombudsman regarding alternative solutions in this situation. The ombudsman may share ideas with a provider who makes a request, however, the nursing home does not become a client of the ombudsman who continues to represent Bonnie's interests as far as possible. The nursing home, more likely and appropriately may turn to legal counsel to advise and represent the facility's interests should a legal remedy be sought. In the event that spousal visits are denied within the nursing home and Bonnie continues to choose to exercise the right of association with her husband, she may choose to see her husband outside of the facility. Should this be the case, the nursing home may alert the adult protective services agency regarding the situation.

Most state licensure and all facilities participating in federal certification have responsibility for the safety of residents that would require the facility's vigilance, documentation, and efforts directed toward resolving problems of resident safety. In this case example where one victim is a nursing home resident, the nursing home has an overriding responsibility for the resident but no responsibility for her husband, a non-resident. Residents of nursing homes are generally considered free of responsibility for other residents; therefore, Bonnie's roommate does not have responsibility for Bonnie's safety. However, it is certainly appropriate for her to mention her own distress to the nursing home staff, and the facility has a responsibility to address her concerns for personal safety and a secure environment.

Professional staff of the facility are governed by professional licensure standards and by regulations governing the facility. They have a responsibility to document observations or reports of concerns regarding a resident's safety. Appropriate follow-up activity is also expected of professional staff to assure resident safety to the extent possible within the circumstances, the resident's expressed choices, and the law. Actions of the facility and resident's responses should also be documented in the resident's records. In the event the facility does not support action by professional staff to address resident abuse, the professional staff may then address the concern to an outside party such as the long-term care ombudsman, the regulatory agency, or adult protective services.

Paraprofessional staff of the facility have a responsibility to uphold the duties of the facility. Generally the staff are expected to report to professional supervising staff rather than documenting a resident's record. State law determines whether or not paraprofessional staff have a mandated reporting responsibility and to whom reports are made. Paraprofessional staff also have the option of addressing concerns to outside parties if the facility is unresponsive to concerns raised. For both professional and paraprofessional staff, many states have in place what is known as a "whistle-blower" law. A law of this type generally provides a legal remedy regarding loss of employment where a staff person has reported a problem to superiors, action has not been taken, and the employee then contacts an outside authority regarding the concern. In addition, the ombudsman and survey agencies accept anonymous complaints and have professional ethical protocols in place which protect the confidentiality of complainants.

A strong case can be made for the nursing home having final responsibility for Bonnie's welfare because of its formal caregiver role and the regulations governing the operation of the facility. This responsibility is the reason that assessment, care planning, and documentation are imperative so that the facility may be protected in the event of negative outcomes resulting from Bonnie's choices. Survey findings or litigation against the facility are possible actions that the facility may guard against. Bonnie, in exercising her rights, needs to be made aware of the scope and limits of the nursing home's responsibility and capacity for care. The facility may determine that it is unable to meet Bonnie's needs and serve notice of transfer or discharge. The experience of the ombudsman shows an increased incidence of transfer or discharge related to behavioral issues. Frankly, this case example fits the profile of a resident who may be transferred frequently from one facility to another. Residents who are difficult to deal with due to personality, dementia, mental illness, organic illnesses, or damage often face transfer or discharge. Federal regulations promulgated as a result of the Nursing Home Reform Act of 1987 (OBRA) require that there be an accepting placement before a resident can be transferred or discharged. This regulation has created an ability to decrease the practice of sending residents home without notice and agreement, or to other nursing homes, or even to homeless shelters, as has been documented in ombudsman practice. It has also created an ability to deal

more effectively with situations where a nursing home sends a resident to
the hospital and then refuses to take the patient back. While these are
positive outcomes of the regulation, a negative effect is the sometime
failure of one facility to fully inform a potential transfer facility of resident
care needs. Federal regulation presumes the needs of these individuals are
appropriate to and can be met by nursing facilities. However, frequently
the reason given for the transfer or discharge is the facility's inability to
meet the resident's needs. Should Bonnie receive a notice of transfer or
discharge, Bonnie might seek representation from the long-term care ombudsman in a transfer/discharge hearing. In this circumstance the ombudsman will again advocate for Bonnie's interests and rights and will use the
facility assessment and documentation regarding the implementation of an
appropriate care plan, consistent with Bonnie's legal rights and the facility's responsibilities, as a basis for representation.

Resident Choice

Bonnie's son is undoubtedly intimately aware of the problems of his
parents and the problems between them. The case example describes him
in terms typical, in ombudsman experience, of children of nursing home
residents who have had long-term substance abuse problems or mental
illness. Often children expect the nursing home to control a situation they
have been unable to control throughout their lives. Although Bonnie's son
has no legal authority over his mother or father, as a visitor and son the
facility may seek his input in conducting a full assessment of Bonnie or in
care plan meetings. If he is aware that his father is visiting his mother, the
son may be expected to communicate his concerns to a staff member. It
should be noted that he has no legal responsibility to share information
with the facility and, unless the son is a guardian or other attorney-in-fact,
his choices for treatment do not outweigh the choices of Bonnie.

Bonnie's husband does not have a right to visit the nursing home. The
right of visitation is Bonnie's. Without Bonnie's agreement her husband
cannot visit. Bonnie and her husband need to be made aware of the nursing
home's knowledge of the abuse and trade of valium, and Bonnie's use of
the drug (as documented by Bonnie's hospitalization). Should Bonnie
express her choice for continued visits with her husband, certain conditions may be placed on visits regarding the transfer of drugs and Bonnie's
personal safety. Possibilities include open-door or chaperoned visits. Bonnie may exercise her choice to have private visits. Both Bonnie and her
husband should be informed of the facility's obligation to report any
further evidence of drug trade or abuse to appropriate authorities. Each of
these actions make use of coercive power and, although they may result in

the desired outcome regarding the husband's visits and possible drug use, they do not set a positive tone for Bonnie's residency in the nursing home. It is likely that the use of such coercive power will result in increased negative behavior from Bonnie and may ultimately result in her receiving a notice of discharge from the facility, or Bonnie may choose to leave the facility. A more positive approach would be a plan of care conference to meet the interests of the facility, the physician, and Bonnie. In the event that Bonnie feels her need for medication is met by the facility but still wishes to see her husband, it is possible that she will agree to open-door or chaperoned visits to meet both her interests and that of the facility.

Bonnie's frequent complaints of missing funds or property have created frustration among the staff of the nursing home. Although staff may feel that Bonnie's claims are unfounded, it does not necessarily mean they are untrue and it does not negate Bonnie's right to request an investigation from other parties such as the long-term care ombudsman. Indeed, Bonnie's reputation as a complainer or the "boy who cried wolf" may actually make it easier for staff or other residents to take her property. With her physical incapacity and no witness, anyone could take property from Bonnie while she watched and then claim she was lying.

> Loss and theft is a prevalent problem in nursing homes. Unpublished findings of Huber in an analysis of ombudsman complaint data from ten states, commissioned by the Institute of Medicine, placed lost or stolen property as the most frequent complaint in the aggregated data. Sixty-five percent of these complaints were verified upon investigation by the ombudsman. (Harris-Wehling et al., 1995)

With Bonnie's consent and the cooperation of the nursing home, steps may be taken to establish safeguards for Bonnie's funds and possessions that will address the concerns and may lessen the complaints. There are resident fund account systems that may be used, as well as lock boxes for jewelry and smaller items. Other solutions may be found to keep the property within Bonnie's immediate control or with some additional control over the facility's system, such as Bonnie holding the key for a lock box which the facility maintains, and which may address Bonnie's need for control and any suspicion she may have of the facility's system. Although the facility may need to take some extra steps in securing Bonnie's property, these actions may reduce the facility's liability.

There is nothing in the case example to indicate that Bonnie does not have decision-making capacity. Clearly, she has a history of making choices that may not be in her best interest. However, Bonnie has recently made choices which are apparently in her best interest, regardless of her motivation, namely those of separating from a physically abusive husband and entering a protective environment capable of addressing her care needs. This deduction is made because it is possible that Bonnie could receive adequate health care services at home with informal caregiver support. It is possible that her husband would not or could not provide the informal support Bonnie needed to stay at home. Added to the institution-alization is the separation from her husband. Bonnie need not separate from her husband to secure her personal funds or to attain Medicaid eligibility. It apparently was the complete removal of two drugs to which Bonnie was dependent (either physically or psychologically) that has led her to choose to obtain the medication through visits with her husband, risking potential physical abuse. Although this is not a choice in her best interest, Bonnie has the right to make bad decisions and to bear the conse-quences of those decisions. Until such time as Bonnie is adjudicated in-competent, or otherwise subject to court order, she has the final authority regarding her welfare.

THE OMBUDSMAN AS TEAM MEMBER

The previous pages have been dedicated to expressing the strong focus of the long-term care ombudsman as client advocate. Ombudsmen must work with and depend upon professionals in many disciplines to actually carry out care and services. The ability of the ombudsman to work with the service providers and other professional disciplines is extremely important to the ombudsman's ability to achieve the client's desired outcomes. One of the most important aspects of the long-term care ombudsman's role is education.

Ombudsmen must first educate themselves. To advocate effectively it is important to know the professions in the field, to know the scope and responsibilities of the various programs or services that may address a given situation, and to know the regulatory structures of the programs and environments. This knowledge introduces the ombudsman to key profes-sionals and networks. With knowledge of programs and those who prac-tice within the programs, the ombudsman can work more effectively with colleagues on behalf of clients. The next component of education is to describe for other professionals the role and scope of responsibility of the ombudsman. Ombudsmen dedicate considerable time to these educational efforts to build stronger working relationships for client advocacy. As with each specialty, there are those professionals who work with each other on a more frequent basis and rely upon established relationships or protocols to serve clients more efficiently.

The ombudsman works with a variety of disciplines. Those disciplines which interact in nursing homes are the best known to ombudsmen, including nursing home administrators, nurses, social workers, nurse aides, nutritionists, activities personnel, and physicians. Often the concerns addressed by the ombudsmen include these same professions who work in other venues with particular mandates or responsibilities. These include hospital discharge planners, hospital physicians, and nurses, adult protective services workers, case managers or case workers, level of care assessors, eligibility experts, reimbursement assessors, regulatory surveyors, etc. Client concerns may also require the involvement of attorneys, judges, administrative hearing officers, law enforcement personnel, mental health professionals, clergy, policy makers, medicaid fraud and criminal abuse units, county prosecutors, ethics committees, and so on.

Examples of these relationships can be drawn from the cases discussed earlier. In the case involving Mary and her sister Martha, the ombudsman would refer the case to an appropriate agency or, in those states where the ombudsman has responsibility to handle home care complaints, would be in contact with the case manager regarding the assessments and recommended services. Mary's goal to stay in the home would be addressed by finding evidence to support her choice and helping the other professionals to recognize and include proper assessment and client choice in their recommendations. The ombudsman would also work to find creative solutions to some of the concerns that emerged during the assessment. This might include working with the church community and any other service providers to be sure that they understood the client's choices and to participate in the implementation of a plan responsive to those choices. In the event that formal services were not meeting Mary's expectations, the ombudsman would, in many cases, make sure that the case manager was aware of these concerns and would potentially negotiate or mediate a resolution. Similar actions would be taken for Martha to assure that her choices were also honored, and efforts would be made to coordinate the services for Mary and her sister or to address their needs separately as choice dictated.

Since the second case example is unlikely to involve the long-term care ombudsman as the facts are presented, a contact with the ombudsman for assistance would be inappropriate. In that instance, the ombudsman would provide education regarding the appropriate service alternatives; APS and law enforcement professionals are the two most likely primary referrals. The ombudsman might also provide information to the caller regarding the dynamics of abusive situations, the roles of various agencies, and choice and autonomy. The ombudsman might take on the role of referring the concern if this were the complainant's wish or empowering the complainant to act and call back if additional assistance was needed or if they felt that services had not been provided appropriately. In the latter circumstance, the ombudsman is more likely to have direct contact with other professionals to determine the validity of concerns. Should this be the case, the ombudsman would work, with client direction, to resolve the concerns or to explain why an agency has acted appropriately, if the situation was not resolved to the satisfaction of the complainant.

The third case offers a mix of institutional and community issues that may be spread more evenly among the responding professionals. The ombudsman may have the greatest scope of knowledge regarding the institutional issues, yet rely on APS for authority in the community issues. Law enforcement professionals who may become involved with nursing home issues often feel unprepared to relate to a "separate" institutional environment and may benefit from the perspective of other professions involved, such as the ombudsman, physicians, nursing home administrators, and licensure agencies. It is possible to see different professionals in charge of the different components of the case.

The most important part of cooperation among disciplines is the knowledge of each discipline's scope of authority and philosophy. This knowledge is an invaluable tool to providing client services. With this knowledge, it is possible to start with an understanding of each area of responsibility, know who needs to, or is available to, address issues and in what manner. Fitting together the "pieces of the puzzle" can help to serve clients effectively and efficiently. This knowledge is also very important when ethical dilemmas arise and a decision must be made. Service providers are better able to work together when they recognize each other's professional ethics and agency expectations. Although knowledge does not provide answers for all of the dilemmas encountered, it does provide the ability to recognize the questions and possible solutions toward resolution of these dilemmas.

BIBLIOGRAPHY

Caplan, A. (1985). Let wisdom find a way. *Generations,* 10 - 14.

Collopy, B. (1988). Autonomy in long term care: Some crucial distinctions. *The Gerontologist,* 28, 10-17.

Harris-Wehling, J., Feasley, J.C., & Estes, C.L. (1995). *Real people real problems: An evaluation of the long-term care ombudsman programs of the Older Americans Act.* Washington, DC: Institute of Medicine.

Hunt, S. (1989). *An Ombudsman's resource paper for effective advocacy: Working through ethical dilemmas in ombudsman practice.* The National Center for Long Term Care Ombudsman Resources, 5-8.

Chapter Seven

A Case Manager's Perspective

Joseph Sonntag, MA

SUMMARY. Case management is playing an increasingly important role in improving access to community based services. The ethical issues and dilemmas in values among clients bring new challenges to this dimension of social work. Public protocols provide an ethical context but ethical practice requires interpreting protocol in social and individual conduct. This chapter will focus on the three case studies of elder mistreatment from the point of view of case management. *[Article copies available from The Haworth Document Delivery Service: 1-800-342-9678.]*

INTRODUCTION

"Rights" as defined by a given society in its laws and constitution are directed toward the common good, but these do not make up the whole basis of our rights as human beings. We give to the courts and law makers authority to make and enforce laws that we consider "ethical." For example, laws exist to protect our basic needs, such as food, shelter, and health care, and our basic rights, such as our freedoms of belief and expression of ideas. No society can demonstrate beyond all doubt that the consensus upon which its laws are built is completely ethical. But, insofar as it

---

Joseph R. Sonntag is Case Manager, Seattle-King County Division on Aging, 618 2nd Avenue, Suite 1020, Seattle, WA 98104.

[Haworth co-indexing entry note]: "A Case Manager's Perspective." Sonntag, Joseph. Co-published simultaneously in *Journal of Elder Abuse & Neglect* (The Haworth Press, Inc.) Vol. 7, No. 2/3, 1995, pp. 115-130; and: *Elder Mistreatment: Ethical Issues, Dilemmas, and Decisions* (ed: Tanya Fusco Johnson) The Haworth Press, Inc., 1995, pp. 115-130. [Single or multiple copies of this article are available from The Haworth Document Delivery Service: 1-800-342-9678, 9:00 a.m. - 5:00 p.m. (EST)].

represents what most of us in a given social system believe to be right, we will support the systems's efforts to enforce the laws and protect us from one another as needed.

As has been pointed out in earlier chapters, the laws and dictums that derive from public protocol are only one part of the whole when we speak of ethical decision-making. In many cultures, ethics pertains also to the realm of individual interpretations and choices. What is right for a given situation can only be fully determined in the depths of one's own conscience, its outcome sought amidst the unique complexity of many other people's needs and rights. In many cases one is guided, not by any legally defined right, but by what the society as a whole perceives to be right ethical choices, which come in some way from a general consensus about human needs and the pursuit of happiness.

So, in discussing specific case situations, we deal with two different dimensions: that based upon the formal protocols of public ethical systems that are set up to protect the rights of citizens and that of the inner realm of personal choice. How "ethical" one is, is seen in some religions and cultures to be determined more by the depth of one's humanity, his or her understanding and compassion, than by adherence to a defined code of rights and laws.

CASE MANAGEMENT

Ethical protocol in case management under the Older Americans Act is derived from Federal and State standards as well as from agency and professional directives. The focus in examining ethics and elder abuse is with those protocols or directives that pertain to clients' rights and the promotion of quality of life among the clients served. Many of these prescriptions for conduct coincide with standards applied generally in the field of social work.

Case management, in the professional standards of social work, is individualized and client-focused, with community concerns and family viewpoints on care plans being secondary. Professional standards also emphasize that the client is presumed to be mentally competent until declared otherwise by a court of law. Directives from the federal guidelines for the Area Agencies on Aging and certain state directives indicate that the goal of case management is primarily to help older disabled adults continue to live independent lives by pursuing the least restrictive alternatives for long term care. In relation to clients' rights, professional protocols include the following important values:

1. the right of confidentiality and privacy
2. equal treatment under the law

3. freedom of choice and the right to refuse services
4. the right to legal representation

Issues of quality of life are also contained in case management protocol: being treated with respect and dignity, self-determination, and participating actively in defining and implementing the service plan.

THE THREE CASES

Mary and Martha

Let us examine the case of Mary and Martha from the viewpoint of public protocol. Legally, family members do not have inherent decision-making authority over other family members. However they can obtain decision-making authority for another family member, for example, durable power of attorney or in cases requiring guardianship through the courts if the family member is judged to be incompetent or (in some state laws) to be too incapacitated to provide for his/her own basic needs.

Martha's and Mary's need for essential health care and personal care are the focus for public intervention, assuming of course that providing basic needs and protection from serious harm are at some level part of the social consensus. Mary's sons may choose not to contribute, nor do they necessarily have an obligation to provide for the needs of Mary and Martha. They have a right to lead their own lives as they want, even to the extent of ignoring their mother and aunt completely. This may or may not be a good ethical decision for both or either of them, depending on their reasons and the context in which this decision is being made. No judgment about the ethical accountability of the two sons can be made without knowing the full circumstances of their personal choices.

Nor do Mary's sons have an inherent right to decide changes for their mother and aunt, including moving them to a retirement home against their wishes. They can work toward convincing them that a decision is in their best interest and for their happiness. They can also pursue legal guardianship and/or better medical and psychiatric assistance for their mother. But often family members make decisions without authorization for an elder family member.

Martha has a right to advocate for herself in keeping her sister as a caregiver. She also has a right to receive care that she is unable to provide for herself. This could present her with an ethical dilemma for herself, given that these two choices may be at odds. It would be here that deliberation and negotiation facilitated by a case manager could be of great value to her.

The basic ethical assumptions contained in the above statements are: (1) In the context of private ethics, "rights" pertain to one's self, to that which each of us deserves and should have as a human being. Outside the realm of public ethics, one does not have "rights" over another person. (2) There must at times be a priority of rights when one must choose between different rights for him or herself, or when one person's rights conflict with those of another person's in a given situation. (3) There is no categorical ethical imperative for caring for other family members, even children or dependent adults. These decisions in ethical practice arise from publicly defined protocols and private ethical decisions. For this reason there can be no general standards of ethics that apply to each and every case.

Confronting the complex reality of private ethics with our clients, we become increasingly aware of the fluid nature of ethical decision-making. As social workers, we would be ineffective without substantial deliberation and negotiation around ethical issues and dilemmas. Ethical practice, forged in the context of a client's private beliefs as well as our own professional protocols, requires such actions. So, ethics goes beyond the limited realm of legally constituted rights as defined by a given society. Ethics, as personal and individual, stretches into the arenas of inner personal growth and changing relationships. It moves us to transcend an isolated self to a loving and socially responsible self.

The obligations that a caregiver feels toward an elderly family member not inconveneniently arises out of an ideology or personal belief system that the person has not examined or reflected on for a long time–perhaps not ever. These unexamined "ought to be" values ("keeping mom at home," "giving up my job to care for dad," and so forth) can leave the caregiver in an especially difficult position unless these values can be brought into the more fluid context of deliberation and negotiation. These processes must include the health and welfare of the caregiver as well as of the client. A sense of guilt that leads one to ignore his or her own physical and spiritual needs will ultimately only drain away the energy that one needs to do good ethical practice.

With regard to reporting abuse, the Meals-on-Wheels program is an example of a publicly funded program, which means that the staff are mandated to report suspected abuse. To be effective in this regard, it is necessary that direct-client workers receive the necessary training to more easily identify the signs of abuse when visiting homes. Meals-on-Wheels workers and others in the public sector, such as the church visitors in this case, should be encouraged to call a central contact number, such as a senior information and referral agency or Adult Protective Services. These agencies can appoint a social worker to do an in-home assessment to determine whether there is a need for further legal or protective services. Another resource is home health services.

Public agencies should have the primary role to intercede on behalf of vulnerable citizens. The courts, legal services, and the criminal justice system in general should be the foundation of any effective reporting system as well as a service-providing one. Leaving decision-making solely in the hands of the family would allow in some cases for continuing abusive situations. The laws themselves, and the enforcement of laws, need to be strengthened. Hospital emergency wards, doctors' offices, and home health visits are arenas for public service, directly involved, by definition, in the physical and mental health of citizens. These providers also have a strong mandate to be involved in protecting the public and many already do so. It is the government's responsibility to require full participation of the medical establishment in protection against abuse and to give these agencies the support and access they require to move expeditiously when they encounter an abusive situation in the home.

To the extent that Mary is not mentally competent, public agencies under legal jurisdiction should receive authority to make decisions on her behalf. Guardianship, if this is the route chosen, need not be primarily a usurpation of one's rights. It can become so if done without careful investigation and proper medical and mental health evaluations, or if done in a slip-shod way through the legal system without careful attention given to the appropriateness of a proposed guardian. If used in a proper manner, guardianship is more a protection of one's rights than a taking away of rights. It is providing incompetent or partially incompetent (or incapacitated) persons with an extension of themselves that can protect them from exploitation and help them make decisions that are in their best interest. Final authority belongs with Mary, through her properly appointed representative.

Family members can, of course, also be invaluable participants in the support system, along with the properly appointed authority such as a legally appointed guardian. However, the guardian needs to determine whether the intent of family members is in the client's best interests and whether they can provide the assistance that they propose to provide. If other family members are to make decisions affecting Mary and Martha without their full consent, this decision-making authority should be given to them by a publicly designated body such as a court. Abuse often occurs when there is an untrained and uninformed family caregiver who does not understand the nature of the client's illness or disability. The following are examples: A demented client cannot remember to take her pills and is berated and threatened for being "obstinate." An Alzheimer's client has become incontinent and is physically punished for this "willful" act. A stroke victim, unable to become motivated to work, is yelled at and called lazy and stubborn.

Whose rights take precedence when there is an ethical dilemma between opposing needs or between opposing parties? We as a society and a responsible public need to seriously reevaluate what qualifies as basic rights and basic needs. Certain areas of need have been seriously minimized in the past. Among these are mental health and spiritual needs. As older people in our society face some of the greatest losses of their entire lives and some of the most challenging changes (e.g., entering a nursing home), we limit our care to checking their blood-pressure and food intake and act as if their inner spirit were of little importance. It is a decided bias of our culture to treat the body and not the spirit and the mind. As Rose Renee Shield (1988) states in her book on nursing home life, the residents "are 'decultured' and brought closer to nature, treated like problem-filled bodies that must be serviced and maintained . . . " (194).

Second, precipitators of abuse should not be allowed to violate the rights or obstruct the basic fulfillment of needs of another for personal convenience or gain. This may sound like an obvious point, but it is allowed in many cases simply because one is "family."

Third, the common good supersedes individual good when basic rights are involved on both sides to an equal degree, in other words in the situation of an ethical dilemma. This is not an easy principal to apply to specific situations, but one point that can be made is that one's wealth or lack thereof should not determine whether one comes in first or second on the priority scale.

Finally, who has the authority to make a decision about Mary's competency? The ultimate authority for such designation of incompetency must lie in the public domain, with government, as worked out through the legal and social services system. Needless to say, this cannot be done effectively without major input from mental health professionals. We should in fact consider integrating mental health evaluations much more directly with the courts.

A case manager assigned to Mary's case would want to investigate the types of tests that she has had for the earlier diagnosis of dementia of the Alzheimer's type, to determine, for example, if tests for other etiologies have been made such as thyroid conditions, nutritional imbalances, or brain tumors. Depression should also be ruled out as the primary cause. If not already done, a thorough work-up involving a full range of tests for physical causes of dementia might be recommended by the case manager. If, after testing, dementia of the Alzheimer's type is indicated, a placement for Mary and Martha is probably unavoidable, unless a home-sharing arrangement can be set up in which a caregiver can move in and provide the needed services in the home. This solution is not likely, however, because until now funding to pay full-time, live-in help for clients with high levels of care needs has been inadequate. If Alzheimer's is diagnosed, it means there will be a continuing deterioration of brain cells and consequently of Mary's physical and mental functioning. It is only a matter of time before she will be even less able to care for herself and her sister.

To recommend the status quo in this case does not seem to be a good position. Both women are in some degree of physical danger in the present situation. Martha is not receiving needed medications and Mary is subject to falling due to apparently increased disorientation. Assisted living might be an appropriate solution. Moving to a regular retirement apartment, as suggested by one of Mary's sons, would probably not be a good move. Alzheimer's clients suffer frequently from increased disorientation and fear when confronted with unfamiliar surroundings. It is doubtful whether the sons would counteract this or provide for the increasing demands related to the women's safety and quality of care in the new location.

We know from experience in the field that frequently a client chooses their perceived happiness over safety. Mary, and possibly Martha also, might refuse to move anywhere away from their present home and continue to minimize the seriousness of their disabilities, until a hospitalization might occur. A competent person has the right to choose happiness as they perceive it over safety, and even a partially competent person making questionable decisions cannot be forced into placement. In a situation like this, a case manager faces an ethical dilemma of conflicting values and must choose between enabling a sometimes dangerous situation and helping to provide at least some needed services under adverse conditions. The services could hopefully decrease the danger potential and provide some comforts for a period of time. Even this, a temporary and piece-meal solution, however, would of course depend on whether Mary and Martha could be convinced that this is a better alternative for them than being hospitalized and having very little choice about placement. An important part of this process is getting to know the clients and learning what has worked for them in the past: What kinds of relationships have they enjoyed? What services have they responded to in a positive way? Many older clients would rather have somebody vacuum their rug or scrub down the walls than get ten hours of free therapy! Maybe this will have to be the starting point.

John and Manny

In case number two it seems clear that John's son Manny is acting outside the law in violating the rights of his father. Manny's physical and mental mistreatment of his father is more than a private family issue. Besides the physical and verbal abuse, the transfer of John's property to the son was very possibly done with coercion or deception and therefore went contrary to both personal and public ethical practice.

In theory, John has, even after the coerced transfer of property if that is indeed what it was, the right to keep his own home, the right to evict his son, the right to file charges against his son, and the right to get appropriate care and nourishment. But it is all too common that the victim of abuse is unable to secure his or her rights, or even recognize them. John is legally (in terms of overall competency) responsible for his own decisions and for securing his own safety and care, but the extended mistreatment and isolation he has undergone have apparently made him incapable of or unwilling to accomplish these objectives. As is often the case, the abused person thinks that he or she is somehow responsible for whatever problems exist, guided by a consciousness that has been robbed of self-esteem. In such a situation, basic rights become a public issue. Adult Protective Services and the hospital have an ethical mandate to assure John's health and safety.

Likewise, Manny himself is responsible for his own welfare, but only to the point that his mental health condition does not render him incompetent to do so–a determination that is usually very difficult to assess. Many of the ethical mores in our society might suggest that Manny's father has primary responsibility for his son's welfare, or vice versa as discussed above, and it is certainly not unreasonable for either of them to have this belief. But these viewpoints, however widespread in a society, cannot be generalized into principles that are applicable to all families and individuals. It is possible, in a given situation, that a positive choice would be not to take care of a son or daughter or parent, if, for example, taking on this responsibility would seriously impact one's own health or that of other family members.

In other words, John does not have an inherent ethical responsibility, just because he is his parent, to take care of Manny, even though his own personal ethics might lead him to do this. It could even be argued that John is not able to effectively care for Manny. It is possible that he does not understand the real nature of his son's needs and thus ends up being more of an enabler toward his son's mental deterioration than a provider of healing for him.

If a case manager believes that care for one's self is a priority value and sees the client harming him or herself for the perceived benefit of another family member, what can be done? Can the case manager impose his or her values on the client? This would not seem like a valid response to the professional protocol, but certainly the case manager can, in the deliberations and negotiations of problem solving, present new values to a client, challenge their scripts, with due respect to the client's beliefs and traditions. It is an interesting footnote that in western Christian society one's own personal rights and needs are often denied to a greater or lesser extent because of a commonly held assumption that love of self (not selfishness) is not a value of equal importance to giving of one's self for a family member.

John's case manager will also be faced with the task of separating preferences from ethical issues in this case. It may be (and the case manager may believe) that it is in John's best interest to regain legal possession of his home and have his son move out and obtain needed treatment under the mental health system; arguably these are not ethical issues but rather preferences to be decided upon by John and his son. Ethical practice in the context of this case would seem to indicate, however, that John not be subjected any longer to mistreatment in his home; this might require that Manny live apart from him until he is stabilized and able to relate to his father in a non-abusive manner.

These strong decisions raise a dilemma, however, for the case manager: Am I an agent for client self-determination (advocate, counselor) or am I an agent of social control (involuntary treatment, criminal justice enforcer)? These two roles do not mix well. It would be advantageous if two separate professional workers were involved, perhaps an Adult Protective Services worker to be a strong advocate for prosecution, thereby pursuing the ethical value of protection of the client's safety, and a case manager whose singular objective is working with the client to interpret and negotiate his or her personal value system or ethics and/or connecting the client with services that will be immediately helpful.

The question is raised: Should the hospital or physician refuse to release John because they are aware that he is returning to an abusive and neglecting situation? My answer would be "yes." They should refuse to release him at least temporarily, and the laws should support this action. An "Adult Protective Services Team" in the hospital, or some other publicly appointed authority, should have the legal right to delay a person's return to what appears to be a seriously abusive environment. The reason for this approach is the nature of abuse and its psychologically damaging character, especially with regard to one's judgment about the abusive relationship itself. Denying John the choice of going home under the above circumstances is based not so much on the issue of John's rights as upon the issue of Manny's illegal activity (abuse). Even if the abuse has not been conclusively documented, the hospital, with substantial evidence provided by professional staff, whether in the hospital or in-home social workers or nurses, should be able to shield John until he is able to clear mentally from the distortions of judgment that commonly accompany abusive treatment. It is not so much depriving him of a right as protecting his right to make a clear decision and to protect him from the continued violation of his rights that has already begun at home.

If John clearly acknowledges the abuse he is receiving from Manny and states that he does not want to change the situation, it may be a somewhat different dilemma for the case manager. In this case, it will require a serious negotiating of realities with all parties involved. Ultimately, at least in the social ambience of this particular case, no one can prevent another from walking off a cliff if the person has his or her full mental capacities.

We have not taken seriously enough the research on the incapacitating results of mental and physical abuse. A person may be mentally competent in almost all aspects of his or her cognition and still be enslaved, so to speak, in one particular dimension, such as subservience to the abuser. The abuser will use many justifications and rationalizations to convince the victim, and everyone else, that no problem exists. Some of the variations include: (1) *Denial of responsibility:* "It was an accident," "I haven't got the time to help him." *(2) Denial of injury:* "I was teasing him a little," "No one really got hurt." *(3) Denial that there was a victim:* "She was just faking it," "He's just stubborn," "He's lazy." (These comments suggest that the victim got what he or she deserved, but nothing excessive.) *(4) Loyalty to the abuser:* because of fear, false loyalty, or convenience, *(5) Defense of victim by necessity:* "I locked her in the basement for her own safety" (Tometa, 1990).

Clearly there is no magic formula for translating these distortions and rationalizations into realizations on the part of an abused client. But this only underlines the importance of the role of the case manager in deliberation and negotiation with clients and their family members. The presumptions which underlie patterns of abuse are often deeply imbedded in the consciousness of the abused and the abuser as well. In John's case, it is possible to raise the question with him, for example, about his apparent loyalty to his son under these abusive circumstances. Only over time will he perhaps begin to see the hurtful loyalty or his unwarranted fear of change.

Situations like John's could possibly be prevented from deteriorating by emphasizing the purpose and role of Adult Protective Services and in educating the community about elder mistreatment. [Only 1 out of every 14 abuse cases come to public attention (Pillemer & Finkelhor, 1988).] The public should be informed that a referral to Adult Protective Services or to a non-APS case management agency for investigation does not require substantiated evidence. There need be no proven or observed mistreatment. When an older adult in the community suddenly becomes isolated, or an abrupt or unexplainable change of lifestyle is noted as in John's case, these are reasons for a referral. It can then be left up to the professional involved to substantiate the abuse or neglect.

Direct observation, "red flags," might reveal risk factors, such as a poor relationship between two people, characterized by poor communication, lack of empathy, and understanding; signs of anger, extreme stress, "wanting out" (could be victim or abuser); or lack of affection and attention shown. I recently analyzed my own caseload of 55 clients on the basis of these red flags and found that 23 of the 55 could be judged as being vulnerable to verbal or physical abuse. Clients with mental incapacity were three times more likely to be in this vulnerability group than those with physical disability only. All of these cases required referrals, if not immediately to APS, to other in-home agencies for increased services and monitoring. A good starter for assessing a situation is simply asking: Would I entrust my mother or father to this person? If not, why not?!

Second, we need to reassess the meaning of guardianship, often thought about just in the context of taking away someone's rights. With careful management, guardianship can be a protection of rights rather than an abrogation of them. We need perhaps a wider and more varied range of guardianship types or voluntary conservatorships defined to meet the different needs of our clients more effectively. The court system needs to shift from only a legal and financial emphasis to one that includes service and care-taking. A representative should be appointed for persons with dementia, whether in or out of nursing homes, to protect their civil and personal rights. *Every* nursing home resident, whether suffering from dementia or not, should have the same. Many are without family support and many are subject to negative family impact.

Third, we have to address the guilt that John feels as a parent, guilt that prevents him from cooperating with a criminal justice solution, if voluntary measures fail. It is not likely that his "logic" regarding his relationship with his son will be affected to any significant degree by a case manager or even a therapist in a short period of time. But he can be helped to see that the only way *to help his son* may be to (1) involve the police, (2) require treatment, and (3) obtain a protective order to keep him from the home. In other words, John will need to understand that, in cooperating with a criminal justice approach, he is attempting to create a better life, not only for himself, but for his son as well.

As social workers and other professionals in the field doing direct client work, we are aware of the difficulty of impacting one's inner convictions about correct or ethical roles in the family. We are dealing not only with the client's consciously stated views but with the complexity of subconsciously held views as well. Very possibly there is a private, subconscious dialogue going on between John and some long past family member that informs him, with little room for doubt, that his duty as a father is to stand by his son, at any cost to himself. Unfortunately, such family values, whether conscious or unconscious, may include abusive and destructive patterns of relationships. The first goal of the case manager or counselor is, not to identify a victim and a villain, but to discover the hidden message in the violence and mistreatment. But since personal change at this level often requires a long and difficult therapeutic process, social control must be brought into play to protect the client first.

Fourth, the legality of the property transfer should be investigated; it could be legally determined that transfers of property require legal representation. Manny would not be able to secure ownership of his father's property without his father having a legal advocate to protect his rights and needs. Finally, an improved nursing home environment would help to dissuade abused patients from returning to abusive situations at home when their primary motivation is to avoid the loss of basic freedoms such as privacy, autonomy, and freedom of choice.

Bonnie

Nursing homes as publicly approved residences have the responsibility to provide for the protection and safety of their residents. However this mandate is considered, from the point of view of the institution or from that of the resident– in either case, legal protection is the goal. As a public institution, the nursing home protects its residents against illegal or harmful outcomes, whether this is a leaking gas pipe, a drug dealer, or an abusive husband. No one should have the right per se to break a law or violate the rights of another person, regardless of whether that other person consents to or even encourages such activity.

From the client's point of reference, clinging to an abusive relationship, for whatever perceived personal advantage, is arguably not someone's right if she/he can be judged to be under coercion, a judgment that could frequently be made based upon psychological studies of abuse. To the extent that a person is not competent to make a decision on behalf of his or her own safety and that decision involves a second party (violator), s/he deserves a legal protector, not just the chance intervention of an aide.

Monitoring for and reporting potential abuse situations is ethically an expected role for the paraprofessional staff, but every nursing home resident should also have a legal representative outside the nursing home with whom s/he is in regular contact and who clearly represents the resident's best interests. Interventions in relation to abusive situations should not be a responsibility only placed on the paraprofessional staff, although involving them on the multidisciplinary teams for the residents would be beneficial.

The role of the son is different from that of a professional staff-person in the nursing home. He does not work for an organization or institution that has the public mandate through specific laws to protect the rights of the residents. It is society's prerogative to require reporting of abuse from whomever, and many states in the United States have laws with wide inclusion in this regard. But most likely, in the son's case, we are dealing with a personal ethical decision as opposed to a legal requirement such as that of the nursing home. If Bonnie is not living with her son, the law will ordinarily not be the primary determinant of his ethical practice. Although it would appear on the surface that the correct ethical decision for the son would be to become involved in protecting his mother, it is not a given. There are situations where such decisions can have a serious negative impact, either on the family member who intervenes (e.g., history of abuse or mental illness himself) or upon a third party (e.g., the spouse or child of the person intervening).

It is certainly within the purview of social workers, counselors, nurses, or other employees who have a mandate to serve the public, to work with and counsel family members in the direction of good ethical decisions for themselves and to help them sort through whatever complexities exist in a given situation. This is not imposing "right" decisions but rather assisting them to make well considered ethical decisions about a family member.

Although it would not be wise to rely primarily on the other patients in a nursing home to monitor and report abusive situations, their reports should be taken seriously and investigated. As mentioned in the other case studies, education (both lay and professional) around issues of abuse should be increased, in or outside of institutional settings, and people should be encouraged to report suspected abuse. Building a strong sense of mutual support and community in a nursing home can be a great protection for all, based not upon legal mandates but upon friendship and caring. Friends will not stand by and allow a person they care about to be abused or neglected without some intervention. Efforts within the nursing home which promote the sharing of people's personal histories, peer support and communication, and other kinds of interactions which promote deeper relationships among the residents are invaluable in providing a milieu of protection and safety. Another factor which contributes greatly toward this end is the developing of regular interactions between the nursing home residents and outside groups and individuals, whether in the context of a political, social, or entertainment activity.

Bonnie's husband should have no legal right to visit her in the nursing home as long as the pattern of abuse continues. Even though he is her husband, he has no legal power over his spouse, and he should be subject to the same restrictions for protection as anyone else. However, a compromise could be reached in this situation if he were willing to cooperate, assuming that Bonnie welcomes his visits. For example, his visits could take place in a more open, public area of the nursing home. Blood tests and other physical examinations of Bonnie could be done routinely after his visits for the purpose of preventing future abuses.

Strictly speaking, Bonnie has a right to allow herself to be abused, but it is a mute point in this case because Bonnie does not have a right to condone illegal activity on the part of another party in the public institution in which she resides. We could also say that Bonnie retains the right to abuse herself to some degree (without, of course, the aid or negligence of the institution being involved). We as professionals strive to improve the standards and quality of treatments for addiction, hoping to provide better incentives to people for choosing health rather than having it imposed upon them (e.g., mandatory alcohol treatment following a DWI conviction). Second, we strive to give maximum attention to the kinds of family and agency interventions that have proven to be successful in the past. Some of these do admittedly involve a degree of moral coercion, but family or group interventions have proven to be a very good compromise with regard to the ethical dilemma of free choice (for self-harm) versus family intervention for healing. Addictive illness deprives the patient to a greater or lesser extent of a true capacity for free choices on his or her own behalf.

In summary, Bonnie herself has primary responsibility for her health and safety. The facility's responsibility is (1) to shield their patient from abuse by another, both from within and from outside the nursing home, (2) to not enable her self-abuse (e.g., over-prescribing valium), and (3) to educate and provide treatment for physical and mental illnesses to allow the patient to reach her maximum level of self-help and recovery. As is true of any citizen, if Bonnie is deemed to be incompetent, she should have a publicly approved legal representative to protect her. A more accurate assessment of mental competence or incompetence is achieved if the legal system relies on an interdisciplinary team which is directly aware of the resident's daily functioning.

As a case manager, I would consider it in Bonnie's best interests, as well as her husband's, to get the therapy and treatment they need as individuals and as a couple. What kinds of therapy or assistance would be most beneficial in a case such as this one would best be determined, once again, if an interdisciplinary team were involved in the deliberations and negotiations. It should be in this context of recovery and rehabilitation (determined by the nursing home following legally prescribed guidelines) that the husband be allowed to visit Bonnie in the future. The nursing home should have the right, even against Bonnie's and her husband's wishes, to forbid his coming if there is no good-will effort to change the pattern of abuse.

The staffing problems of this nursing home chain are critical before any enduring solutions can be achieved in a situation like Bonnie's. The work of the aides in many nursing homes is greatly undervalued and underpaid, and the resulting turnover, lack of work satisfaction, and poor training result in predictable patterns of patient neglect and poor problem-solving on their behalf.

One of the best preventative measures we could take against the neglect of disabled older adults, whether they are living in a nursing home or in the community, would be to put aides on a solid employment basis with good pay and benefits. This is more an ethical issue for the nursing home administrator and the state ombudsman than for the overextended aide. Also, government overseers need to focus more on the quality of life and relational issues in nursing homes.

CONCLUSION

The case manager has a difficult role. While it clearly includes definite core functions such as assessment and service plan development and implementation, the above discussion of three cases show that these functions do not come easily in the context of individual people's lives. The role of the case manager will be most effective when it becomes a coordinative role, skillfully drawing in the expertise of medical professionals, mental health counselors, lawyers, nutritionists, social service agencies, and others with whom the client is involved or will be involved.

The goals are maintaining client independence and autonomy, protecting client rights, and providing access to needed services, while respecting and abiding by individual differences and values. The goals are achieved by good listening and good understanding and a knowledge of the resources available. The limitations faced by a case manager are as varied as the human beings served and the social system that tries to be of service. Where to draw the line between the lack of a quality of life and an abusive situation is very complex in any society, and we must rely to a greater or lesser extent upon the protocols of our profession. Nevertheless, there will always be a place in case management to interpret and implement, to translate theory into practice; and in so doing we have the opportunity to interact with other persons and impact their lives in a unique way.

REFERENCES

Pillemer, K. & Finkelhor, D. (1988). The prevalence of elder abuse: A random sample survery. *Gerontologist, 28* (1), 51-57.

Shield, R.R. (1988). *Uneasy endings, Daily life in an American nursing home.* Ithaca, N.Y: Cornell University Press.

Tomita, S. (1990). The denial of elder mistreatment by victims and abusers: The application of neutralization Theory. *Violence and Victims, 5*(3), 171-184.

Chapter Eight

A Legal Perspective

Candace J. Heisler, JD
Mary Joy Quinn, RN, MA

SUMMARY. Even experienced practitioners in the field of elder abuse and neglect have had limited experience with the American civil system. This chapter explains the overall goals of the criminal and civil systems, the rules governing them, their processes, and the ways in which they can prevent and combat elder mistreatment in an ethical context. Practical application of the goals, rules, and process of each system is described in the sections on the three cases. This chapter represents one of the first attempts to view the criminal and civil legal systems conjointly and to advocate for the cooperation of the two systems in individual cases of elder mistreatment. It also describes the role of the two legal systems in relation to practitioners in the health and social services context and advocates for a multidisciplinary approach to elder mistreatment. *[Article copies available from The Haworth Document Delivery Service: 1-800-342-9678.]*

INTRODUCTION

Most practitioners working with older adults have had limited experience with the American legal system. As a result, it is underutilized in the

---

Candace J. Heisler is Assistant District Attorney for the City and County of San Francisco, 880 Bryant, Room 322, San Francisco, CA 94103. Mary Joy Quinn is Director of Probate Court Services, San Francisco Superior Court, 633 Folsom Street, Room 303, San Francisco, CA 94107.

[Haworth co-indexing entry note]: "A Legal Perspective." Heisler, Candace J., and Mary Joy Quinn. Co-published simultaneously in *Journal of Elder Abuse & Neglect* (The Haworth Press, Inc.) Vol. 7, No. 2/3, 1995, pp. 131-156; and: *Elder Mistreatment: Ethical Issues, Dilemmas, and Decisions* (ed: Tanya Fusco Johnson) The Haworth Press, Inc., 1995, pp. 131-156. [Single or multiple copies of this article are available from The Haworth Document Delivery Service: 1-800-342-9678, 9:00 a.m. - 5:00 p.m. (EST)].

prevention and resolution of elder mistreatment. For those reasons, this chapter provides basic information about our legal system and its two primary components: the civil justice system and the criminal justice system. The larger part, the civil justice system, deals with such matters as divorce and child custody, personal injury and contract disputes, and guardianships. In civil law, the losing party generally must pay money damages to the other side. In the criminal justice system, if the person charged with a crime is found guilty, he or she loses personal freedom, frequently must serve time in custody, and may lose civil rights. The sentence may result in probation conditioned on the defendant complying with various requirements such as participation and completion of a rehabilitation program on substance abuse or anger management or both and/ or psychiatric treatment.

Goals of the Legal System

The civil and criminal legal systems approach the prevention and resolution of elder mistreatment matters with common *goals* and certain *rules* that govern their handling. The *goals* of the legal response to elder mistreatment are to: (1) Stop the unlawful, improper, or exploitive conduct that is being inflicted on the victim; (2) Protect the victim and society from the perpetrator and further inappropriate or illegal acts; (3) Hold the perpetrator accountable for the.conduct and communicate a message that the behavior is unacceptable and exceeds societal norms; (4) Rehabilitate the offender, if possible; (5) Make the victim whole by ordering restitution and/or the return of property as well as the payment of expenses incurred by the victim as a result of the perpetrator's conduct.[1] The two parts of the legal systems also seek to act in ways that create the least disruption or invasion into the victim's life, that take into account that person's individual situation, competency, wishes, and desires, and that keep the situation from becoming worse.

Rules of the Legal System

While the *goals* of intervention describe what is sought, the *rules* dictate what must be done to achieve the goals. These rules are broadly described as standards for prevailing in the case or the level of burden on the accuser for proving the case to the satisfaction of the judge or jury: due process, i.e., the extent to which the law requires that perpetrators and victims are informed of their rights and how to exercise those rights, for example, the right to be represented by an attorney. Other rules include legal protections and notice, i.e., the extent to which the law requires that people involved in a case are officially notified of the various legal steps in the case. Additional rules include legal duties imposed on various individuals to report elder mistreatment to the proper authorities. The last broad rule governs the role and legal authority of the people involved in the case, especially the victim. While these broad categories generally apply to both civil and criminal law, their precise applications differ greatly between the two systems. For instance, in both civil and criminal courts the party making the accusations must provide evidence that proves in the mind of the judge or jury that they are correct to some degree of certainty. In civil courts, which deal with lawsuits and guardianships, depending on the type of case, there are two distinct levels of proof. The first is *preponderance of the evidence* which is the lowest level of proof, or slightly over 50% certainty that the accusations are true. The next higher level of proof is termed *clear and convincing evidence* and means that the accuser has the burden of providing evidence that the accusations are true so that a judge or jury is *convinced* that the evidence proves that the accusations are correct. Finally, because the potential consequence to the criminal perpetrator is the loss of personal freedom and civil rights, the criminal law imposes the highest level of proof on the state or government bringing the action–guilt *beyond a reasonable doubt*.

Process in the Legal System

In both the criminal and civil courts, the party who brings the action must prove each element of their case. On the civil side, elaborate procedures permit the parties to collect information about the issues and from each other. Typically, those formal procedures are used when lawsuits are filed. The exception is in guardianship matters where courts are usually provided with relatively little evidence on which to base their decisions. However, that situation is changing as various states amend their guardianship laws to provide that court employees and/or court appointed attorneys furnish neutral information to the court. On the criminal side, the prosecuting attorney must generally provide the defense attorney with all evidence that may tend to lessen the guilt or mitigate the sentence of the perpetrator ("exculpatory evidence") as well as the evidence that the prosecuting attorney will use to establish guilt ("inculpatory evidence"). In criminal cases, the perpetrator cannot be forced to testify and may remain silent throughout the case. No comment or negative inference can be drawn from the failure to testify. Most criminal defendants are entitled to counsel. If the suspect is indigent, the court must appoint counsel for him or her. On the civil side, many states now provide for free counsel in guardianship matters if a proposed ward cannot afford to pay for an attorney. However, in other kinds of civil cases such as lawsuits, there is no right to free counsel.

Both civil and criminal law require that the accused is given notice of what they are alleged to have done. Giving notice is required as a matter of fairness, to determine the facts and to make decisions about accountability.

The legal system is adversarial in nature. In the clash between the parties in a search for the truth, the legal system mandates roles for the participants. On the civil side, the person who files the lawsuit is termed the plaintiff and that person must meet one of the two legal burdens previously described in order to prevail. Because the lawsuit generally concerns the interaction of two or more parties, the parties themselves retain control over the case. The plaintiff and the defendant can settle the case, come to agreements, and otherwise direct what takes place. Where guardianships are concerned, the person filing the case is typically termed the petitioner because traditionally, guardianship hearings have not been adversarial. Rather, there has been an assumption that the petitioner is acting on behalf of an older adult who needs help. Traditional views are giving way to many system reforms as it is realized that sometimes persons seeking guardianship are acting in their own interests rather than to assist an elder in need. The result is that guardianship proceedings are becoming more complex and, at times, adversarial in nature. Legal rights of proposed wards are protected to a greater degree than occurred previously.

The adversarial nature of the legal system is markedly different in criminal proceedings. There are two parties, the prosecution side that represents the state or the government or "the people" and the defense side that represents the perpetrator, called a defendant. The prosecution has no specific client. Rather, it represents society at large and is the chief law enforcement officer in the jurisdiction.[2] The crime victim is a witness, although elder mistreatment victims, like other victims, are not always required to testify. Decisions concerning charging and final disposition of the criminal case are made by the prosecutor acting as a representative of the state and exercising his or her legal discretion to decide how to act. The criminal defendant or perpetrator is most often an individual who is represented by an attorney totally committed to representing the best interest of the client. The defense attorney is required to "maintain inviolate the confidence at every peril to himself to preserve the secrets of his client."[3]

Inherent in these goals and rules of the civil and criminal legal systems are both legal and ethical issues. Legal issues are those that are defined by law. Ethical issues are of a higher standard than the law and can be loosely defined as selecting the right thing to do among several alternatives. For instance, historically, segregation was legal in many states but it was not ethical. Ethical decision-making involves balancing goals with facts, balancing the needs and desires of the victim with the defendant's interests and seeking the achievement of justice for all parties. The law establishes the threshold for when and how actions may be taken. For instance, certain standards must be met before a guardianship petition or lawsuit can be filed in the civil courts. On the criminal side, this means no matter how heinous or egregious the facts may be or how evil the perceived perpetrator may appear, a case may not be prosecuted unless there is evidence sufficient to prove every element of the case beyond a reasonable doubt.

In deciding whether, who, and what to charge, clear professional ethical protocols guide prosecutors. The charging process is exclusively within the province of the prosecution and consists of two separate evaluations. First, does sufficient evidence exist to support a charge?[4] Second, if so, is it in the interests of justice to file the case?[5]

While all attorneys are expected to act with honor, propriety, and dignity, prosecutors (and indeed all other officers of the court) must also promote confidence in the law and the legal system and avoid impropriety and the appearance of impropriety. Prosecutors must seek justice, not just convictions. This duty exists because: (1) the prosecutor represents the government and therefore should use restraint in the discretionary exercise of governmental powers, such as in the selection of cases to prosecute; (2) during trial the prosecutor is not only an advocate but may also make decisions normally made by an individual client, and those affecting the public interest must be fair to all; and (3) in the American system of criminal justice, the accused is to be given the benefit of all reasonable doubts. [6]

ETHICAL ISSUES

The ethical issues most apparent in legal proceedings with elder mistreatment are: (1) promotion of autonomy and (2) least restrictive alternative. Ethical dilemmas arise when evaluating these issues in light of an older adult's mental competency.

Autonomy

American legal and ethical values place a high priority on autonomy. The issue is self-governance: "being one's own person, without constraint either by another's action or by psychological or physical limitations." [7]

The high value placed on autonomy is reflected in the Constitution and the professional ethical protocols of the medical, legal, and nursing professions.[8] Autonomy may be an idealized notion given the very real interdependence most elders have within their families and their communities and given the reality of high levels of impairment in old age. [9]

The issue of autonomy is always present whether the older adult is in the civil or the criminal justice system. In the criminal justice system, the issue of autonomy comes into play when the elder is informed and consulted about the various options available to keep him or her safe and when the sentencing of the offender is under consideration. It is not a victim's responsibility to determine if criminal charges will be brought against an offender and in many jurisdictions, victims are not asked to "press charges." The prosecuting attorney, as the state's representative, makes that decision in order to communicate the message that the conduct is criminal, not simply a "private matter," and to ensure that the victim is protected, rather than manipulated, exploited, or threatened.

In guardianship matters, autonomy is the main issue when an adult is thought to be incapable of managing his or her affairs, whether due to abuse or neglect by self or others. In guardianship, decision-making is placed in the hands of surrogates. With changes in state laws and the dissemination of current gerontological thought, courts now carefully consider autonomy and the wishes of the elder as expressed in the past, the present, and for the future. Forward looking courts seriously consider these expressions in their deliberations, regardless of the mental status of the older adult.

Ethical practice requires that practitioners are careful not to err on the side of failing to take action to protect an elder. Blind adherence to the concept of autonomy can lead to resolutions that fail to ask even the most basic questions and can result in the abandonment or death of a client who declines the first offer of help or who has an unpleasant personality or is "difficult."

Least Restrictive Alternative

The concept of the least restrictive alternative, a legal doctrine first articulated in the field of mental health, has gained wide acceptance among courts and service professionals. It creates an ethical duty for practitioners to fashion individualized solutions that are least intrusive upon their client's personal freedom. The concept applies to the personal and the environmental care of the elder and the handling of material resources. It recognizes that elders may have capacities in some areas and lack capacity in others. Ideally, the more restrictive the option, the greater the due process protections and the opportunities for the individual to object and state preferences.[10] The doctrine is primarily civil in nature, though on occasion it is applied in criminal matters, particularly in the placement of persons found to be criminally insane.[11]

In civil law, legal options begin with the client handling their own affairs and then move up the ladder to more restrictive options in the following manner: client signs name to checks but someone else fills out the checks, direct deposit to bank accounts, representative payee arrangements for certain checks, joint tenancy on bank accounts and/or real property, trusts, the various powers of attorney, protective orders (for placement or medical treatment), guardianship of estate, and, lastly, involuntary placement in a locked mental health facility. [12]

Legal alternatives to guardianship are used more frequently, especially since 1987 when the Associated Press conducted a nation-wide investigation into the guardianship system and found it woefully lacking in protections for frail elders. In most cases, a neutral person never spoke to elders or advised them of their legal rights despite the fact that a guardianship often deprives them of many rights such as the rights to vote, to make a will, to select a physician, or to control finances. Following that investigation, most states amended their guardianship laws.[13] Also as a result of the investigation, practitioners began relying on less restrictive legal options, sometimes without fully considering their benefits and burdens. For instance, there has been heavy reliance on powers of attorney with little understanding that there is no bonding, no notice to other relatives, no monitoring by a third party, and no way to regain misappropriated or mishandled assets short of a civil law suit. There has also been reliance on trusts that may be beneficial financially in some situations but make no provisions for personal care or abusive trustees. Additionally, individuals who become trustees or attorneys-in-fact seldom understand what is required and as a result, they assume responsibilities that they are not prepared to handle. Ethical practice requires that practitioners in the position of recommending legal options have basic knowledge of the benefits and burdens of each legal option and mandates that practitioners fully discuss all available options with the client.

The concept of least restrictive alternative is not easily transported to the criminal justice system. It is not a guiding principle for the criminal system though most courts decide sentences by balancing what a perpetrator did with available sentencing alternatives while attempting to protect the public, hold the offender accountable, and protect the victim and society at large. The concept of least restrictive alternative can be seen in criminal matters that are relatively minor and may have elements which are both civil and criminal in nature. Interventions may begin in the civil arena and move to the criminal side if the offender does not comply. For instance, the offender may first be warned and urged to make changes, then officially admonished, then cited, and eventually arrested. This process is sometimes used in situations involving public nuisances or neighborhood disputes. Finally, the least restrictive alternative approach is applied in the criminal justice context with those found criminally insane. Persons are placed in facilities according to the amount of treatment and control they need and the degree of protection the community requires.

Competency

The issue of competence is critical in the legal context. It determines whether a witness will be allowed to testify in a criminal case, if a guardianship will be imposed, and if a lawsuit is "winnable" based on the allegations and evidence a victim produces. And yet, the term is as poorly understood in legal circles as it is in mental health and clinical gerontological settings. Marin et al. note in their chapter, that there is growing recognition of the difference between *legal competence* and *clinical competence*. All adults are thought to be *legally competent* until a court of law rules otherwise. This means they can execute legal documents, make medical decisions, decide where to live, and in general, have full control of their lives. *Clinical competence* relies on observations of health and social services practitioners. It is task and time specific. It is interesting to note that recent guardianship reform laws have tended to incorporate concepts of clinical competence into the law.

Over the years, competency has been variously measured by old age, the quality of decision-making, medical or psychiatric diagnosis, risk of impoverishment through heedless spending, and physical endangerment.[14] In truth, the search for a commonly accepted definition of competence can be likened to the search for the Holy Grail. The journey is ongoing but as yet there is no mutually agreed upon conclusion. Each discipline functions with its own definition. For instance, the legal profession focuses on what an elder is *incapable* of doing while psychology looks at what the elder is *capable* of doing. [15]

Many state laws provide that a guardianship can be imposed on an individual who is "subject to undue influence" but that concept does not appear in the medical or psychiatric reports upon which criminal prosecutors and civil attorneys must rely. It does not appear to be a concept that is familiar to practitioners outside the legal field. Undue influence situations can occur even when an elder is alert, oriented, and capable of carrying out activities of daily living. Undue influence has been defined as the substitution of one person's will for the true desires of another. It can be accompanied by fraud, duress, threats, or the application of various types of pressure on susceptible persons including frail elders. [16]

Current trends conceptualize "competency" in ways other than simply evaluating the quality of the elder's decision-making. There is growing reliance on a constellation of factors to determine competency. There is more focus on what the older adult *actually does* to take care of the needs of daily living including the management of material assets. There is consideration of the elder's past decision-making. For example, was the elder in the habit of giving large sums of money to perfect strangers or is this new behavior? Medical and psychiatric diagnoses offer valuable information as to conditions that impinge on mental functioning and are able, with some measure of accuracy, to predict the course of a given condition. There is recognition that mental and physical functioning is subject to a variety of factors such as nutritional status, the presence of mental illness such as clinical depression, the time of day, isolation, grief states, substance or medication intake, relationship status, and self esteem. There is also recognition that "competence is" dependent on the types of personal and environmental support an older adult may be receiving. [17]

Given all these complexities, it is understandable that there is no single tool to determine competency. Nevertheless, practitioners working with frail older adults who are the victims of elder abuse and/or neglect must try to determine if their client is "competent," often in order to take decision-making away for what are usually good and benevolent reasons.[18] In general, practitioners look for two elements when assessing competency: (1) Does the individual have the capacity to assimilate the relevant facts? and (2) Can the person appreciate or rationally understand his or her own situation as it relates to the facts at hand? Relevant questions include: Can the person make and express choices regarding his or her life? Are the outcomes of these choices "reasonable?" Are the choices based on "rational" reasons? Does the person understand the personal implications of the choices made? [19]

The reality is that dealing with competency is less about creating the perfect definition and more about working with the characteristics of the individual older adult.[20] Practitioners must deal with the definitions that are set forth in their respective laws and disciplines while understanding the everyday realities of "competence." For instance, the criminal prosecutor or civil attorney may realize that the elder victim is less cognitively clear in the afternoon and therefore will attempt to have him or her testify in the morning. Those working within civil and criminal courts may attempt to ensure that judges who hear elder mistreatment cases are familiar with their special dynamics. In the absence of valid tools to accurately measure the various features of competence, we must rely on a variety of pieces of knowledge about elders and the conditions that affect them. Ethical practice demands no less.

THE THREE CASES

These case examples contain both civil and criminal issues. While the presenting facts and issues are often the same, cases have, for serendipitous reasons, ended up in either the civil or the criminal part of the legal system. In the future, it is likely that more cases of elder mistreatment will be simultaneously handled by both systems as civil and criminal agencies work more cooperatively.

Mary and Martha

Criminal Justice System Perspective

It must be recalled that the criminal justice system may not intervene unless criminal behavior, as defined by law, is occurring or has occurred. This is true no matter how extreme the conduct may be. In this matter, unless Mary's actions constitute one or more possible crimes, the criminal justice system's role is limited to assisting other agencies or cross reporting to Adult Protective Services if law enforcement discovers reportable conduct. In this sense, what is legally required and ethically appropriate coincide.

Assuming that a basis for criminal intervention is identified, who are the potential victims? There are at least two: Martha and society at large, especially those living near Mary's home who see and smell the garbage being distributed around the property and must endure any related animal and vermin infestations. It is unlikely that Mary is a victim unless further facts were disclosed that showed she was the victim of criminal acts by her sons (or others). Criminal justice system intervention may be appropriate to ensure that Martha and society are protected from further victimization. Indeed, if Mary is competent to make her own decisions, live independently, and provide caregiver services for Martha, unless there is legal intervention, the conduct will most certainly continue.

The facts suggest the possibility of two different types of criminal conduct: creation of a public nuisance and caregiver neglect. There may be caregiver neglect of Martha, a crime in many states. [21] The available information strongly suggests that Mary has assumed the role of caregiver and is unwilling to relinquish her position. Indeed, she became defensive and annoyed when it was suggested she was unable to adequately care for her sister. She also demonstrated short term memory loss and could not recall that she had fallen and incurred injuries. Her ability to care for herself, her surroundings, and her impaired sister are markedly affected by her poor judgment which could be due to medication mismanagement or to dementia. Martha is unclean, malnourished, probably improperly medicated, and is completely helpless and unable to even ask for help. While there is a serious issue of Mary's intent, that is, whether she actually intends to neglect her sister, until that issue is fully resolved, intervention by the criminal justice system is unlikely. If Mary is unable to provide care because of her own physical or mental infirmity, she cannot be guilty of criminal neglect as she lacks the requisite intent. At a minimum, law enforcement should work with Adult Protective Services or other service providers to ensure that Martha's needs are assessed and the need for guardianship or services short of guardianship are evaluated.

The other potential criminal conduct is creation of a public nuisance, that is, a situation which is injurious to the public health and welfare. The facts indicate that Mary is failing to maintain her property and is either herself distributing garbage around the property or is allowing her sons to do so. Because of the likelihood that garbage will attract animals, rodents, and vermin and will release unpleasant odors if sufficient amounts collect, it will certainly constitute a public nuisance. Nuisances are matters that are sometimes brought to the attention of the criminal justice system.

Given Mary's age and disabilities, a continuum of responses over time is likely beginning with the least intrusive measures. Initially, a police officer or a health department official would view the property, interview Mary and her neighbors, and attempt to determine who is responsible for the nuisance. An attempt would be made to have the responsible party abate and remediate the problem although as the property owner, Mary is ultimately responsible. Efforts would be made to encourage Mary to correct the problem. Were that to be unsuccessful, a letter advising Mary of the possible legal consequences would be sent, followed, if necessary by a stronger letter mentioning possible criminal consequences for failure to act. Law enforcement would attempt to work with Mary's friends, Adult Protective Services or other agencies, Mary's attorney, or other authorized representative, or her sons, to settle the problems. If there were still no resolution, the matter might then be referred to the prosecutor's office for action, often by way of alternative dispute resolution through an office hearing or mediation often conducted by an agency outside the criminal justice system.[22] Finally, if all else failed, a prosecution might be commenced.

Assuming that Mary is Martha's caregiver and is both legally responsible for Martha and capable of forming criminal intent, then she might face criminal charges if the evidence establishes the elements of criminal neglect beyond a reasonable doubt. Alternatively, or in addition, assuming that Mary is legally responsible for the creation of a criminal nuisance and unwilling to correct the situation short of the filing of a criminal charge, then Mary might be prosecuted if the evidence established every element of the offense beyond a reasonable doubt. The neglect matter would allege Martha as the victim. A key goal of prosecution would be to protect Martha and ensure that her needs are met. It would not be necessary (or indeed possible) for Martha to ask that charges be filed, that she testify, or that she cooperate with the prosecution. The fact that she is legally incompetent to testify would not preclude the case from being prosecuted at all or to a successful conclusion. [23]

Were the crime of nuisance charged, there would be no particular individual alleged as the victim because it is the public that is the victim. The crime would be prosecuted based on the available evidence: what police or health department officials saw; Mary's statements, if she choose to provide information, and if any had been identified; neighbors and townspeople who had seen the garbage or smelled the odors. In both cases, the prosecutor, required to act in the best interests of the entire community, would decide whether to charge Mary and, if so, with what crimes.

Other potential criminal charges warrant mention. Every state has a reporting statute. Most mandate reporting some forms of suspected elder mistreatment; others merely authorize it. There is usually civil and criminal immunity for good faith reporting, even if the report is erroneous. States with mandatory reporting provisions generally criminalize the failure of a mandated reporter to report. However, prosecution for failure to report is extraordinarily rare. Persons not mandated to report have no legal duty to do so. Such persons typically include private citizens, family, visitors, and friends, and public employees who are not in mandated professions. While Meals-on-Wheels had been delivering food to the sisters, there is no indication that they saw or made contact with Martha or could see the garbage around the property. Further, in many states, they are not mandated reporters. It is hoped that Meals-on-Wheels staff members are trained to recognize elder mistreatment and encouraged to report it for appropriate follow-up even when not mandated by law. Ethical community intervention in these cases requires that those who routinely interact with older adults become "gatekeepers," i.e., persons who look out for and report suspicious observations.

Once Adult Protective Services (APS) learned of this case, they should have promptly cross reported to law enforcement where required by local reporting laws. This case and others like it are simply too complex for APS to attempt to resolve alone. The opportunity to work with law enforcement using their investigative and enforcement tools to reinforce APS' service delivery, prevention, and protection services are the means most likely to assure a successful resolution of this matter. In addition to the interventions already described, this matter, given the relationship between Mary and Martha, the uncertain role of the sons, the obvious needs of Martha, the potential and as yet undefined needs of Mary, the unwillingness of Mary and Martha to accept services, and the undefined role of friends and church members, is appropriate for consideration by a community multidisciplinary team. All public and private groups, including law enforcement, should be part of the discussion and ethical decision-making process.

The legal responsibilities of the sons also require discussion. Generally, adult children are not required to provide care or services for their aging relatives, unless there is a specific legal relationship such as trustee, guardian, or other fiduciary arrangement or unless the children are providing caregiver services for the parent or other family member. [24] In this case, the facts suggest that the sons do not adequately provide for their mother and aunt. There is no legal role; the sons only visit monthly and apparently provide no financial support. Their insight into Mary's and Martha's needs are poor. They are neither willing nor apparently able to be more involved, and their plans are ill-formed. It is very doubtful if they will be active and capable participants in providing for Mary's and Martha's needs. This however, is not a criminal matter. It does, however, raise serious civil law questions.

Civil Justice System Perspective

Because both sisters are moderately to severely impaired, they meet the criteria for guardianship in most states. However, their ties to their church suggest that there may be a possibility of a less restrictive alternative. There may be a particular ministry to the aged or homebound in the church or a reliable church member who would be willing to take informal or formal responsibility (power of attorney) for the sisters if they would cooperate. There may even be someone who would serve as guardian of person and estate. Certainly action needs to be taken to tend to the bills and ensure that there is ongoing health assistance and at some point in the near future, assistance with housekeeping and cleaning around the property. Mary will need to be helped to see that her sister must be bathed and that their environment needs attention. She may respond to "plain talk" about the seriousness of her situation if it comes from people she knows and is delivered in a tactful, persistent fashion. These same familiar people may have more success in getting services to the sisters than a professional would.

The least desirable solution to the sisters' problems appears to be the appointment of Mary's sons as guardians. Most state laws require judges to give preference to the appointment of family members as guardians absent evidence that they are incapable of undertaking the responsibility. All too frequently, legal practices do not require that a court employee or representative conduct a neutral investigation which focuses on the capacity of the family member to provide appropriate care. Further, those who may be familiar with the situation may be reluctant to convey information to the court. The result is, the judge is never provided with critical information with which to make an informed ruling. To date, the sons have exhibited some concern but little appropriate or adequate action. Hopefully, if they petitioned to be appointed as guardians for their mother and aunt, the visiting nurse and other concerned parties would make certain that the judge was informed of the activities of the sons as well as their proposed solution to the elderly women's problems, that is, to move them from their long time home, something they fear. Appointment of the sons would appear to be appropriate only if there were strict court monitoring and court orders that would require the sons/guardians to keep the sisters in their familiar surroundings with needed assistance and to assure that their personal and financial affairs were handled correctly. Not all states provide this type of court monitoring, and, for that reason, the better guardian might be a neutral party who lives in the community and is both capable and willing to act as guardian, possibly a church member, a respected accountant or attorney, or if available, the Public Guardian. It is likely that Mary will object to having a guardian appointed. Although she is becoming progressively less competent, she is entitled to object, to be represented by an attorney, and to state her preference as to who will act as her guardian. Most likely, she will ask that her sons serve as guardian. However, if the court is furnished with reliable information about the actions of the sons and presented with an acceptable alternative candidate for guardian, the likelihood of the neutral party being appointed is enhanced. Much will also depend on the vigor with which the court appointed attorney presses Mary's wishes and desires including the desire to remain in her home.

Another civil system possibility, though rare, is that neighbors may file a lawsuit against the sisters, especially Mary, for creating a health hazard that affects them. Alternatively, there may be repeated referrals to law enforcement and/or health authorities.

John and Manny

Criminal Justice System Perspective

This case has clear criminal conduct. John has been the victim of numerous illegal acts: theft of possessions and money; financial exploitation; improper transfer of title to the house; assault and battery; and where provided for as a separate crime, elder abuse.[25] There are many forms of abuse present: financial, physical, and psychological. Indeed, the psychological and physical abuse appear to be the means to convince John to allow Manny to take control of his person and his assets. John has become Manny's prisoner.

Manny's actions are a reminder that elder abuse, especially by family members, often takes several forms. Criminal justice practitioners, like all other persons and groups assisting older adults, must remember to search for more than just one form of abuse and to recall that elder mistreatment includes a pattern of conduct, often using terror, isolation, and physical and emotional abuse to facilitate taking financial advantage of an older person. Manny's personal history is typical of many abusers: he is unemployed, financially dependent on John, has a history of mental illness, and lives with the person he is abusing. Likewise, John has traits and behaviors often found in victims: he is frail with physical disabilities resulting from his stroke; he is old, has assets, has decreasing cognitive functions, is isolated; and has concern for and acts to protect his son to his own detriment. John's personal ethics include parental responsibility for his child including a need to shield him. The result is that John protects and covers for Manny. [26]

The criminal legal issues that arise in this matter are: (1) How will law enforcement learn of this case? (2) Can and should the case be filed without John's consent? (3) Can the case be prosecuted without John's cooperation; and if John refuses to testify, should the case be filed nonetheless? (4) What is the criminal justice system's responsibility to protect John? and (5) What, if anything, should be done to address Manny's needs?

The conduct here is serious, even life threatening. Because John has been taken to several hospitals and because most states mandate that doctors, nurses, and other health care practitioners report physical elder abuse, many if not all of these instances should have been reported directly to law enforcement and then cross reported to APS, or vice versa. The failure to report may constitute a crime.[27] Even more seriously, the failure may well have resulted in the release of John to his abusive adult child, Manny. It could also have resulted in the appointment of the abusive adult child to serve as the trustee or legal guardian.

Once John's case is reported to law enforcement, a criminal investigation should commence. Ideally, the investigation will be a cooperative one involving APS and law enforcement. The criminal investigation should focus on identifying witnesses and evidence to establish whether Manny has committed criminal acts against John, attempting to separate John and Manny in order to keep John safe, and on providing services and protection for John to meet his present and future needs. The criminal justice system, APS, and other service providers who address John's needs must each attempt to protect John from future physical abuse, threats, and financial exploitation. Law enforcement may be able to secure an emergency protective order and freeze bank accounts and other financial assets. Once a criminal action is filed, the prosecutor can request, and the court can order, that Manny have no contact with John. The court can also find that Manny is a danger to the community and order that he be held in custody on high bail. Should a court wish to release Manny from custody, it can release Manny on condition he enter a psychiatric facility or comply with other reasonable conditions. If Manny is convicted, the court may order him to enter a psychiatric facility, commit him to jail or prison, order him to have no contact with John while on probation, and require that he replace or restore the items that have been taken and return ownership of the house to John.

In investigating this case, criminal justice agencies will evaluate whether John's participation will be required. Because the conduct is clearly criminal in nature, a decision to file will be likely made by the prosecutor. While John's desires will be considered, the prosecutor's decision should not rest on John's shoulders. To put such a responsibility on John is to disregard the reality that society at large, in addition to John, is entitled to protection from Manny. It is also to place John at risk; if Manny believes that John is "in charge" of deciding whether he (Manny) will be charged with criminal acts and then how the case will proceed, Manny will manipulate, threaten, and even do harm to John to encourage him to "drop charges." The criminal justice system will still consider John's wishes. He will be consulted and empowered by involving him in determining whether a criminal order of protection will be sought, identifying what restrictions are appropriate if Manny is released prior to trial, and deciding what conditions should be requested if Manny is placed on probation. John will be further empowered by being listened to, consulted, and having his experience as a crime victim validated. John will be consulted about his wishes by the prosecutor and the probation department prior to sentencing, but ultimately the court will decide the appropriate sentence based not only on John's desires but a review of the facts and Manny's criminal, mental health, and employment histories, as well as the threat Manny poses to John and the community at large. And finally, in a number of states, John may address the court at the time of Manny's sentencing in order to state his desires.

The prosecution will proceed with the matter if the available evidence supports the charge(s) beyond a reasonable doubt. John's capacity to give evidence will be evaluated. He is legally competent to give testimony if he is able to distinguish truth from falsity, understand his duty to testify truthfully, and is able to perceive, recollect, and communicate his information.[28] Where capacity to testify is in issue, a prosecutor will generally request that a mental health assessment be completed prior to deciding whether to call John as a witness. Even if John is incompetent to testify, the prosecution may proceed with the case if other sufficient and compelling evidence exists. In this case, it is critical that the case be filed even if John is incompetent to testify so the state can carry out its goal of protecting John, attempting to make him and his estate whole, protecting assets so they are available to support John in the future, releasing Manny's hold on John and his assets, separating Manny from John, holding Manny accountable for what he has done, and attempting to rehabilitate him by ordering treatment for both his mental illness and his abusive behavior. If the criminal justice system declines to act where serious criminal acts have occurred and where those acts can be proven, society does not fulfill its responsibility to protect its members from criminal harm.

There may be some feeling that if Manny is mentally ill, he should not be prosecuted. It is worth observing that many mental illnesses do not constitute legal insanity. Further, criminal conduct is excused when committed by one who is criminally insane. However, the criminal justice system still acts by committing a criminally insane person to a mental health authority for treatment and there is well-established linkage between the criminal justice system and the mental health system. Given the serious nature of these acts, the criminal justice system should act to protect John and society and to determine if Manny is legally responsible for his actions. Deferring prosecution because Manny *may be* mentally ill does nothing to protect society at large and John in particular.

Civil Justice System Perspective

As early as the first hospitalization, but certainly by the second, this matter should have been recognized as a complex situation requiring multiple, coordinated responses. Criminal, civil, and guardianship legal issues are intertwined. Public agencies, law enforcement, family members, friends, church members, and medical practitioners all have roles to play. Meeting John's needs would most effectively have been accomplished through a multidisciplinary meeting where the many concerned parties and agencies could agree on a plan and approach to present to John. Had this occurred, John might well have better understood his situation and possible options. Once John became mentally incompetent, the multidisciplinary response could still have guided the development of an effective and ethical service plan which gave him the greatest degree of autonomy appropriate to his level of functioning. It was clear that John was in a high risk situation; he was being urged to separate from his son. Instead, he was sent home to continue living with his son with no provisions for monitoring. It does not appear that his sister, who originally made the APS referral, was contacted at that juncture. She or another member of the family might have been available to serve as guardian. Granted, John was found to have the mental capacity to understand his situation, but there was no apparent understanding on the part of the professionals involved that Manny was exerting undue influence on his father. Many state laws provide that a guardianship can be ordered if there is undue influence. It appears that there was enough evidence to convince a judge that a guardianship was appropriate. John might have objected but a petition for guardianship could have been filed against his will and he could have been represented by an attorney. His attorney may have been able to negotiate the return of John's assets, an allowance for Manny, and provisions for household help. John may have welcomed this type of intervention; he may have been relieved that decision-making was being taken out of his hands. Manny most certainly would have objected to the guardianship petition. If the court had independent investigators to interview all the parties prior to the guardianship hearing, Manny would have had a chance to tell his story and most likely, would have revealed symptoms of his mental illness to the investigator. Other parties such as the sister and professionals involved in the case would have been contacted and a solid case built that would dictate the appointment of a neutral party as guardian. Even if there were no investigation prior to the hearing, it is likely that Manny would have come to the hearing and there revealed his mental illness and inability to care for his father.

A guardian could have arranged for in-home attendant care that may have stopped the abuse by providing a monitor in the home in the person of an attendant. At the very least, the attendant would lessen the isolation and would serve as a witness to Manny's mental illness and the dynamics between father and son and would be able to report back to authorities. Possibly a guardian could have arranged for day care that would have given respite to Manny and again, lessened tensions. That may have helped John feel more comfortable since he was uneasy with his son providing his care. A guardian, with court permission, could also have provided an allowance for Manny (if John had sufficient assets) thus fulfilling John's wish to provide for his son whom he knew was impaired and "under stress." This allowance could have been given to Manny whether or not he continued to live with his father.

A guardian could also bring a civil action to restore all of John's belongings to him including title to the house. In many states, there are legal provisions that permit guardians to take these actions.[29] If necessary, a guardian could file a lawsuit against Manny for the restoration of John's belongings although that would be costly and time consuming. Many states now have laws that provide for civil lawsuits against financial abusers permitting attorney fees and recovery of damages even after the older adult has died.[30] If John continues to be abused by Manny, despite the various provisions for John's care, and if Manny refuses to return John's belongings to him, it would be necessary to separate them. It might be necessary to obtain a civil protective order to protect John. Law enforcement might have to be involved to remove Manny from the house. Even then, however, supervised visitation would probably be appropriate in the future since this is a father-son situation and John strongly identifies with his perceived parental role.

The issue of who should serve as guardian bears discussion. Manny had indicated that he thought he should serve as guardian; this is not unusual. Abusers, family or not, but especially if they are family, usually assume they should serve as guardians. It is not clear if other family members were available to serve as guardian for John. The Public Guardian was appointed but not until John had suffered a great deal more and lost mental capacity. Where there is no Public Guardian or where the Public Guardian cannot take every case referred to the agency, professionals concerned about the surrogate management of elders' personal and financial affairs can create resources. Many states permit non profit organizations such as family service agencies to serve as guardians of person and/or estate. Agencies that are "for profit" may also be able to serve and there may be reputable practitioners who are interested in becoming private professional guardians. A caveat is needed where any private sector professional guardian is involved. Governmental agencies, such as Public Guardians, by their nature, usually have higher accountability systems than do private guardians, and thus are less prone to becoming abusive when they act as guardians. It is recommended, therefore, that careful thought be put into promoting private guardians, especially if there is no strong court monitoring available.

Bonnie

Bonnie's case presents a number of criminal and civil issues: (1) Are there reporting violations? (2) Is the skilled nursing facility properly discharging its duties to protect and care for Bonnie and its other patients, and if not, is it guilty of civil and/or criminal misconduct? (3) Can, and should, Bonnie's husband be prosecuted for abusing and drugging her? and (4) What role should and can Bonnie play?

In states where there are mandatory reporting statutes, abuse occurring in skilled nursing facilities often must be reported to the Long Term Care Ombudsman (LTCO). In this case, there are strong indications that physical abuse and drugging were ignored as were Bonnie's allegations that she had been the victim of theft. Not only was the LTCO never contacted, but because she was a difficult and manipulative patient, Bonnie was denied protection and actually suffered further. Such conduct may well subject the facility to civil and criminal liability including lawsuits to compensate for Bonnie's suffering, loss of the state license necessary to do business, and criminal code sanctions. So long as the facility accepts responsibility (and money) to care for Bonnie, they must protect her.

It is evident that the facility failed to properly discharge its duties to care for and to protect Bonnie and secondarily, other patients who might be victims of the husband's acts or Bonnie's clandestine use of drugs. Bonnie is a vulnerable adult with significant physical and mental disabilities. She is manipulative and abusive to staff and other patients. She regularly accuses others of theft, though it is worth noting that it is impossible to tell whether any of these allegations are true: none were ever investigated.

The facility failed to obtain appropriate social information at Bonnie's admission. They never inquired about her relations with her son or husband although it is clear she was capable of providing information. Even after they suspected Bonnie was obtaining drugs, they did nothing to monitor her access to drugs or consider the possibility of a restraining order against her husband who was supplying the drugs. When they learned of suspicious interactions with him, they failed to act. They failed to inquire into Bonnie's accusations of theft. Even after staff saw that

Bonnie was bruised and were told the husband had taken her money, they did nothing. On the day of the serious final incident, they failed to conduct a medical examination and only acted after Bonnie had problems breathing. Only then did they discover that she had sustained fractured ribs and had overdosed on valium.

As Bonnie's caregiver, the facility owed a legal duty of care to her. Their negligence and failure to act may constitute criminal neglect by a caregiver as well as improper or unfair business practices if the conduct is part of a pattern.[31] There may be also be federal Medicaid violations if Bonnie is a Medicaid funded patient.

In deciding whether to prosecute the facility, the prosecutor would have to decide if the record keeping and care provided met the community standard for appropriate care. It is often difficult for prosecutors to find well-informed and unbiased witnesses to establish these elements, and investigations of nursing facilities are costly, time-consuming, and extremely difficult. Few prosecutors and investigators are skilled in handling such matters which will need to extend beyond Bonnie's treatment to see if there is a pattern of mishandling patients. It is possible, however, that this information could be provided by those investigators who routinely investigate nursing homes and other facilities licensed by the state.

Adding to the difficulties is the issue of whether prosecution will improve the care provided to Bonnie and other patients or will cause the facility to close down leaving Bonnie and other patients without necessary care. Skilled facilities able to serve patients like Bonnie are few in number and relocating Bonnie, who is not a private pay patient, may not be easy.

What about the abuse by her husband? It is evident that there is a long history of domestic violence in the relationship and that Bonnie is completely unable to protect herself. The husband's abusive conduct is made more serious by his access to valium; it is likely he is supplying Bonnie with illegal drugs.[32] He lacks any insight into his own conduct and seems unable to be with Bonnie without abusing her. In this case, proving abusive conduct may not be difficult; there are medical findings as well as the observations of the roommate and the nurse. Whether or not Bonnie wants the charges filed, they should be in order to protect Bonnie, other patients, and staff members who attempt to protect Bonnie and to address her husband's behavior and attitudes that allow or cause the abuse. Because domestic abuse is a pattern of behavior that recurs and escalates without intervention, it will not stop just because the facility may now be more vigilant. [33]

Whether or not there has been prior "mutual battering," the criminal court should not close its door to Bonnie and thereby deny her protection now. Additionally, though it may be desirable to attempt to treat Bonnie's allegedly abusive prior conduct and her drug abuse problems, the criminal court cannot order her into treatment. She is not charged with any crime and is not subject to criminal court jurisdiction. There may be some thought given to charging Bonnie. It is extremely unlikely that sufficient underlying facts could be developed to allow for prosecution. Verbal abuse of other patients is not a crime; proving her alleged illegal use of drugs would be impossible in the absence of drug screens, seizures of illegal drugs, witnesses to her drug taking, and complete documentation of her actions by nursing home staff. And, finally, since no one documented or investigated her accusations of theft, it is impossible to show that these acts did not happen. Ordinarily, false accusations of crimes are only criminal if they are part of a scheme to extort money or if the accusations are made to law enforcement.

Consideration should be given to whether it is necessary, desirable, or possible to call Bonnie as a witness in the event a criminal case is brought against her husband or the facility. A mental health assessment should be conducted to see if Bonnie is legally competent to testify. Both prosecutions appear to be possible even without her participation if a complete investigation is conducted to gather evidence and identify other witnesses. Thought should be given as to whether both sets of prosecutions should be undertaken and in what order. Since the prosecution of Bonnie's husband might well require the calling of nursing facility staff who might also be the persons accused of caregiver negligence and neglect, it may be difficult to compel their testimony. Were these persons to assert their constitutional rights against self-incrimination, it might be legally impossible to call them in the husband's case at least without granting them immunity against prosecution. Were immunity given, they could not be prosecuted though their employer and other employees could still face criminal charges. The prosecutor might well have to weigh the importance of filing charges against him and perhaps against some or all of the nursing facility staff and/or administrators.

Civil lawsuits might also become a factor if Bonnie or her son explore the reality that she should have been protected in the nursing home. The issue of guardianship is less compelling in this case, primarily because Bonnie does not appear to have mental impairments. She is alert and able to make her own medical decisions although it is questionable if she would voluntarily enter a drug rehabilitation program. The level of her placement appears to be appropriate. There appears to be the very real possibility that proper supervision in a nursing home would provide for Bonnie's needs. There is no estate to be handled; Bonnie is a Medicaid patient and the facility receives her benefits directly. It would be important to ascertain if she is receiving her personal need allowance, however.

CONCLUSION

This chapter represents one of the first opportunities to evaluate ethical issues related to elder mistreatment from the perspective of the criminal and civil justice systems. The two systems, while sharing the common goals of protection, prevention, and accountability, address intervention from very different approaches. Effective and ethical legal responses require that the two systems work cooperatively, each using its tools, to continue the effort to reduce and combat the growing problem of elder mistreatment. The authors are hopeful that this chapter will encourage practitioners in each legal system to recognize that effective and ethical interventions are often joint and cooperative efforts by both systems.

NOTES

1. Modified from J. Carter, C. Heisler; N.K. Lemon, *Domestic Violence: The Crucial Role of the Judge in Criminal Court Cases*. Family Violence Prevention Fund, San Francisco, 1991; Heisler, C. "The Role of the Criminal Justice System in Elder Abuse Cases," *Journal of Elder Abuse & Neglect* 3(1), pp. 5-33 (1991).

2. National District Attorney's Association (NDAA), *National Prosecution Standards*. First Ed. 1977, Chicago, p. 23.

3. California Business and Professions Code Section 6068 (e).

4. A prosecutor should file a complaint only when the following exists:

(a) Based on a complete investigation and a thorough consideration of all pertinent data readily available, the prosecutor is satisfied that the evidence shows the accused is guilty of the crime to be charged; (b) there is legally sufficient, admissible evidence of a corpus delicti; (c) there is legally sufficient, admissible evidence of the accused's identity as the perpetrator of the crime charged; (d) the prosecutor has considered the probability of conviction by an objective fact-finder after hearing all the evidence available to the prosecution at the time of charging and after hearing the most plausible, reasonably foreseeable defense that could be raised under the evidence presented to the prosecutor.

California District Attorneys Association (CDAA), *Uniform Crime Charging Standards*, p. II-1, 1989; cited in CDAA, *Ethics and Responsibility for the California Prosecutor*. Third Ed. 1992, p. 84.

5. NDAA, Standard 9.3 "Considerations of Charging," p. 131, provides:

"The prosecutor is not obligated to file all possible charges which available evidence might support. The prosecutor may properly exercise his discretion to present only those charges which he considers to be consistent with the best interests of justice. Among the facts which the prosecutor may consider in making this decision are:

1. The nature of the offense;
2. The characteristics of the offender;
3. The age of the offense;
4. The interests of the victim;
5. Possible improper motives of a victim or witness;
6. A history of non-enforcement of statute;
7. Likelihood of prosecution by another criminal justice authority;
8. Aid to other prosecuting goals through non-prosecution;
9. Possible deterrent value of prosecution;
10. Undue hardship caused to the accused;
11. Excessive cost of prosecution in relation to the seriousness of the offense;
12. The probability of conviction;
13. Recommendations of the involved law enforcement agency; and
14. Any mitigating circumstances.

NDAA, Standards 9.2 Factors which may justify a decision not to file include:
A. Doubt as to the accused's guilt;
B. Undue hardship caused to the accused;
C. Excessive cost of prosecution in relation to the seriousness of the offense;
D. Possible deterrent value of prosecution;
E. Aid to other prosecution goals through non-prosecution;
F. The expressed wish of the victim not to prosecute;
G. The age of the case;
H. Insufficiency of admissible evidence to support a case;
I. Attitude and mental state of the defendant;
J. Possible improper motives of a victim or witness;
K. A history on non-enforcement of the statute at issue;
L. Likelihood of prosecution by another criminal justice authority;
M. The availability of suitable diversion programs;
N. Any mitigating circumstances; and
O. Any provisions for restitution.

NDAA Standard 8.2 Improper bases for charging include:
(a) The race, religion, nationality, sex, occupation, economic class, or political association or position of the victim, witnesses, or the accused;
(b) The mere fact of a request to charge by a police agency, private citizen, or public official;
(c) Public or journalistic pressure to charge;
(d) The facilitation of an investigation, including obtaining a statement from the accused; and
(e) To assist or impede, purposely or intentionally, the efforts of any public official, candidate, or prospective candidate for elective or appointed public office. See also, CDAA, *Uniform Crime Charging Standards,* II-1-II-2.

6. California Rules of Professional Conduct (Cal.RPC) 5-110, 5-200; ABA Model Code of Professional Responsibility Ethical Considerations (ABA EC)7-13. See also, ABA Model Code of Professional Responsibility Canon (ABA Canon) 5; Berger v. United States (1935) 295 U.S. 78, 19 L.Ed. 1314; United States v. Cianciulli (E.D. Pa. 1979) 482 F. Supp. 585; and ABA Standards for Criminal Justice Standard 3-1.1(a) 2d Ed. (1980).

7. Beauchamp, T.L., Childress, J.F., *Principles of Biomedical Ethics*, 2nd Edition. Oxford University Press, New York, 1983.

8. American Nurses Association, *American Nurses Association Code for Nurses*, 1950; Wood, E.F., "Statement of Recommended Judicial Practice," Adopted by the National Conference of the Judiciary on Guardianship Proceedings for the Elderly. Commission on Legal Problems of the Elderly, American Bar Association and the National Judicial College (1986); American Medical Association, *American Medical Association Principles of Medical Ethics*, 1980.

9. Caplan, A.L. "Let Wisdom Find A Way," *Generations* 10(2), 10-14 (1985); Moody, H.R. "Ethics and Aging," *Generations* 10(2), 5-9 (1985).

10. Quinn, M.J. "Elder Abuse and Neglect," *Generations*, 10(2), 22-25 (1985); Quinn, M.J., Tomita, S.K., *Elder Abuse and Neglect: Causes, Diagnosis, and Intervention Strategies*. Springer Publishing, New York (1986).

11. See, e.g., Calif. Penal Code Sections 1026 et. seq.

12. Quinn, M.J., Tomita, S.K. *Elder Abuse and Neglect: Causes, Diagnosis, and Intervention Strategies, supra.*

13. Keith, P.S., Wacker, R.R. "Guardianship Reform: Does Revised Legislation Make A Difference In Outcomes For Proposed Wards?" *Journal of Aging and Social Policy* 4(3/4), 139-155 (1992).

14. Quinn, M.J. "Everyday Competencies and Guardianship: Refinements and Realities," in Snyder, M.A., Kapp, M.B., and Schaie, K.W. (Eds.), *Impact of the Law on Older Adults Decision Making Capacity*. Springer Publishing Co., New York (In Press).

15. Willis, S.L., "Assessing Everyday Competence in the Cognitively Challenged Elderly," in *Impact of the Law on Older Adults Decision Making Capacity*, Ibid.

16. Grant, I.H., Quinn, M.J. "Guardianship and Abuse of Dependent Adults," in Zimny, G.H., Grossberg, G.T. (Eds.), *Guardianship of the Elderly: Medical and Judicial Aspects*. Springer Publishing, New York (in press).

17. Willis, S.L. *supra.*

18. Caplan, A.L., *supra.*

19. Kapp, M.B, *Geriatrics and the Law: Patient Rights and Professional Responsibilities*, 2nd Ed., Springer Publishing, New York (1992); Gutheil, T.G., Applebaum, P.S., *Clinical Handbook of Psychiatry and the Law*, 2nd Ed. Springer Publishing, New York (1991); Roth, L.H., Meisel, A., & Lidz, C., "Tests of Competency to Consent to Treatment," *American Journal of Psychiatry*, 134, 279-283 (1977).

20. Moody, H.R., "Ethics and Aging," *Generation*, 10(2), 5-9 (1985).

21. See, e.g., California Penal Code Section 368(a) and (b).

22. "Criminal Mediation: A Concept Whose Time Has Come," *California Lawyer*, State Bar Report, Dec., 1992, 68-70.

23. California Evidence Code Sections 700-701; Federal Rules of Evidence 601; Heisler, C.J. "The Role of the Criminal Justice System in Elder Abuse Cases," *Journal of Elder Abuse & Neglect*, 3(1), pp. 5-33 (1991).

24. California Civil Code Sections 206, 242; Penal Code Section 270c.

25. See, e.g., California Penal Code Section 368. Heisler, C.J., Tewksbury, J.E., "Fiduciary Abuse of the Elderly: A Prosecutor's Perspective," *Journal of Elder Abuse & Neglect* 3(4), pp. 23-40 (1991).

26. Wolf, R.S., Pillemer, K.A., *Helping Elderly Victims: The Reality of Elder Abuse*, Columbia University Press, New York (1989).

27. See, e.g., California Welfare and Institutions Code Sections 15630 et seq., 15634, 15634(d); Nebraska Statutes 28-372, 28-375, 29-384; Colorado Statutes 26-3.1-102, 12-36-135, 18-8-115; Virginia Statutes 63.1-55.3; South Dakota Statutes 22-46-6 (not mandatory, but immunity if do report).

28. California Evidence Code Sections 700-701; Federal Rules of Evidence 601; *State v. Lufkins* (S.D., 1986) 381 N.W. 2d 263; SDCL 19-14-1-2.

29. See, e.g., California Probate Code Sections 2462; 2900.

30. See, e.g., California Welfare and Institutions Code Sections 15657-15657.3.

31. *People v. Casa Blanca Convalescent Homes, Inc.* (1984). 159 Cal.App.3d 509; California Business and Professions Code Section 17200; California Penal Code Sections 368(a), (b).

32. Slade, M., Daniel, L., Heisler, C.J., "Application of Forensic Toxicology to the Problem of Domestic Violence," *Journal of Forensic Sciences*, 36(3), May, 1991.

33. Carter, J., Heisler, C.J., Lemon, N.K., *Domestic Violence: The Crucial Role of the Judge in Criminal Court Cases*, Supra, pp. 90-93, 1991.

Chapter Nine

A Religious Perspective

Rhonda Eugene Johnson, Jr., PhD, MDiv

SUMMARY. Even though religious persons cannot rely on a *generally* accepted protocol for ethical decision-making, every religious person has a particular tradition out of which he or she speaks when making ethical choices in a given situation. This chapter describes a Christian perspective on the three cases. *[Article copies available from The Haworth Document Delivery Service: 1-800-342-9678.]*

As far as I know, there is no such thing as a generally accepted protocol for ethical decision-making among "religious professionals" in the same sense that there are protocols for physicians and attorneys. To begin with, the whole idea of a "religious professional" in the same sense as a mental health professional is a highly debatable one. Secondly, the "religious perspective" on ethical issues might vary as much between Buddhists and Muslims as between Adult Protective Service workers and physicians. Even among people who count themselves "Christian," there will also be, of course, a wide range of views. Nevertheless, that is the perspective from and about which this chapter speaks, all the while acknowledging that, while it tries to be true both to the Bible and to Christian tradition, what it offers as a protocol for "Christian practitioners" is far from a majority opinion.

The Rev. Rhonda Eugene Johnson, Jr. is Senior Pastor, Church of the Holy Cross, United Church of Christ, 440 West Lanikaula Street, Hilo, HI 96720.

[Haworth co-indexing entry note]: "A Religious Perspective." Johnson, Rhonda Eugene, Jr. Co-published simultaneously in *Journal of Elder Abuse & Neglect* (The Haworth Press, Inc.) Vol. 7, No. 2/3, 1995, pp. 157-167; and: *Elder Mistreatment: Ethical Issues, Dilemmas, and Decisions* (ed: Tanya Fusco Johnson) The Haworth Press, Inc., 1995, pp. 157-167. [Single or multiple copies of this article are available from The Haworth Document Delivery Service: 1-800-342-9678, 9:00 a.m. - 5:00 p.m. (EST)].

As the Christian sees it, God is always the initiator of my (the individual's) service. Christian ethics is an ethics of response. For the Hebrew Scriptures as well as the Christian Gospel, the primary proclamation is that God moves toward us before we move toward God. It is because of God's primary action in creation, liberation, and preservation that we are motivated to act, empowered to act, and know how to act.

All Christian action is, therefore, understood as a response to God's prior action. The "law," the explicit regulations contained in the Hebrew and Christian scriptures represent those principles for governing human relationships that have come out of hundreds of years of Jewish and Christian reflection on the question: "What does God require?" as an appropriate response to what God has done and is doing. But the law in this sense is not only those principles that are stated as such but those principles for human relating that can be derived from the main narratives of both the Hebrew and Christian Scriptures.

Ultimately, however, the question is "What does God require?" That is, Christians will follow Jesus in believing that because God is higher than God's law, there are times when the "spirit" of the law will take precedence over the letter. That is, a Christian must believe that, in the last analysis, it is God who reveals my neighbor to me. Any written protocol can serve this end; but it does not contain it.

Most of the time, perhaps, the means that God uses to do this will be through the law, but this is not always so. If one is to live with this kind of ethics, one has to have faith that God will reveal God's will to the community or the individual. This implicit gift of priority to subjectivity makes many people within, as well as without, the church extremely uncomfortable. In fact, it is most disturbing when it *does not* make believers uncomfortable, when they *do not* make their decisions to go beyond the law "in fear and trembling."

The other, especially the needy other, does have a claim on us. This is an inextricable part of what it means to understand the other as, like oneself, a child of God, and to understand one's self as a follower of Jesus Christ. We are called upon to give whatever it takes in situations where God shows us a needy neighbor.

THE THREE CASES

Mary and Martha

In the first narrative, we have a specific tie to the church community. This does not mean that Mary and Martha are more properly an object of its concern but that, therefore, there should be no way that the church can fail to see their needs.

"Who is my neighbor?" was a question put to Jesus Christ. It is also a question which the church is compelled to answer in the same way as Jesus gave an answer to the one who questioned him. The story was the well-known one wherein a despised (from the point of view of Jesus' listeners) Samaritan man stops to help a badly beaten man whose cries for help had previously been ignored by two respected religious practitioners of the day, a priest and a Levite. The point of the story is that the neighbor is any particular person God shows me as in need of my care.

Christian ethics will not only expect responsibility from the other parties involved but it will also expect the same or more from itself. Only when all the alternatives have been exhausted should it consider going beyond either religious or secular law. At the same time, Christian ethics feel free to challenge these laws when it understands itself to be led on. For example, it may have no legal right to intervene in Mary's case and, in fact, any intervention might possibly be rejected by the sons, the case manager, or Mary herself. But if the church concludes that she is being abused or neglected by her other caregivers or that she is abusing or neglecting herself or her sister, then it is obligated to do all it can to address the situation.

But the church can not do this from a perspective outside of the family dynamic, as a judge or presumably impartial judge, for example. It always acts as one engaged in the situation and does not ask someone else to do that which it is unwilling or unable to do if they refuse. For example, if the sons try to force the sisters to move to a high-rise apartment and the sisters continue to strongly reject this option, and the church supports them in their rejection, it should do so only to the extent that it can take on or see that someone else takes on the responsibilities for the care and protection of the sisters that *would have been* available if they had moved to the high rise.

This approach raises the whole issue of the "authority" of the religious person or group to act in a given case. From within its own perspective, the church is "authorized" to act, in fact it *must* act, any time God shows it a needy neighbor. However, it is not naive enough to expect that the other caregivers will necessarily accept this authority.

Christians are in the "business" of providing support and not judgment. But, just as the Samaritan as well as the priest and the Levite had to decide whether to stop and help the man or continue on with their presumably important and meaningful service, when there is more than one needy person involved, there will inevitably be a question as to whose needs/

rights take priority and whether or not a win/win situation can be worked out.

What are the goals for the sisters in this case: what would a win/win situation for both the sisters and Mary's sons look like? It would be a situation which would: (1) preserve Mary's health and self-respect, (2) preserve Martha's health and self-respect, and (3) allow the sons to have the security of knowing that their mother and aunt are being cared for.

What can the church do to try to achieve these goals? It can increase the frequency of its contacts with the sisters. "Permission" to do this should be easy for it is, in fact, something Mary values. While visiting, the members can check on whether or not there is garbage around the house and if there is, they can even clean it up. They can also monitor bill-paying and pill-taking to make sure that these concerns are met regularly and consistently. Further, such regular visitation will better equip them to observe changes in mental and physical health and work on responding to these with the others who are involved in their care.

But any church will have limits on the amount of time its members are able to devote to these tasks. Such limits are, of course, set by the number of volunteers and their available hours and also the demands of other needy people and projects. If the church finds itself unable to supply Mary's and Martha's needs, it can still advocate for them, provide a voice for them. Still, its sense of responsibility to all the parties involved should discourage it from acting/speaking for "their" point of view, if such advocacy might cause the sisters to be denied basic needs which others are able to supply or conditions that they consider intolerable.

For example, it might come to the point where Mary and Martha are, in fact, no longer able to provide for their own basic physical needs at home. The sons are willing to take responsibility for providing these basic physical needs by moving them to a high rise building. If the church agrees with Mary and Martha that this move would be destructive to their quality of life, it should only intervene to the degree that it is willing to supply what such a move would provide.

The assumption, here, is that such basic physical needs take precedence over quality of life needs to the extent that the second builds upon the first. If it appears that the sisters cannot look after themselves, then they challenge the church in the way the man set upon by robbers challenged the priest and Levite. These good religious people, one might legitimately assume, were on their way to important tasks. Since there are limits to what they can do, their choice is whether to exchange the task in which they were engaged for the task presented to them.

What Jesus *seems* to be saying, by implication, about their response, is that they were not showing love of *this* neighbor. But what he *definitely is* saying is that the Samaritan *did* show love for *this* neighbor. The priest and the Levite, as much as the Samaritan, have to rely on God's showing them who their neighbor is in a given situation. And they have to take the consequences, which for the priest and Levite has meant two millennia of being the "bad guys"–even though they might well have been going about the task of being neighbors to some others. The most faithful church, the most faithful Christian will always, necessarily, ignore some poor souls groaning in the ditch since, in the foreseeable future, there are going to be more needy persons than persons to care for them. Therefore, unless we are sustained by a faith that God will *show* us the ones to whom *we* should respond and *empower* that response, we will be plagued by guilt over what we *have not done* to the point where it inhibits what we might and should do.

The Christian assumes that we are acting as part of the "body" of Christ in the world–that we are acting as Christ's agent, continuing his work of healing and transformation. As a corollary, Christian ethics begins from the awareness that the individual Christian and the individual church are not alone in this process, that "before" it is our commitment it is God's commitment and that as extremely important as it is that we take responsibility for doing our part, it is *not* true that "the only hands that God has are our hands."

Thus, any church and any Christian will not presume to be the only actor in this drama. The work of Christ preceded and follows as well as *is present in* the work of any particular church or Christian. Thus, the question is not so much "What would Jesus do?" as "What is Jesus doing?" The judgment about what we are to do in this situation is based on understanding what he has done and on faith that the Holy Spirit is informing and empowering the actions of the faithful community to be a part of that work in a given situation.

Also, respect for Mary demands recognizing her limits as well as those of her sister and her caregivers. Mary lives in a particular body, which has its limits as all of our bodies have limits. If the church expects her to transcend the limits of that body, it might give up on her when its hopes for her "recovery" fail to materialize.

But the church, as a community that proclaims a God who loves us enough to submit to the limitations of our physical selves, should follow the example of its God in meeting her where she is, at any given point in time, even if that point recedes further and further from where she "was." It is perfectly understandable that we might be tempted to say that "the real Mary" (meaning Mary as we have "always known her") is no longer here. But since ours is a faith that celebrates One whose way to world-transformation was by giving up his prerogatives, it is particularly incumbent upon us to meet others where they are *now*.

In a particularly revered and often quoted passage from one of his New Testament letters, the Apostle Paul advises Christians to imitate their God in identifying with, in literally becoming, one of the needy and abused. The point is not that he accepted these abuses as unchangeable but that his way of having a transformational impact was through identification rather than executive over-ruling.

Thus, the primary act of Christian faithfulness is identification with the other person, especially the person in need. The task is to try to see the world through her or his eyes rather than interpret the world of the other through one's own eyes.

New Testament ethics will also see every person equally as a child of God and hence entitled to the freedom of self-determination, as long as her or his freedom does not infringe upon that of others. Since its primary duty is obedience to the will of God, New Testament ethics will understandably have a great concern about the possibility or danger of the church itself "playing God."

In Mary's case, this involves the church's resisting the temptation to identify the "real" Mary with the one who was more intact, as if the present Mary is somehow less important. An incarnational theology will affirm–and act upon–God's presence with and empathy for persons in whatever state they are. Getting to know the Mary who is now will involve spending more time simply listening to her talk. This listening will not be an attempt to humor her or to use such listening as a strategy, a springboard to something else, but as an end in itself. It will help Mary understand *who* she is, now, through putting herself in words in a supportive atmosphere.

However, trying to understand Mary from within her own perspective does not mean unreflectively capitulating to the demands she makes which may be destructive to herself and others. Mary's responsibility for her own fate is circumscribed by her dementia. Her caregivers must pick up the responsibility her condition has forced her to abandon, but such assumption of responsibility must always *be held in tension with* the attempt to understand Mary from within her own perspective.

From this perspective, for example, "I," Mary, see myself as a person under attack for things I don't feel really guilty of. There seems to me perfectly good explanations for why garbage is sometimes near the door, why the bills are sometimes unpaid. Why don't others see this in the same way? I have always been a good housekeeper and I still am or would be if other things and people didn't get in the way. As for my neglecting Martha, that is simply not true. I can care for her as I have cared for many others all my life.

My boys have the best of intentions, but they don't realize how lost we'd be in that high rise, away from all of our friends and in a situation unlike any we've ever know. We'd *just die!* It's *good* that they can't afford to send us away!

Unrealistic as we might consider such an interpretation to be, it is still *her* or as close to her as we can get, taking into account all of the "facts" that we can obtain. It is as much a distortion to fail to recognize that *all* of our interpretations are more or less subjectively distorted as it is to assume that, because they are, they are all equally far from the truth.

John and Manny

The application of biblical injunctions is much clearer in this case than in the former. Knowing what the *reader* of Case Two knows (which is, of course, more than any first person observer "on the scene" would know), Manny, for whatever reason, is clearly not "honoring" his father's humanity. Thus the first obligation of the church in this case would have been to advocate on John's behalf for the recognition of and protection of his freedom of self-determination, with John himself, first, then with his son, then, if there was no response, with his sister, and then with APS.

An identification with John's perspective might take into account his blaming himself for Manny's actions (he was not a good parent and so forth) or his guilt for failing in his parental obligations or even guilt for having been the sole inheritor from his wife. The church should respect John's right to make his own decisions but must, at the same time, recognize those factors that affect his decisions. Only thus can it have any degree of objectivity. However, in the conflict between what, presumably, is best for John and what he chooses for himself, the effort to identify with John's interest, as he saw it, would put his right to make his own decision above considerations of his personal safety.

Here, we can see one of the real advantages of a team approach. John's right to self determination is obviously going to be impinged upon by his ability or inability to think rationally. This does not mean that John should make judgments that we would agree with but that it should be determined that he is capable of rational thought. The church cannot make that decision but, at the same time, mental health professionals who can make such judgments need to be reminded that their own standards are not purely objective. For all of us, no matter how scientific we consider ourselves and our criteria to be, the demarcating line between "rational" and "a judgment I can understand and with which I can agree" is a fine line, indeed.

Manny also is a victim. He is a victim of his mental disability if nothing else. However, an identification with him and an effort to see things from his point of view would not mean a complementary refusal of an attempt to see things objectively any more than it would in the case of John. The church can, in good conscience, support John in his desire for self-determination and in his desire to be a good parent; but it cannot have the same support for Manny if it appears that he is abusing his father and consciously maneuvering to get rid of his father and to profit from it. The church need not condemn Manny–and it *should* not do this–in order to do all that it can to keep him from harming his father.

On the other hand, the church *can* make a judgment about *Manny's* interest, which is different from Manny's own. It can conclude that it is in Manny's ultimate long-range best interest to treat his father decently and humanely because the kind of abuse he is inflicting on his father is also doing terrible moral damage to his own humanity. Protecting John against Manny would have to take precedence over allowing John to (permit Manny to) destroy himself because it serves the long-term best interest of two people: the son as well as the father. Allowing *Manny* to destroy his father, knowing all the while his diminished psychological and/or moral condition, would be on the order of allowing a child in a room full of other people to play with a bomb, about whose destructiveness she/he knew nothing.

Since, in the beginning stages, John's capacity for handling his own affairs is not in doubt, helping him with the details of managing his life's needs may not be a principal concern. But with his second stroke, his church, which bears some appropriate guilt for not having responded sooner, should work with his sister to see that his needs are being met and should provide constant support and monitoring itself.

While separating John from Manny is critical, it has become increasingly clear that Manny, too, is a casualty of *his own* illness. He needs the church's advocacy and support as much as his father does. The church should not only refrain from demonizing him but, recognizing that the interests of the hospital and the public guardian will be focussed on the father, the church should try to see that Manny's interests are protected and that he receives the kind of care he needs. Manny, as well as his father, needs to be heard sympathetically by someone in the church. This is for his own best interest but it also should serve to yield a better understanding of his father's situation. Again, the joint imperatives of the church–to identify with the church and not to judge at the same time as trying to see and understand the total situation–would require it to see Manny as a person in need of care as much as his father.

For John's part, it is more important than ever that the church not give up on him when the public guardian takes on legal responsibility. The public guardian does not have the resources to try to provide stimulation and interest. By contrast, perhaps, the church could provide regular visitors recruited from its Men's Fellowship, with whom John might play cards, swap stories, and the like; or, if there is a senior day care center at this church or elsewhere, it can make it possible for him to attend. John's deterioration is not necessarily irreversible; but it might *become* so if his guardian and others responsible for him assume that it is or if, in fact, his deterioration is allowed because of the lack of stimulation and encouragement.

It is also important the someone from the church, a clergy person or some other trained person, help John talk and work through his "parental responsibility" issues, especially as these relate to his faith. The idea is not to talk him out of his own ideas but to give him a chance to air his views and, where appropriate, to help him see how he might have behaved more "responsibly," even within the criteria provided by his own system. Possibly he could be helped to understand his present situation in alternative ways that are, however, equally compatible with his faith.

Bonnie

The manner in which the church became involved in Bonnie's situation is not spelled out in the case narrative. Let us assume that her roommate has regular visitors from her church and she reported to them what she suspects to be going on in Bonnie's case. It seems to be a case of mutual abuse with the husband's past history of inflicting violence on his wife and Bonnie's past history of abusing herself. Since it is Bonnie who seems to be most liable to harm and who has the least flexibility to protect herself in this case, her needs are primary. The choice to identify, first, with her, however, does not clarify the situation for it is clear that there is a tacit exchange with her husband; he "buys" the right with the valium he brings her not to have her report his attacks on her.

On the other hand, the church has a number of assets but is fearful of any temptation to "play God" even when it is acting as the "body of Christ." It also has the privilege of being able to consider more "angles" than other practitioners who, of necessity, have to look at the situation from the perspectives imposed by their discipline or the parameters of their legal responsibility. Led by both this concern and this privilege, the church might try to take a second look at the *relationship* between Bonnie and her husband, in addition to the *individuals in* the relationship, and to look at it *from within* the relationship as well as from without. This perspective is something that the church has to offer to an interdisciplinary team whose members might not consider themselves as being "allowed" to look at the situation from a *lay* point of view.

To reduce the relationship between Bonnie and her husband to an exchange of one negative for another is to reduce it unconscionably. To describe their relationship as one where the husband is doubly abusive (in bringing her the drugs as well as in abusing her physically) is perhaps accurate but not exhaustive. Given the way Bonnie treats everyone else, is it not reasonable to assume that he *gets* as well as *gives*. Why does he keep coming back? Does he now have her where he wants her–in such a state of dependence that he can abuse her, and she has no recourse? Or is there something "good" in their relationship to go with all the bad?

Might there not be some way that the relationship issue can be addressed by the church? Perhaps the husband can be engaged in conversation by a church member skilled at this sort of thing who *just happens* to run into him in the facility cafeteria. This person's ear can become his and the church's point of entry into understanding and, possibly, helping to heal the dynamics of their relationship.

In this case, the roommate provides the eyes through which the church has seen the neighbor. Once seen, Bonnie has as much a claim on the church as if she were a member. This is the church's point of view, however, and not that of the nursing home or the husband, both of whom could construe the church as meddling.

This claim is true as long as the needy one is mentally competent, which Bonnie seems *not* to be, at least on occasion. Again, the church is not in the business of judging people for their faults but in helping them when they need help. Since it has no connection with Bonnie, however, it either must try to establish one, through developing contacts with her when her roommate is visited or using the roommate as an "excuse," i.e., being the representative or mouthpiece of the roommate in insisting that Bonnie's legal rights are being met.

Again, it is appropriate to take a graduated approach, a value strongly recommended to the early church in several places in the New Testament; Matthew 18:5-10 being one of the most notable of these. The first objective should be conversation with the husband, not accusing him but drawing him out as much as possible with regard to his feelings about the situation, trying to really get to know him as a person in his own right irrespective of Bonnie's needs. If this fails to have any impact on Bonnie's case, then overtures might be made to the son, again, investing enough time in the son to try to understand his own history, his own place in the family, not just leaping in with a judgment about what "should be done."

Next, the nursing home administration and finally APS should be approached. Once more, the nature of the church's involvement makes it ideally suited to participating in a team project.

Another disadvantage, because the church as an institution has no legal authority to intervene, is that there *are no* rigid protocols regarding procedure and time. The church is not likely to be carrying as heavy a "case load" as a given APS worker and therefore can, and should, take the time to approach, not just Bonnie, but the family of which she is a part. Having the confidence that this is God's project as well as its own, gives the church a sense of urgency but also hopeful patience. It will be willing to include as many perspectives both to get as close as possible to the truth of the situation and also to be as fair and respectful as possible to all who are concerned.

Compassion and justice are the two living principles underlying everything the church does. Compassion is the prompt toward identification and withholding of judgment. Justice is the absolutely necessary complement to this, maintaining an outside, more objective view. These principles are always in tension but they do not project conflicting goals. Instead, they reveal two sides of the same goal. In Bonnie's case they establish a "bottom line" for what the church seeks. Given Bonnie's inability to look after her own case, someone must see that she receives the protections granted her by the law.

Part of service to others is meeting their needs insofar as it is possible to do so. An equally important part of service is seeing that those needs are not being denied by others. No one, least of all Jesus, asks the church to be naive. If thirsty persons need water, the church is a poor steward if it keeps filling the glass all the while ignoring the fact that someone else keeps emptying it before the thirsty one can drink. "Be as innocent as doves and as wise as serpents" Jesus advises in the Gospel of Luke. If no one else is willing to take up this responsibility for Bonnie, the church, having had her put into its care, must do so.

In summary, the church and the Christian come to our caregiving "with fear and trembling," strongly motivated but also hesitant about overstepping our bounds. Our authorization will vary considerably from case to case; but even where such external authorization is lacking, the church may act in response to what it feels is a clear call from God to respond to a neighbor in need.

When it does respond, it will always keep in tension the necessity to see the situation from within the perspectives of everyone involved and the equal necessity to see it in totality, from as objective a perspective as possible. This commitment to subjectivity is one of the primary gifts of a "religious perspective" to an interdisciplinary team. Objectivity is a gift it receives in return.

Chapter Ten

Multidisciplinary Ethical Decision-Making: Uniting Differing Professional Perspectives

Martha Holstein, MA

SUMMARY. This chapter suggests a reconceptualization of autonomy as a way to think about developing options for a client suffering from mistreatment. It suggests ways for a multidisciplinary team to function despite differences in professional orientation and values. After describing the financial and other constraints that team members encounter in making recommendations for clients, the chapter closes with suggestions for immediate action despite these serious constraints. *[Article copies available from The Haworth Document Delivery Service: 1-800-342-9678.]*

The ethical problems that arise in situations of elder abuse and neglect appear, at times, to be almost irresolvable. First, social, financial, and other constraints limit the options available for clients. Second, clients and professionals bring a history of values, beliefs, and life experiences to the bracketed moment that creates the need for an intervention. Third, clients bring to the particular situation, a long history of addressing simple and complex ethical problems. The team enters a situation already filled with meaning for the clients. They have formed identities that shape the possibilities, both practically and emotionally, that are available to them.

Martha Holstein is a doctoral candidate in Medical Humanities, Institute for Medical Humanities, University of Texas Medical Branch, 1311 Ashbell Smith Building, Galveston, TX 77555-0132.

[Haworth co-indexing entry note]: "Multidisciplinary Ethical Decision-Making: Uniting Differing Professional Perspectives." Holstein, Martha. Co-published simultaneously in *Journal of Elder Abuse & Neglect* (The Haworth Press, Inc.) Vol. 7, No. 2/3, 1995, pp. 169-182; and: *Elder Mistreatment: Ethical Issues, Dilemmas, and Decisions* (ed: Tanya Fusco Johnson) The Haworth Press, Inc., 1995, pp. 169-182. [Single or multiple copies of this article are available from The Haworth Document Delivery Service: 1-800-342-9678, 9:00 a.m. - 5:00 p.m. (EST)].

169

The moral problems that team members face also have definitional complexities. For example, while the authors in this volume and, by extension, other professionals in similar roles agree that client autonomy, protecting the client from harm, and alleviating suffering must be fundamental ethical tasks, they differ in how they understand these goals. In addition to uncertainty about how to understand autonomy (see Agich, 1992; Collopy, 1988), there are other definitional complexities that make team reflection and decision-making difficult. What is harm and what is suffering? Neither harm nor suffering, for example, are necessarily physical. What then does it mean to protect a client from harm or to ameliorate suffering? Reconciling these differing frameworks and, at the same time, taking the client's definitions as pivotal often create serious tensions.

Unfortunately, one ethical theory cannot reduce complexity, facilitate resolution, or overcome differences in fundamental values. To do this work will require many theories and approaches, an inherent flexibility to find solutions to what are really problems in living that are exacerbated by age or poverty or family dysfunction or a number of other familiar problems. Thus, this concluding essay will focus on three themes. First, it will explore a way of "doing" ethics that resonates with Tanya Johnson's discussion of "communicative ethics" and takes into account the differing perspectives of team members. Second, building on Paula Mixson's essay, it will consider how external forces such as public policy and resource constraints can and do constrain desirable ethical actions. Our most significant ethical challenge may lie beyond the day-to-day activities that so consume us. In conclusion, the essay will explore options for action within constraints.

AUTONOMY AND ITS LIMITS: "DOING" ETHICS

In each of these papers, client autonomy is a recurrent and appropriate theme. Autonomy is one of the most powerful ideals in American culture; it supports rights-based claims and the ethical procedure of informed consent. It is also the foundation for such legal documents as *Durable Powers of Attorney for Health Care* and *Living Wills*. It tends to work the best in certain settings, like the acute care hospital where a competent patient must make a decision about a specific treatment. As traditionally understood, it works less well in long-term care. For these reasons, this section will look briefly at these traditional definitions (which have been well covered in other chapters) and propose another way to think about autonomy.

Autonomy has often become conflated with respecting persons. In this thinking, we respect persons by leaving them alone to pursue their own plans and projects. As a result, autonomy, literally defined as self-direction, has emphasized non-interference. This position assumes that individuals have the capacity and the resources to make such choices and that, in most situations, society has only a minimal stake in what individuals choose.

While this conception has been important for elders, (it has welcomed them into the moral community as decision-makers), it has important limits. One result is that bioethics has tended to focus on the "minimization of harm" over the "maximization of good" (Fox & Swazey, 1984, p. 664). To maximize good would require explicit attention, for example, to the preconditions that permit the exercise of choice. Further, an atomistic view of autonomy rarely reflects the way most people make actual choices in the real world. For example, most of us are embedded in families and communities of meaning; it is important to us that our choices are acceptable to these significant individuals and groups (Taylor, 1984). People want to live lives that they can respect or at least tolerate on moral reflection. What would this mean for Mary or Martha or John? Is there a way to permit John to be a parent and also safe?

Viewing autonomy, in Daniel Callahan's (1984) words, as a moral obsession rather than a moral good, can endanger other important ethical values, such as the common good, maintaining relationships, caring, and justice. For clients approaching the end of their lives, moral values, often in keeping with their past history, may be far more important than autonomy. Hypothetically, for example, in the case of John and Manny part of our ethical response may be an exploration of what values define John's identity and how he might have used these in the past to solve other problems with his son.

As George Agich (1993) notes, the traditional view of autonomy "supports an abstract view of persons as independent, self-sufficient centers of decision-making . . . and [omits] fundamental concern or sympathy for the other . . . " (p. 90). Instead, Agich develops a view of autonomy that takes seriously the social context of moral life and the concrete conditions that support or negate the possibilities for autonomy. In this view, actual as opposed to abstract autonomy is revealed in the interstices of human life, in our ability to live in ways that conform to our moral concerns and to the stories we tell about our lives. To act autonomously is "to strive and to experience the world in a precarious dialectic of habit and choice, necessity and reason" (Agich, 1993, p. 90). This new thinking in ethics and aging is consistent with and contributes to a broader critique of bioethics by feminists, casuists, moral psychologists, and others. This critique, now increasingly familiar, emphasizes particularity over generalizable rules, cases over theory, and our fundamental links to others throughout our lives. They, for example, remind us that generalized rules, while important starting places, often ignore the particularities that help each of us answer the question: "Who am I?" In this view, we would think about autonomy as self-direction in moments of choice but as the complex working out of a life, at whatever stage we have reached, that lets us be who we think we are. This does not mean ignoring the ravages of dementia or other forms of diminished competency. It does mean, however, that within that context we try to reinforce what remains of the person's identity.

Recent ethical thinking has also raised questions about the approaching bioethics primarily as an analytical and procedural enterprise. The goals in this approach have been to clarify conceptually the issues in any moral dispute and develop methods of resolution that do not impose a particular moral view on an unconsenting person. With this view, any moral dilemma could be resolved by ordering or reconciling the relevant moral principles and following the appropriate action-guide or rule (for a discussion of this background, see Cole & Holstein, forthcoming). In this approach, beneficence would be viewed against autonomy. Can a client ever be denied autonomy in order to enhance his or her well-being?

As attention turned to ethical problems and aging, the limits of this approach emerged. These limits were most sharply perceived in long-term care where decision-making is ongoing, incremental, and often involves a number of other people in addition to the patient. In such environments, small and large decisions are made on a daily basis; they rarely involve the life and death choices that ethical analysis has tended to address. Only occasionally are immediate decisions required.

Issues of older adult abuse and neglect emerge in just these kinds of settings. Moreover, the difficulties that arise are biographically and situationally complex. In such circumstances, ethical analysis demands the widest possible vision and the systematic exploration of possibilities that transcend the simple dichotomy between autonomy and beneficence. While both are useful as commonly agreed-upon guideposts to open discussion about morally troublesome situations (Churchill & Siman, 1986), they often cannot take us far enough. For example, a patient or client may make an autonomous choice to reject certain actions or treatments. These decisions may seriously trouble social workers, physicians, family members, or others. Yet, the moral responsibilities of the practitioner rarely end at the point when the client says "no." Honoring autonomy does not preclude probing for the values underlying a choice or helping to clarify the client's or patient's anxiety and awareness of what is at stake (Miles, 1988; Klever, 1989). Respect for autonomy, in its enriched form, does not mean that others detach themselves from an elder's decision-making process (Agich, 1993). Persuasion and continued conversation are also ethically valid choices.

In this way, informed consent, the practical expression of autonomy in practice settings, becomes part of an ongoing, open-ended conversation in which all the relevant participants reach a provisional consensus about care (Brody, 1989; Katz, 1984). It offers a "medium of progressive acknowledgment and adjustment among people in search of a common and habitable moral world" (Walker, 1993, p. 35). The main tasks in this endeavor are to keep the conversation going, to create moral space (Walker, 1993), and to mediate conversations taking place within that moral space. This approach is essentially dialogic, where different individuals (and the state or the institution) have a stake in the outcome. What the elder might want is very important but it is not the singular determining factor in resolving the problem.

Thus, a client may resist transfer to a nursing home, yet, her family may have reached the limits of their ability to provide care. All other options such as hiring home care workers for an adequate number of hours are closed because of resource constraints or, in some communities, the unavailability of workers. While the real culprit may be public policy, the client and the family pay the penalty. An enriched view of autonomy negotiates the particular social situation in which choices are inevitably made. The case manager (or other team member) is not faced with a problem of client autonomy; what the client wants the most is not available to him or her. Working with the family and the client, the responsible professional would carve out the space for each person to express what are the most important values they wish to preserve. The "best" solution, though not necessarily the "right" solution would respond to these values.

Working within long-term care, however, may offer positive features not available in an acute care setting where the need to make decisions is often immediate and discrete. Problem resolution in long-term care may involve a series of trial runs, the testing of possibilities. "Different resolutions will be more or less acceptable depending on how they sustain or alter the integrity of the parties, [and] the terms of their relationships. . . . (Walker, 1993, p. 35). It also permits what McCullough and Wilson (forthcoming) call "preventive ethics." By anticipating what may come next and what realistic options are possible, the client, her family, and the professional workers can plan prior to the crises. While this anticipatory planning may also be relevant in acute care settings, it is almost always so in long-term care. For these reasons, family conferences become important vehicles for communication and planning.

What then do these shifts in thinking about autonomy and the process of ethical decision-making mean for the APS worker, the physician, or the attorney involved in an elder abuse or neglect situation? In essence they suggest approaching ethics through dialogue, a conversational model in which the goal is not an "ideal" solution but one that each of the key parties can live with. These shifts remind us that moral problems are episodes in ongoing histories of "attempted mutual adjustments and understandings among people" (Walker, 1993, p. 35). The parties to the conversation ask questions, encourage discussion, facilitate storytelling, propose solutions, justify recommendations by putting forth their best "arguments." They obtain facts, define the problem, involve the clients, consider options and alternatives, understand long- and short-term consequences of choices, articulate the ethical values at stake, develop a plan, and communicate it to all key parties (Bayley, 1993). Participants take seriously the particular social situation in which the problem emerges and seek to understand the relationships of the involved parties, how they understand themselves and each other, and what circumscribes their choices. As Iris Murdoch (1970) put it, "visible acts of will emerge at intervals and in ways that are often unclear and often dependent on the condition of the system in between the moments of choice" (p. 54). If a family, such as John's and Manny's, has always functioned in a particular way, it would be unrealistic to expect a radical departure at the moment of choice. Instead, given what may be a history of "dysfunction," how can a team negotiate differences? This model does not require discarding traditional ethical principles; rather it means that they serve as starting rather than end points, important ideas to bear in mind rather than to apply in codelike fashion (Walker, 1993).

The chapters in this volume suggest an important ingredient for working through ethical problems–the involvement of a multidisciplinary team. While each team member might begin with the values or ethical norms of their discipline, that is only the beginning. To move beyond specific disciplinary approaches, it is important that team members educate each other about their perspectives. In this way, the risk of misunderstandings is reduced. To develop a unified plan, it is often useful for the team to have a "mediator." This person does not assume a value-neutral position but rather assures that different points of view are reflected in the conversation, that important questions are considered, and that varied approaches are explored. The task is to develop as many options as possible.

Thus, with the case of Mary and Martha, the "rights language" so familiar to us may limit the ability to find solutions. Instead, the team might try to elicit stories from each person involved, both together and separately. Although I will highlight a few directions for such questions, the team's own experience will be the best guide. They might consider asking Martha and, to the extent possible, Mary to tell their stories. The questions they might ask include: What was their life like prior to the current situation? How did the sisters relate in the past and how did they interact with Mary's sons? What is important to them? What values and cultural norms seemed to guide their lives? While the sisters should be part of any team meeting, talking to them individually might yield suggestions of what alternatives to the current situation might be acceptable. Respecting Mary's and Martha's perspectives requires a moral give-and-take, "a sometimes painful process of mutual deliberation, judgment, and criticism, and an occasional accounting for one another's views and deeds" (May, 1986, p. 48).

To handle immediate problems, the team might bring other key people or organizations into the discussion to address the problems of the trash or meals or bills or medications. Can the sons be asked to make a more modest but specific commitment? It seems clear that matters cannot be left exactly as they are in the present. This makes the team's task one of determining as many options as possible in accord with what the sisters want or, at a minimum, what they might be willing to accept.

The conversational or dialogic approach tries to resolve disagreements by exploring, for example, why a client or patient like John has made a certain decision, whether that person grasps the consequences or might re-consider it in the light of the concerns of others (see Moody, 1988 for a discussion of negotiated consent). The goal of this approach is to open possibilities for decisions that respond to the sisters, the sons, the community, and the laws and regulations that guide the team's work. The result will, in most cases, be a compromise and, if possible, a new set of goals that meet needs in a previously unanticipated way. The result will not reflect any single actor's "ideal" outcome. This resolution will rest on a clear assessment of what is at stake, how each party understands the situation, and a robust deliberation that leaves everyone reasonably comfortable. Though the decision might not have been each person's choice, they can nonetheless accept it because the deliberative process was so rich.

In cases of elder mistreatment, we often lack good alternatives (see next section) to offer clients. Let us, however, assume that we have engaged in the kind of dialogic process described above. What possibilities may have emerged that enlarge the scope of choices beyond autonomy and benefi- cence? In the case of Mary and Martha, for example, we cannot obligate the son (or nephew), the church, or the community to step in. We can, however, appeal to deeply held American values of responsibility for members of one's own community. An organized effort, with either rotat- ing or singular leadership, would mean that no one person would have to assume full caregiving responsibility. At the same time, we might find a task or tasks for Martha and Mary to do to reciprocate for the help she and her sister are receiving. The same goal might also work for John. Is there a way for him to be a responsible father to his son (or to another person) without the risks he now faces? Reciprocity is a key value that we often ignore when faced with an elder who is severely disabled. Not only auton- omy but full membership in the moral community entails responsibilities as well as rights at whatever level such responsibility can be displayed (Blythe, 1979; Jameton, 1988; May, 1986). If caregivers or practitioners deny Martha or even Mary the opportunity to be responsible, they are further isolating them from their family and community. Further, they are eroding their sense of self-worth (Agich, 1993) already damaged by chronic impairment. The team might also consider ways to reinforce what remains of Mary's self-identity. Even if she has Alzheimer's disease, re- cent clinical research suggests that behavioral interventions can reinforce self-esteem, a sense of being a morally choosing agent, and social confi- dence (Kitwood and Bredin, 1992). These efforts, as insistently ethical as treatment choices, might facilitate her willingness to accept help.

RESOURCE AND OTHER CONSTRAINTS

In a society dominated by efforts to reduce social and medical care spending, the "best" options for elders are rarely available. As Paula Mixson (this volume) points out, "what *should* be done and what *can* be done all too often are drastically different realities." They constrain both team development and the options the team can make available to clients. Constraints restrict the ability to do comprehensive assessments or other "fact" finding activities. They also reinforce the already existing orga- nizational barriers to anticipatory planning.

The Multidisciplinary Team

For a team to function well, the members must meet regularly and come to know and trust one another. Until that is done, it may be impossible to overcome problems caused by differing professional identities, hierarchy, status, and unequal power relationships. The dominance of one professional group or another can hinder open communication and frequently silence the voice of the patient or client. Yet, a communicative ethics requires free and open communication unhindered by power relationships. For this reason, the team can benefit from the presence of an outsider, perhaps an "ethicist" whose primary role is that of listener, observer, mediator. Moreover, the narrative approach to ethics requires time to hear stories unfold, to examine options informed by those stories, to test possibilities, and to re-visit the problem, more than once if necessary. Yet, even if resources permit the team to function, they rarely are sufficient to encourage the optimal conditions for successful operation. Working with clients in situations such as the case examples each author has considered takes time. Of all constraints, that may be one of the most difficult to overcome as budgets are cut and staff reduced.

Options for Clients

Resource constraints and the allocation of existing resources also limit the options that may be available to meet a client's needs. In many communities, the choices are narrowed to two: remain at home or enter a nursing home. Either choice might harm the patient. While state policy assumes that informal caregivers, generally women family members, will provide most care to disabled elders, little practical assistance may be available to them. The team, therefore, can provide the family member who assumes primary responsibility for caregiving with minimal help. Yet, some steady relief or even payment for the care may be interventions that mitigate the dangers of abuse. Adult day health, geriatric day hospitals, or Alzheimer's programs are still unavailable in many communities. Interventions like representative payees or limited guardianships may not be available.

While it is beyond the scope of this chapter to consider in detail the problems that patients in nursing homes experience, it should be noted that society's unwillingness to expend additional public dollars sharply reduces the ability to improve nursing homes. Nursing homes, emerging from the 19th century almshouse, have earned a reputation that frightens most older people. They are rarely entered as the result of a positive choice even when care and conditions are exceptional. For this reason, the ombudsman and other team members encounter specific problems with a patient like Bonnie. As Jo Ellen Walley points out, nursing home regulations often limit options. While designed to protect the patient, regulations can impede a patient's ability to live according to life-long habits.

Preventive Ethics

While many communities have well-functioning teams, this is not always the case. Frequently, social and medical services are compartmentalized. Moreover, the limited involvement of either system in home visits impedes the possibilities for "preventive ethics." Home visits by a team of medical, social work, and nursing professionals can uncover problems long before they become unmanageable. Yet, few geriatric or primary care teams conduct regular home visits. They are costly, use personnel that can be more efficiently used elsewhere, and sometimes do not have an immediate outcome. For those who make such visits, however, insights into the family, how they live their lives, and what is important to them can yield long-term benefits if difficulties arise (personal communication, Family Medicine Team, University of Texas Medical Branch, October, 1994). At a minimum, such visits reveal the many ways people choose to live their lives over time, perhaps progressively adapting to disabilities in ways that meet their needs but may seem alien to the outsider. Observations over time provide information about sudden changes in patterns or new and different dangers as individuals become more disabled.

There are problems even in communities where home visits are frequent. If, for example, the APS worker does not have regular contacts with practitioners who go into patients' homes, it becomes very difficult to anticipate the problems that might be festering. Neither the APS worker nor the legal system become involved in problems until they are at a crisis or near crisis stage. While many older people are not recipients of social services, most do have primary care physicians. These practitioners may be the most important link in a chain of anticipatory planning to avoid crises.

"Fact" Finding

Comprehensive assessment of patients, recommended in the chapter by Robert Marin and his colleagues and essential for the "fact" based information that teams need, is not available to many older people living far from academic medical centers or other large medical facilities. This lack means that the team often makes decisions based on inadequate information; yet, the first step in any ethical analysis is to be certain the "facts," including medical information, are known to the extent possible.

If time and financial constraints limit the team's ability to go into people's homes, investigate complaints, work closely with the court to achieve the "least restrictive" solution for the client, and conduct follow-up views and interviews, then the team may work with inadequate "facts."

EXTENDING THE DEFINITION OF THE "ETHICAL"

These social and other constraints to good decisions for abused and/or neglected clients are pervasive and familiar. They are also fundamentally ethical. Creating the conditions in which people can live more fully autonomous lives cannot be relegated to the ethical sidelines. Feminist and other scholars have pointed out that contemporary bioethics has tended to focus on adjustments within an acceptable system. A more robust view of ethics, however, involves institutional and social criticism as well as analysis of individual dilemmas (Noble, 1988; Sherwin, 1992; Weston, 1991). It is hard to know, given the constraints so commonly experienced, just how the professional is to engage in such larger scale criticism. Moreover, it is equally hard to know where to draw the line between what is relatively unalterable and that which is subject to change (Brock, 1989).

Philosophers have historically been concerned with questions of justice; more recently this concern has tended to focus on the allocation of resources in conditions of scarcity. Yet, these concerns have rarely been translated into action-oriented stances. For professionals working in situations of elder mistreatment, where the choices for prevention and protection are always less than optimal, the advocacy stance (to try to change what can be changed) may be morally compelling. Yet, here too, constraints appear. For example, while time may be the most visible, organizational location, APS services or court investigator units may effectively impede advocacy-oriented action. If located within the structure of state government, advocacy-oriented action is sharply limited.

WHAT TO DO WHILE AWAITING THE MILLENNIA

To "do" ethics in the ways set forth in the opening section of this essay depends first and foremost on well-informed and thoughtful professionals who take the client seriously as a partner in the deliberative process. While recognizing the seriousness of the constraints, also described above, that narrow choices, a start can be made by thinking of ethics differently. It is not necessarily a series of dichotomous choices between principles such as autonomy and beneficence but it is rather an engaged conversation among equal partners seeking to establish a habitable moral world. Ethical deliberation then becomes a process of negotiation among less than optimal choices. What is important is that the process of reflection is as sustained and open as constraints allow.

Some partial measures are possible. To the extent possible, professionals involved in questions of elder mistreatment might benefit from regular exchanges with one another. An example of such an exchange is the San Francisco Consortium for Elder Abuse Prevention. Team members might also join with professionals who work in related areas to establish a community-based ethics committee. Functioning like a hospital ethics committee, this kind of a structure would bring together people from different human service settings to learn from one another. In this way, team members can expand their experiences with ethical problems and potential solutions through education and the exchange of ideas about cases either retrospectively or prospectively. The goal in establishing a consortium or a community-based ethics committee is to bring in new conversation partners in an environment where limits of the possible can be tested and ideas floated in a non-emergency and non-judgmental atmosphere. If possible, advocacy-oriented coalitions can be formed to suggest changes within any given community. While ideally these alternative means to get together to discuss ethical problems, which meet only occasionally, are best paired with an established multidisciplinary team, they can stand alone. As such, they represent an immediate avenue for discussing ethical problems while serving as an example of communicative ethics in practice.

CONCLUSION

In modern society, we face a constant struggle between the ideal and the possible. Practitioners, however, rarely have the luxury of working in ideal circumstances. For those who work with abused and neglected older adults, the likelihood of achieving an ideal solution is slim. While the public may be appalled at newspaper descriptions of elder mistreatment, that dismay rarely translates into political action. Despite outrage, few understand the roots of problems that lead to elder abuse and neglect and, therefore, few assume responsibility for activities designed to address these deeper causes. Educational campaigns may be a starting point, but who is to conduct them and how will one find the time are questions for which answers are not easily forthcoming. It is unlikely that this picture will change in the immediate future.

Thus, those of us who are concerned with the mistreatment of older adults are left with a difficult assignment: to behave as ethically as we can with and toward frail and disabled clients and their families (for even those who abuse are often also victims). In closing, I recall the fictional voice of Alice Bell, a very old, very poor woman, who had suffered a devastating stroke (for a detailed study of this novella and its use in gerontology, see Holstein, 1994). Her son wanted her placed in a nursing home as did the social welfare authorities. They saw her only as a dependent burden; they could not see what she gave to the neighbors who helped her. But most of all they wanted her safe and clean. However, from Mrs. Bell's point of view, they did not really see her. "They" could not believe that this "slobbering, glugging thing that could not make its wants known was a human being. . . . If only they would let her be! But they wouldn't. They were too kind" (Barker, 1984, pp. 231, 235). For Mrs. Bell, as for the patients and clients described in the three cases, their disability, illness, and what flowed from them are particular instances in a life narrative. How any particular instance of mistreatment fits into that life story is critical. Part of our ethical task is to hear the voice of the older person, to situate it within his or her narrative, to hear from all those involved in the case, and out of that mix, to arrive at the best decision we can within whatever constraints we face.

REFERENCES

Agich, G. (1993). *Autonomy and long-term care.* New York: Oxford University Press.

Barker, P. (1984). *Union street.* New York: Ballantine Books.

Bayley, C. (1993). Commentary: How best shall we serve (Case Study). *Hastings Center Report, 23,* 30-31.

Blythe, R. (1979). *The view from winter: Reflections on old age.* New York: Harcourt Brace Jovanovich.

Brock, D. (1989). Biomedical ethics: Some lessons for social philosophy. *Journal of Social Philosophy, 20,* 108-115.

Brody, H. (1989). Applied ethics: Don't change the subject. In B. Hoffmaster, B. Freedman, & G. Fraser (Eds.), *Clinical ethics: Theory and practice.* Clifton, NJ: Humana Press.

Callahan, D. (1984). Autonomy: A moral good, not a moral obsession. *Hastings Center Report, 14,* 40-.

Churchill, L. & Siman. (1986). Principles and the search for moral certainty. *Social Science and Medicine, 23,* 461-468.

Cole, T. & Holstein, M. (forthcoming). Ethics and aging. In R. Binstock & V. Marshall (Eds.), *Handbook of aging and the social sciences,* 4th ed.

Fox, R. & Swazey, J. (1984). Medical morality is not bioethics: Medical ethics in China and the United States. In R. Fox (Ed.), *Essays in medical sociology.* New Brunswick, NJ: Transaction Books.

Holstein, M. (1994). Taking next steps: Gerontological education, research, and the literary imagination. *The Gerontologist, 34*, 822-827.

Jameton, A. (1988). In the borderlands of autonomy: Responsibility in long-term care facilities. *The Gerontologist*, 28, Suppl., 18-23.

Katz, J. (1984). *The silent world of doctor and patient*. Glencoe, IL: The Free Press.

Kitwood, T. & Bredin, K. (1992). Towards a theory of dementia care: Personhood and well-being. *Ageing and Society*, 12 (Pt. 3), 269-288.

Klever, L. (Ed.). (1989). *Dax's case: Essays in medical ethics and human meaning*. Dallas: Southern Methodist University Press.

Lidz, C., Fischer, L. & Arnold, R. (1992). *The erosion of autonomy in long-term care*. New York: Oxford University Press.

May, W. (1986). The virtues and vices of the elderly. In T. Cole, & S. Gadow (Eds.), *What does it mean to grow old? Reflections from the humanities*. Durham: Duke University Press.

McCullough, L. & Wilson, N. (forthcoming). Managing the conceptual and ethical dimensions of long-term care decision making: A preventive ethics approach. In L. McCullough & N. Wilson (Eds.), *Ethical and conceptual dimensions of long-term care decision making*. Baltimore: Johns Hopkins University Press.

Miles, S. (1988). Paternalism, family duties, and my aunt Maude. *Journal of the American Medical Association, 259*, 2582-3.

Moody, H. R. (1992). *Ethics in an aging society*. New York: Oxford University Press.

Moody, H. R. (1988). From informed consent to negotiated consent. *The Gerontologist, 28*, Special Suppl., 64-70.

Murdoch, I. (1970). *The sovereignty of the good*. Boston and London: Routledge and Kegan Paul.

Noble, C. (1981). Ethics and experts. *Hastings Center Report*, 12, 7-9.

Sherwin, S. (1992). *No longer patient: Feminist ethics and health care*. Philadelphia: Temple University Press.

Walker, M. U. (1993). Keeping moral spaces open: New images of ethics consulting. *Hastings Center Report, 23*, 33-40.

Weston, A. (1991). Toward a social critique of bioethics. *Journal of Social Philosophy, 22*, 109-118.

Index

Haworth
DOCUMENT DELIVERY
SERVICE

This valuable service provides a single-article order form for any article from a Haworth journal.

- *Time Saving:* No running around from library to library to find a specific article.
- *Cost Effective:* All costs are kept down to a minimum.
- *Fast Delivery:* Choose from several options, including same-day FAX.
- *No Copyright Hassles:* You will be supplied by the original publisher.
- *Easy Payment:* Choose from several easy payment methods.

Open Accounts Welcome for . . .
- Library Interlibrary Loan Departments
- Library Network/Consortia Wishing to Provide Single-Article Services
- Indexing/Abstracting Services with Single Article Provision Services
- Document Provision Brokers and Freelance Information Service Providers

---

MAIL or *FAX* THIS ENTIRE ORDER FORM TO:

Haworth Document Delivery Service
The Haworth Press, Inc.
10 Alice Street
Binghamton, NY 13904-1580

or FAX: 1-800-895-0582
or CALL: 1-800-342-9678
9am-5pm EST

PLEASE SEND ME PHOTOCOPIES OF THE FOLLOWING SINGLE ARTICLES:

1) Journal Title: _____

    Vol/Issue/Year: _____ Starting & Ending Pages: _____

Article Title: _____

2) Journal Title: _____

    Vol/Issue/Year: _____ Starting & Ending Pages: _____

Article Title: _____

3) Journal Title: _____

    Vol/Issue/Year: _____ Starting & Ending Pages: _____

Article Title: _____

4) Journal Title: _____

    Vol/Issue/Year: _____ Starting & Ending Pages: _____

Article Title: _____

(See other side for Costs and Payment Information)

COSTS: Please figure your cost to order quality copies of an article.

1. Set-up charge per article: $8.00

                 ($8.00 × number of separate articles) _____

2. Photocopying charge for each article:

                 1-10 pages: $1.00 _____

                 11-19 pages: $3.00 _____

                 20-29 pages: $5.00 _____

                 30+ pages: $2.00/10 pages _____

3. Flexicover (optional): $2.00/article _____

4. Postage & Handling: US: $1.00 for the first article/

                 $.50 each additional article _____

            Federal Express: $25.00 _____

            Outside US: $2.00 for first article/

                 $.50 each additional article _____

5. Same-day FAX service: $.35 per page _____

                            GRAND TOTAL: _____

METHOD OF PAYMENT: (please check one)

❑ Check enclosed   ❑ Please ship and bill. PO # _____

          (sorry we can ship and bill to bookstores only! All others must pre-pay)

❑ Charge to my credit card: ❑ Visa; ❑ MasterCard; ❑ Discover;

                ❑ American Express;

Account Number:_____ Expiration date:_____

Signature: ✗_____

Name: _____ Institution: _____

Address: _____

_____

City: _____ State: _____ Zip:_____

Phone Number: _____ FAX Number: _____

MAIL or *FAX* THIS ENTIRE ORDER FORM TO:

Haworth Document Delivery Service	**or FAX:** 1-800-895-0582
The Haworth Press, Inc.	**or CALL:** 1-800-342-9678
10 Alice Street	9am-5pm EST)
Binghamton, NY 13904-1580	